TO
HONOR
AND
OBEY

TO
HONOR
AND
OBEY

Lawrence Taylor

WILLIAM MORROW AND COMPANY, INC.
NEW YORK

Library of Congress Cataloging-in-Publication Data

Taylor, Lawrence, 1942–
    To honor and obey / by Lawrence Taylor.
      p.   cm.
    ISBN 0-688-09854-1
    1. Murder—New York (N.Y.)—Case studies.   2. Rape in marriage—
New York (N.Y.)—Case studies.   3. Fratt, Louann.   4. Fratt, C.K.
Poe.   I. Title.
HV6534.N5N39   1992
364.1′523′097471—dc20   91-22454
                                                                                                              CIP

Printed in the United States of America

First Edition

1   2   3   4   5   6   7   8   9   10

BOOK DESIGN BY M&M DESIGNS

To Julie

CONTENTS

PROLOGUE:
November 22, 1988

A lone figure turned the corner of Seventy-eighth Street and entered the dark and silent emptiness of Park Avenue. The woman, wearing a beige raincoat and trailing a tiny dog on a leash, hesitated for a moment. Then, with short, hurried steps, she walked on into the lonely night.

Park Avenue is quiet at 3:15 in the morning, quiet and friendless. Tall, narrow brick and granite buildings, blackened by decades of decay and pollution, stand pressed against one another in endless procession to the north, toward the strange and hostile lands of Spanish Harlem. To the south, the dismal old buildings march in staid formation down into the vulgar mid-Manhattan world of commerce, gradually merging with ever higher towers of glass, steel, and concrete.

But on the elegant Upper East Side, Park Avenue is a broad, tree-lined enclave of discreet wealth, an ageless bastion of gentility. Its stained but somehow gracious old brownstones, unchanged since the twenties, are home to chic art galleries, fashionable restaurants, and polished brass plaques quietly identifying the offices of physicians to the rich. In the buildings above these small concessions to commerce are hidden the homes of the wealthy, the sanctuaries of the privileged. In the safety and privacy of the upper levels of the old brick and granite fortresses lie the multimillion-dollar co-ops and condos of bankers, lawyers, stockbrokers, doctors, corporate directors.

Unlike in the predatory jungles to the north, or the frenzied industry to the south, those in the genteel cosmos of Park Avenue go about the business of living with tasteful restraint. It is still New York, however, and even leisure is pursued with some intensity. There is a gentle buzz of activity along the avenue as it traverses the Upper East Side. Taxicabs deposit elderly matrons at art galleries, maids walk dogs and push baby carriages, elegant wives chat over espresso with other elegant wives.

At 3:15 in the morning, however, Park Avenue is dark, lonely, and deserted. Or almost deserted.

The woman wore a pink Ellesse sweatshirt and powder blue sweatpants, covered by a beige raincoat, and white Reeboks. In one hand she carried a brown and gold Louis Vuitton bag, in the other a leash attached to the tiny Shih Tzu. She was slender and fair, in her mid-fifties, with a narrow patrician face, delicately chiseled features, fine ash-blond hair styled in a girlish bob, and clear blue eyes. At one time she had been a strikingly beautiful woman, but that beauty was now eroded by lines deeply etched across her brow and around her mouth, tightly pressed lips permanently curled into a hard, thin grimace, and a nose just beginning to swell and vein from alcohol. Garishly bright red lipstick and carefully applied mascara bore witness to a desperate attempt to hide the erosion. But it was in the eyes, the clear blue eyes, where beauty had first died. Age had caused the inevitable sagging under those eyes, but something more than age had created the heavy lids, the empty stare, the vacant look of disillusionment and numbing weariness. She had been a bright and lovely woman once, filled with faith, spirit, and purpose. Now she was a slightly pathetic figure, aging gracelessly, fighting to find meaning and worth in a drawer full of creams, paints, and powders.

The woman turned right at Seventy-ninth, continued walking hurriedly down the tree-lined row of old brownstone buildings. She stopped for a moment as the dog halted its mincing prance to relieve itself next to a tree, then continued on. At Lexington Avenue she paused, then crossed the eerily silent intersection to a fourteen-story building of blackened red brick on the northeast corner. A dark green canvas awning jutted out to the curb from a door of glass and polished brass bearing the number 151. Neighboring the building to the north on Lexington stood the venerable Unitarian Church of All Souls, built in 1819; to the east, on Seventy-ninth, a sign discreetly announced the location of the Elliott Galleries.

As the woman approached the narrow building on the corner, a doorman in uniform appeared from inside and quickly opened the door. He was a little man in his middle years, possibly Puerto Rican, and he greeted her with a broad grin and a slight bow as she entered. She responded with a mechanical smile that disappeared immediately, then followed as the doorman hurriedly led her to the elevator, opened the doors, and stepped aside.

The woman and her toy dog rode in silence up to the fifth floor. She stared straight ahead, unseeing, her expression still vacant and expressionless. When the elevator eased to a halt and the doors opened, she stepped out into the spacious foyer of a fifteen-room co-op occupying the entire level. An expensive Persian rug lay spread out over a polished hardwood floor. The woman walked through the foyer and into a huge living room. The room had been furnished and decorated with a quiet and understated elegance, with large, well-upholstered chairs and a couch arranged around another Persian rug in the center of more polished hardwood. There had been no attempt to impress with stylistic interior designers; rather, the emphasis was on tasteful comfort and the luxury of space.

The woman put the Vuitton bag down on a chair, then unsnapped the leash from the Shih Tzu's collar. She took off her raincoat, walked over to a closet door, opened it, and carefully hung the coat on a hanger. Then she walked across the room again, through a hallway and into a large bathroom, the tiny dog bouncing after her.

The woman stood before a large mirror mounted above an ornate counter and sink. She looked into the mirror, studying the deep lines and weary eyes staring back. She closed her eyes and just stood there for a long moment. When she opened them again, she avoided looking at the the mirror. She leaned down and began taking off her white leather sneakers, arranging them neatly by the door. With deep exhaustion in every move, she began pulling the pink sweatshirt over her head. She neatly folded it on the counter, then peeled off the blue sweatpants and carefully folded them as well. Then she walked over to the bathtub and turned on the faucet. She waited for a few seconds, tested the temperature of the water coming out. Satisfied, she stepped back, took off her bra and panties, and draped them neatly across the sweatsuit.

The woman stepped into the bathtub and gently lowered herself to her knees. Slowly, she leaned forward and down until her head was under the warm running water. She stayed there, bent over and her head under the faucet, until her hair was thoroughly soaked. Then she opened a nearby bottle of shampoo and began working the fragrant liquid into her fine ash-blond hair. She continued like that for a while, slowly, almost hypnotically, massaging the cleansing foam through her hair.

Finished, she rinsed her hair out under the faucet, then towel-dried herself. Stepping out of the bathtub, she picked up the bra, panties, and sweatsuit and put them back on. Then she began blow-drying her hair in front of the mirror. Slowly, carefully, she worked the hair with a brush, her eyes never leaving the cheerless face in the mirror.

Satisfied at last, the woman walked out of the bathroom and into the living room, the Shih Tzu again tagging along behind. She sat down in a chair next to the telephone, picked up the receiver and dialed 911. The toy dog jumped up into her lap.

She waited quietly, stroking the tiny animal. When she finally heard a voice on the line, she spoke.

"I've stabbed my husband," she said simply. Then, very calmly, she added, "I believe he's dead."

PART ONE:
ENIGMA

CHAPTER 1

"It was in his neck, I believe. Yes, I stabbed him in his neck."

"In his neck."

"Yes. The first time," the woman said calmly. "I believe it was in his neck."

"The first time?"

"Yes. Well, you see, he backed away at first, after I stabbed him in the neck. He seemed surprised. I think there was a lot of blood. In any event, he was blocking the way out of the apartment."

"He was between you and the door."

"Yes. And then he said . . . I believe the words were, 'You're not getting out of here alive.' "

Michael Dowd nodded, wrote down something on a legal pad. "Please go on, Mrs. Fratt."

"Well, Poe was standing there, preventing me from getting out, from escaping. Then he struck me again. In the face. And then again." She spoke without feeling, detached, as if explaining a vaguely distasteful event. "He struck me three or four times, as I recall." She paused, as if waiting for a cue.

"And what happened next?"

"I was swinging the knife. Back and forth. Trying to make him get away from the door. But he just kept backing up, toward the door. And then he turned and reached for something."

"He reached for something?"

"I believe it was a clock, or a letter opener. On a table. That's when I stabbed him the second time, when he turned away. In the back."

The lawyer nodded, scribbled some more notes on the pad.

"Then Poe fell. He fell to the floor. No," she corrected herself, "first he tried to grab for the knife. He grabbed the blade, I believe. Then he fell to the floor."

Again, a pause. "That's when you left?" Dowd asked.

She nodded. "I wasn't trying to kill him, you understand."

"I understand." Michael Dowd leaned back slightly in his green leather chair, his pale blue eyes peering over the tortoiseshell reading glasses perched near the end of his swollen Irish nose. He was a big man, heavyset, but with a gentleness accented by a round, cherubic face and a soft, ruddy complexion. His straight brown hair fell loosely across his face like a schoolboy's and was beginning to gray. But the eyes still sparkled mischievously, as if he were recalling some terribly funny prank. The schoolboy image was reinforced by clothes that were perpetually rumpled and ill-fitting. He was wearing a white shirt, frayed at the collar and cuffs and only half tucked into his pants. A muted red tie hung crookedly to one side. His dark gray pants were baggy and continually rode down his ample waist, causing the pants cuffs to slip under his shoes as he walked. A matching dark gray coat was carelessly thrown in a chair along with a tan trench coat. There were those, in fact, who suspected that he never changed these clothes, since he always wore a dark gray suit, white shirt, and muted red tie.

At forty-eight years of age, Dowd resembled nothing so much as an aging, overgrown schoolboy.

It was startling, then, when Dowd spoke, for the voice that came out of that gentle, impish face was deep, strong, and resonant—the voice of a William Jennings Bryan.

"I understand," he repeated.

"And I left. I placed the knife back in my bag and I left."

"The kitchen knife you had brought with you to your husband's apartment."

"Yes."

"The one you always carry with you when you walk the dog at night, for self-defense," Dowd said, jotting down another note to himself.

"Yes."

"And the dog?"

"The dog?"

"Where was the dog during the . . . altercation?"

"I couldn't really tell you, Mr. Dowd. My mind was on other things."

"I understand. You did leave with the dog?"

"Of course."

"On a leash?"

"I beg your pardon?"

"Was the dog on a leash when you left?"

"Well, I assume so. Yes, I'm sure he was."

"You had taken the leash off when you had arrived at your husband's apartment, hadn't you, Mrs. Fratt?"

"I . . . yes, of course. Poe was quite fond of our dog. He had the run of the apartment."

"Uh-huh. So after you, uh, stabbed Mr. Fratt, and he fell to the floor, you found the dog."

"Yes."

"And you put the leash back on."

"Yes."

"And recovered your bag."

"Yes."

"And replaced the knife in the bag."

"Yes."

"And left."

"Yes."

"Uh-huh. Please go on."

Dowd studied the woman sitting on the other side of his desk as she continued telling her story without apparent feeling. She was wearing a plain black wool suit, simple and very expensive, together with a gray and white silk scarf and black pumps. She sat straight up in the green leather chair, her posture perfect, hands folded in her lap, knees pressed discreetly together. Straight ash-blond hair cut neatly in a bob, every strand in place. Fingernails manicured, makeup perfect. Calm, cool, collected. Yet, her face seemed sad, tired, as if she had been fighting a losing battle for a very long time.

Louann Fratt. Age, fifty-five. Residence, 151 East Seventy-ninth Street. Housewife, socialite. Three children, ages twenty-six, twenty-seven, and twenty-eight. Married, for thirty years, to C. K. Poe Fratt.

Charles Kennedy Poe Fratt. Age, fifty-seven. Wealthy senior partner in Peat Marwick Main and Company, largest accounting firm in the nation. Football All-American nominee at Cornell in the fifties. More recently, a director of the National Democratic Committee, top presidential fund raiser, and national convention delegate. Separated from his wife, living in a studio apartment at 52 East Seventy-eighth Street. Recently deceased.

Dowd recalled the sensational headlines in the New York newspapers. WIFE STABS TOP EXEC TO DEATH, the *Post* had announced in bold print across its pages. EXEC BUTCHERED, WIFE BOOKED, blared the *Daily News*. Even the staid *New York Times* carried the story prominently, though with more restrained headlines: EXECUTIVE SLAIN; WIFE IS ARRESTED. And in the days following, the banner headlines continued: NO BAIL FOR WIFE IN SLAYING; D.A.: KILLER WIFE CARRIED KNIFE TO MATE'S APARTMENT; KIDS SPRING MOM IN DAD'S SLAYING. Even the ongoing Joel Steinberg-Hedda Nussbaum trial could not push the story from the headlines. The public was, as always, fascinated by the fall of the rich and powerful.

The reported details had been sketchy. Detectives had responded to a 911 call from Mrs. Fratt. At her residence, she told them she had stabbed her husband. Then she handed over the murder weapon, an eight-inch kitchen knife; she had washed the blood off the knife. When asked why she had stabbed him, Mrs. Fratt replied that he had beaten her after an argument about their pending divorce. The detectives escorted her to her husband's apartment, three blocks away. There, just before dawn, they broke in the door and found his body lying just inside in a pool of blood; he had been stabbed to death. Mrs. Fratt was arrested and charged with second-degree murder. At the arraignment, she was ordered held without bail. She spent the following day at Rikers Island before a higher court judge reversed the decision and released her to her children on $25,000 bond.

Now she was in Dowd's office, asking him to defend her. But what bothered the lawyer was not that the prosecution had the murder weapon, fingerprints, and a confession. It was not that any strategy of self-defense would be destroyed by the simple fact that she took a knife to her husband's apartment. What bothered him was that Louann Fratt appeared to have absolutely no remorse about killing her husband of thirty years. In fact, she seemed to have no feelings about the killing at all. How could she be so cold, so matter-of-fact, in describing being beaten by her lifelong partner? How could this woman feel nothing when recalling how she stabbed the father of her children to death? More important, Dowd thought to himself, how would a jury react to such an attitude?

"... called the nine-one-one operator. I explained that I had stabbed my husband—"

"Mrs. Fratt," Dowd interrupted, "let's start over." He studied her for a moment. "Let's go back to the beginning."

"The beginning?"

"Tell me about yourself."

"I'm afraid I don't quite understand."

"Tell me about yourself," he repeated. "Where you came from, your family, how you met your husband—Poe? Tell me what your marriage was like. . . ."

"I see." She thought for a moment, still uncomfortable with baring her private life to this stranger. "Very well. I was born and raised in Aberdeen, Washington. A small lumber town," she added, a touch of contempt in her voice, "near Seattle. My father owned a mill there. After high school, I attended Mills College. In California." Dowd had heard of Mills, a West Coast version of Vassar. "Then the University of Washington. After graduation, I worked for United Airlines. As a stewardess," she added hesitantly. "It was soon after that I met Poe."

"When was this?"

"Nineteen fifty-five. January of 1955."

"Please tell me about him."

"Poe?" Again she thought, her mind going back more than thirty years. Dowd thought he saw, for the first time, the slightest suggestion of a smile.

"He was . . . well . . . tall, strong, very handsome. He had played football at Cornell, you see. And . . . dynamic." She lowered her gaze self-consciously.

"Dynamic," Dowd repeated.

"He had a . . . strength about him, a . . . forcefulness. He was a very strong, forceful person, Mr. Dowd. Masculine, I suppose you would say. He knew where he was going, what he wanted." She thought for a moment. "And he always got it."

"Uh-huh. And his background?"

"Poe was born in Seattle. His parents . . . His mother was Laura Emory." She emphasized the last name, half expecting Dowd to recognize it. "The Emorys are quite well established in Seattle."

Dowd nodded.

"Poe's father, Norbert Fratt, came from a family of some reputation in New England. The grandmother was a Poe. Edgar Allan Poe?"

Dowd nodded again.

"Of course, Poe—my husband, that is—was named after the family. In any event, we saw each other off and on after that. He had just graduated from Cornell, and he was spending three years in the army, in Virginia." She added, as if it weren't necessary to explain, "He was an officer."

"At some point the two of you decided to get married?"

"Yes. Poe didn't want to get married until he could support a family. It was in September of 1958. He completed his obligation to the army, and we were married. I quit the airlines, and we moved to Palo Alto, in California. You see, Poe wanted to get a master's degree in business administration. He had been accepted at Stanford."

"I understand you have children."

"Soon after Poe received his M.B.A., he accepted a position with a company in Seattle. And William was born. A year later, Laura. She was named after Laura Emory, you see. Then Poe Junior."

"Go on."

"After that, we moved a good deal. Let me see, Poe took a position as a management consultant in Palo Alto in 1962. Then it was in 1965, I believe, that he joined Peat Marwick. It was Peat, Marwick, Livingston then, and Poe became partner-in-charge of the Los Angeles office."

"Were you working at all during this time?"

"Me? Oh, no, Poe would never permit that."

Dowd nodded, again studying the sad-faced woman over his horn-rimmed glasses.

"Then other assignments. The San Francisco office. We had a lovely home in Piedmont. In . . . I think it was 1978, Poe was named partner-in-charge of European operations, and we moved to Paris. We had three lovely years in Paris."

"Mrs. Fratt, how would you characterize your marriage?"

"I'm afraid I don't know what you mean."

"Was it a happy marriage?" he asked. "Were the two of you happy?"

"Happy," she repeated, examining the word. "Yes," she said hesitantly, "I think you could say we were happy."

"Were there any incidents of . . . unhappiness?"

Louann Fratt looked back at Dowd, trying to decide something. "Nineteen seventy-five," she said simply. "California. Poe had . . . an affair. It didn't really amount to anything. I was quite upset at the time, though. I consulted a divorce attorney."

"And what happened?"

"Poe apologized, begged me to forgive him." Her eyes left Dowd's, began staring intently at a spot on the wall just behind him. "I did."

"Uh-huh." He wrote something down, then looked back at the woman. "Please go on. What happened after Paris?"

"After Paris," she repeated to herself. "After Paris, Poe was transferred back to the United States. New York City. We bought the co-op on Seventy-ninth. . . ."

Dowd continued to study Louann Fratt as her voice droned on without feeling. Who was this woman? What had really happened that night in her husband's apartment? And why had she come to him? Why had a widow worth millions of dollars come to a tiny office in Soho, to a lawyer who had gained fame defending poor people free of charge?

He kept watching the woman as she talked. This cultured lady from another world was clearly uncomfortable and out of place in his office. This was not Park Avenue. The office was not a modern, expansive designer suite located in the World Trade Center. And he was not a high-priced tax lawyer in a three-piece pinstripe. This was a small, cluttered room on the twelfth floor of an old, disintegrating building in a seedy Soho neighborhood. And Dowd's people were murderers and thieves.

Yet, Dowd's working home was a strangely pleasant one. When clients stepped out of the dreary, rickety elevator, they were confronted with a small but bright and cheery reception area. True, the oddly zigzagging walls and obtrusive columns of this onetime storage area lent a Kafkaesque atmosphere, reinforced by a confused jungle of exposed pipes, conduits, and supporting beams hanging from the high ceiling. But Dowd and the two lawyers with whom he shared the space had had these painted white, then offset by creative track lighting. The hardwood floors, blackened by decades of grime, had been laboriously sanded and varnished until the original light ash color had returned. Green plants grew from pots everywhere, and colorful paintings and prints hung on the white walls.

The reception area led off into four small rooms. In one was the communal law library, doubling as a conference room and coffee area. The second was an office, home to Ellen Yaroshefsky. An attorney now in her forties, Yaroshefsky had worked in Seattle as a zealous advocate for the Center for Constitutional Rights. Now she limited her practice to criminal law and feminist causes, particularly sexual harassment matters—usually pro bono. The third room held the offices of JoAnn Harris, an attorney in her early fifties. Harris had served as the chief of the fraud section while with the United States attorney, prosecuting mostly white-collar cases.

Dowd inhabited the fourth room. Like the reception area, the walls ran at crazy angles, water heaters jutted out obtrusively, and the high ceiling was crisscrossed with pipes and conduits. And like the reception area, everything had been painted white and the floor sanded to a beautiful blond grain. In the middle of the room stood a maple veneer desk with green leather inlay, surrounded by green leather chairs. The desk was littered with files, law books, and months-old correspondence; a huge glass ashtray was piled high with cigarette ashes spilling over onto the desk. More files were stacked high in the one chair not currently being used and on the floor against the wall behind Dowd. A bookcase against another wall held yet more files, books, pleadings, notes; on top of the bookcase was a bronze statue of the blindfolded woman holding the scales of justice. A number of plaques hung on the walls, including Dowd's diploma from St. John's University law school, an "Irishman of the Year" award from the Emerald Society, and a tribute from the St. Patrick's Society of Queens "in appreciation for his legal efforts on behalf of Irish Freedom and Unity." On another wall was an artist's rendition of Dowd arguing to the jury during his defense of Eamon Meehan, charged with running guns for the Irish Republican Army.

Dowd leaned back in his chair and looked past the woman and out the large window beyond. The window covered most of the opposite wall, giving him an impressive southerly view of downtown Manhattan. From here he could see the Brooklyn Bridge, the Manhattan Bridge, and even the scene of his many battles, the Criminal Courts Building.

". . . when the last of the children moved out. Poe Junior is at Cornell now, getting his master's in business."

Dowd's gaze returned to the dignified woman seated so primly in front of him. Louann Fratt could have gone to the high-priced lawyers, the superstars. But she had come to him. Why?

He briefly searched through the debris piled across his desk, found the pack of Salems he was looking for. Absently extracting a cigarette, he put it in his mouth and lighted it.

"Mrs. Fratt . . ."

"Yes?"

"I . . . Look, the district attorney has charged you with murder. They have the knife, the prints, the confession. There's no question you killed him, killed your husband."

"Yes."

"The only possible defense I can see is . . . self-defense."

"I understand."

"No, you don't understand." He sighed. "Let me explain the law of self-defense here in New York. You're only permitted to use deadly force to defend yourself if you yourself are threatened with deadly force."

"Yes," she said. Then, patiently, "He struck me. Four or five times."

"Hitting you with his fists is not using deadly force."

"Poe is . . . was a very large man, Mr. Dowd."

"I understand that. But the law still says you can't kill him if he's only hitting you with his fists."

Louann Fratt stared at Dowd for a moment. Then, slowly, she looked down at the carefully folded hands in her lap. She sat like that in the awkward silence.

"I'm sorry, Mrs. Fratt", Dowd said finally. "I—"

Louann Fratt said something almost in a whisper.

"What?" Dowd said.

"He was trying to rape me," she repeated quietly.

CHAPTER 2

At the time Louann Fratt walked into his office, Michael G. Dowd had defended a number of women accused of murdering their husbands—and had won a stunning series of courtroom victories. As a result, he was rapidly gaining a reputation as a champion of women.

But Dowd is an unlikely champion. The son of a mailman, he was raised in a traditional Irish Catholic home in Queens, in a world where the man sat on a throne and women were relegated to keeping house and having babies. The word "chauvinist" was unknown in the Dowd family, but there were few environments more oppressive for a woman than a conservative Irish Catholic household.

Dowd's strict religious education reinforced the traditional attitudes he had learned at home. After twelve years of Catholic elementary and high schools, he enrolled at Fordham University in Manhattan, a Jesuit institution. Three years later he was married, then accepted for legal studies at St. John's University. St. John's, a Catholic college whose law school was in Brooklyn, was considered with some derision in the legal profession as a blue-collar facility. Many of the students labored at jobs during the day and attended classes at night; Dowd himself worked part time at his uncle's law practice in Manhattan to help make ends meet. The big Wall Street law firms largely overlooked the graduates of St. John's, leaving them to scratch out a common living in general practice or in the sordid world of criminal law.

When Dowd graduated and passed the bar, he joined his uncle's firm and spent the next four years learning the business of being a lawyer. When this apprenticeship period was over, he left his uncle to form his own firm with two friends in his old neighborhood of Queens. The three young lawyers settled down into a small, low-key general practice of drafting wills, handling divorces, and generally representing anyone who walked through the front door. Because neither of his partners wanted to deal with the distasteful business of criminal cases, Dowd found himself with a steadily increasing number of seedy-looking clients. More than anything, though, Michael Dowd was just a small-town lawyer who happened to practice in New York City.

Not surprisingly, Dowd grew up to be a big, fun-loving, hard-drinking Irishman who viewed women as subservient creatures. When he and his friends went out for a night on the town, the women stayed home. The men got drunk, talked politics, and occasionally engaged in a recreational brawl. A story from one of them about slapping his wife around for complaining about his carousing would bring gales of laughter from the men. Women were a source of endless amusement, and Dowd gave little serious thought to them.

Despite this insensitivity to women, Dowd was at heart an idealist. And it was not long before this intensely idealistic nature began to show itself. A loyal follower of John F. Kennedy in the sixties, he soon became very active in city politics. This political fervor culminated in his running Mario Cuomo's New York mayoral campaign against Edward Koch in 1977. The particularly dirty nature of that campaign disillusioned Dowd, however. He quit the political arena and turned his attention back to his law practice.

But Dowd was still an idealist and, reflecting the "curse of the Irish," a believer in lost causes. It did not take long before his lifelong commitment to one of those causes, Irish nationalism, led him to one of his most controversial cases.

Patrick Mullin had been born in Ireland. The small, quiet, mild-mannered forty-three-year-old resident of Queens was well known for his philanthropic work in raising money for the starving people of Biafra. More recently, however, he had turned his attention to another, more violent, crusade: gun-running for the outlawed Irish Republican Army. However, the F.B.I.'s new Anti-Terrorist Task Force had an informant who had been selling guns to the I.R.A. for over twenty years and had finally been caught. The informant had agreed to expose Mullin and the gun-smuggling ring in exchange for getting his ten-year prison sentence cut in half.

Dowd, ever the intensely committed Irishman, agreed to represent Mullin without charge. At trial, he and the attorneys for three codefendants presented an incredible defense: Unknown to the F.B.I., the informant had been working with the C.I.A. in selling the guns to Mullin and his ring. When the jury finally recessed to deliberate, the issue was clear: The defendants had readily admitted running weapons to the I.R.A.—but had they been acting with the sanction of the United States government? The jury returned with its verdict: "Not guilty." The audience broke into cheers. The trial judge turned to the jurors, saying, "I stand in awe of you! I salute you!"

Dowd subsequently represented a number of other I.R.A. figures without fee, including Chiefs of Staff Eamon O'Dougherty and Joe Cahill, as well as the Meehan brothers, Eamon and Colum; the Meehans had been tortured in a British prison and had later won a judgment against the British government from the European Commission on Human Rights.

Dowd's penchant for lost causes took a very different turn one bleak winter day when a young, destitute cleaning lady walked into his office in Queens. She told him that she had hacked her husband to death with a machete.

And Michael Dowd's life was changed forever.

The woman seemed frightened, withdrawn, her eyes fixed on the floor. Her clothing was old and badly worn; oddly, her left arm was in a cast. Dowd introduced himself to the wretched-looking figure. He asked her to tell him what had happened.

Slowly, hesitantly, in a barely audible whisper, Ann-Marie Brown told him exactly what she had already told the police: She was growing old, she had lost her figure (she had had a baby three weeks before the murder), she was ugly, and so her husband was going to leave her. So she waited until he fell asleep on their couch and then killed him with a machete. She had broken her wrist on the way out of the apartment, slipping on the bloody floor. She could not recall how she had gotten the bruises on her face and body—probably from the fall.

The case appeared hopeless, but Dowd could not say no to this pathetic woman.

Months later, Dowd was still trying to figure out what to do with the Ann-Marie Brown case when he saw a television program on battered wives. There seemed to be vague similarities to the facts in the Brown case. Curious, he began probing into something called "battered wife syndrome." He met Dr. Julie Blackman, a psychology professor at Columbia University's Barnard College. Dr. Blackman listened, agreed to talk with Ann-Marie.

After meeting with Dowd's client, Dr. Blackman was suspicious of her story. She decided to hypnotize the woman. And under hypnosis a very different story came out than the one she had told Dowd. Ann-Marie's husband had abused her regularly: He had denied her food, hidden her clothing, and beaten her on a regular basis. On the evening of the killing, he had beaten her badly, then taken their three-week-old baby by the heels and, swinging it in the air, threatened to throw it out the window. When Ann-Marie tried to stop him, he broke her wrist. Then he told her that he was going to take a nap—and he was going to kill both her and the baby when he woke up. It was only then, in desperation, that she killed him.

Dr. Blackman explained to a stunned Michael Dowd that Ann-Marie's earlier "confession" was simply what her *husband's* version of the facts would have been: Ann-Marie's self-esteem had been so thoroughly destroyed by the sustained physical and emotional abuse that she no longer perceived things from her own perspective but only from that of her husband.

Dowd had long talks with the psychologist, began reading articles and books about abused women. Slowly, he learned about such things as the recurring three-stage "battering cycle"—first, the escalation of violence, then the explosion, and finally the contrite (and effective) begging for forgiveness. He discovered the "learned helplessness" syndrome. The husband—and society—convinces the woman that she is worthless, incompetent, stupid, and incapable of surviving without masculine help and direction. Emotional abuse—far more devastating than the physical—undermines her self-esteem. All of this is reinforced by the woman's financial inability to support herself and the children without the husband. Finally, society expects her to be nurturing, loving, forgiving; abandonment by the husband would mean failure as a woman.

And Dowd read about "traumatic bonding"—how physical abuse paradoxically brings a woman closer to a man: Hurt, vulnerable, and dependent after a beating, the woman gratefully accepts the inevitably contrite man's apologies and comfort because she has no one else to whom to turn for love and caring. As the violent cycle is repeated, the woman's self-esteem is destroyed, she feels isolated and helpless, and she loses all hope of changing her situation.

Dowd had two reactions to this new world of the abused woman. "I was *horrified!*" he recalled later. "I mean, I could so easily have missed the truth about her!" He thought for a moment. "And guilt," the big, hard-drinking Irishman added quietly. "Society tolerates this kind of thing—because of men like me." He recalled the moment of his conversion. "I was driving to court one day, and then it happened. I just suddenly saw the world through her eyes, through the eyes of a woman. And I was overwhelmed by a sense of guilt, of responsibility for her life. I'd been a part of this injustice. By my silence, I'd condoned it. I remember the moment so clearly. I remember I cried."

He decided not to charge Ann-Marie a fee.

In February 1981, the trial of Ann-Marie Brown began in

the New York Supreme Court in Brooklyn. Dowd was in his element now. "I feel comfortable in the courtroom; it's like. . . . I'm home." In his element, and at a new level of intensity: "It's hard to explain. Everything is sharper, clearer, faster. I feel like I'm on a 'high' during trial."

It came time for Ann-Marie to testify. Frightened, her eyes still to the ground, she reluctantly took the stand. Dowd tried to get her to tell what her life with her husband had been like, but she could not say anything bad about him; she repeatedly expressed deep love for him and, oddly, continued to speak of him as if he were still alive. When Dowd pressed her for the truth, she refused to answer. Finally, the judge stepped in and ordered her to answer her own attorney's questions. Cornered, Ann-Marie broke down on the stand and cried uncontrollably. Then, haltingly, painfully, came the truth. . . .

While the jury was deliberating, Dowd saw Ann-Marie staring at a photograph with tears in her eyes; he knew it was a photo of her baby, and he knew what she was thinking. He held her in his arms for a moment. "You're a nice man," she said finally. "Thank you." There was quiet resignation in her voice.

The jury finally returned with its verdict. Dowd and his client stood as it was read: "Not guilty." Ann-Marie collapsed in tears in Dowd's arms.

Dowd won that murder case. Since then, there have been many others—fascinating cases, each unique and yet each sharing the common thread of a frightened, desperate woman alone in an ignorant and uncaring world.

A hard-drinking, chauvinistic Irishman who defended terrorists becomes a gentle, compassionate champion of oppressed women. How did Dowd get from defending terrorists to defending battered women? What is the link? Possibly the answer lies buried in the heart of an Irishman—in the tragic Irish weakness for hopeless causes, born of battling for centuries against English tyranny. And, perhaps, in the love of a good fight. What does seem clear is that, to the depths of his soul, Michael Dowd is a committed defender of the oppressed, the downtrodden, the underdog.

For centuries longer than the Irish, women have been

oppressed—many violently. And Dowd had defended some of those who had risen and slain their oppressors. But the wealthy and privileged Louann Fratt was certainly not a battered wife.

What did this Park Avenue socialite want from him?

CHAPTER 3

"Mrs. Fratt," Dowd said, trying to hide the doubt in his voice, "you're telling me that when you killed your husband, he was trying to . . . rape you?"

The woman nodded slightly.

The room was silent for a long moment.

"Mrs. Fratt . . . Ah, there was no mention in the newspapers of an attempted rape."

"No."

"I mean, you apparently didn't tell the police at the scene that he tried to rape you?"

"No."

"You just told them that he'd hit you with his fists, after an argument."

"Yes."

"And you didn't mention it during your nine-one-one call to the police?"

"No."

Dowd sighed. "I'm sorry, Mrs. Fratt. You're going to have to explain that to—"

Once again examining her folded hands, she said in a

34

cold, detached voice, "I was too . . . embarrassed. I . . . It was so . . . degrading."

Dowd stared at the woman seated across the desk. After another awkward silence, he said, "You're saying that . . . after thirty years of marriage . . . your husband tried to rape you."

Quietly, "It wasn't the first time, Mr. Dowd."

The lawyer waited for a moment. "Mrs. Fratt," he said finally, unsure of what he had here. "I think maybe we should back up a little bit."

Louann Fratt lifted her chin sharply. "Yes, of course." She paused for a moment. Then she began, recalling events as if she were describing a slightly boring social event. "In May of last year, Poe came home one evening and suddenly announced that he . . . he wanted a divorce. I was . . . stunned. I couldn't understand why, after thirty years . . . I thought it was a good marriage. I couldn't understand why he wanted to leave."

"And he left?"

"No. Not at first. We each consulted with attorneys, retained attorneys. But Poe stayed for a while. He just . . . lived there. Then, about six months later, he moved out. He moved into an apartment three blocks away, the one on Seventy-eighth, the one where . . ."

"Uh-huh."

"In any event, after that, he would come by occasionally. To discuss business matters . . . finances, the children." She stopped for a moment. "To pick up his mail." She seemed to stiffen again. "It was during one of those visits . . ."

"I'm listening."

"July first of this year. At ten o'clock in the evening. Poe came by to pick up his mail. I invited him to sit down. I remember we sat down on a loveseat in the living room. I joined him. We talked for a few minutes. I don't recall now what it was we were talking about. Nothing terribly important. I remember I'd been playing tennis, and I still had my tennis outfit on. We talked. And then suddenly he . . . suddenly he grabbed me . . . and he tore at me, tore my tennis shorts off . . . and then he . . . and then he raped me."

Dowd was astonished—not that this woman had been

raped by her husband; to a criminal lawyer little was shocking. What amazed him was that Louann Fratt described how she had been raped in the same way she would describe the condition of her stock portfolio. There was absolutely no emotion, no feeling, nothing to indicate she even cared.

"I know this is difficult, Mrs. Fratt—"

"On the loveseat. I recall at one point we fell off, we fell to the floor."

"Uh-huh. And what happened after this?"

"When he was finished, I ran into my bedroom and locked the door."

"Did your husband leave then?"

"I don't know. I don't know when Poe left."

"You don't know?"

"I didn't come out of the bedroom until the next day."

Dowd continued studying the woman, trying to understand what kind of an animal this was. She had been so frightened that she had locked herself in a room and stayed there until the next day—and yet she described it calmly, objectively, as if it had happened to someone else.

"Poe called a day or two later. He apologized, of course."

"What did you say?"

"I told him that if he ever did that again, I'd tell the children."

"Uh-huh. How much does your husband weigh, Mrs. Fratt?"

"Two hundred and twenty pounds."

"Please go on."

"I saw Poe three more times, I believe, before the night of . . . the night he died."

"Tell me about that evening again."

"The evening of November twenty-first," she sighed. "Very well. At approximately six-thirty, Poe called on the telephone. He wanted to pick up his mail. I agreed. I remember that I wanted to discuss an investment with him, some stock we held in Carol Oil Corporation. In any event, by eleven-thirty that night he hadn't yet come by. So I called him. But his line was busy."

"Uh-huh."

"I called a number of times. Finally, at one-fifteen in the

morning, I reached him. And he said . . . he told me that he
wanted me to bring his mail to him."

"He wanted you to deliver his mail to him at his apartment," Dowd repeated.

"Yes."

"Do you have a car?"

"Poe has a Ford Taurus. He lets me use it when I need to."

"But you didn't have the car that evening?"

"No. No."

"So your husband wanted you to walk to his apartment
with the mail."

"That's correct."

"Alone, at one-fifteen in the morning."

"That's correct."

"Uh-huh. And you went."

"Yes. I put on a red sweatsuit. And I put the mail in a bag.
And, as I explained, I put the kitchen knife in the bag as well."

"For protection."

"Yes."

"On the streets."

"Yes."

"Anything else in the bag?"

"Some cigarettes."

"Uh-huh. Please go on."

"I left. Oh, and of course, our dog. He has to be taken on
walks quite often. He's twelve years old, you see. He has a
bladder condition."

"Uh-huh."

"In any event, we walked the three blocks to Poe's apartment. When we arrived, Poe let us in, and he offered me a
glass of wine. I remember he told me to pour myself a glass.
The bottle was in the kitchen. I drank the glass of wine, and
then we sat and talked for a short while."

"Do you remember what you talked about?"

"Oh, nothing terribly important. I do recall we talked quite
a bit about the football game. He had been to the game the
previous weekend."

"What game was that?"

"Cornell-Penn," she replied, as if the answer were evident.
"He had met some friends there. And our youngest son, Poe

Junior, was at the game. We talked about Poe Junior, and about the friends, and the game."

"Uh-huh."

"And then he tried to rape me," she said simply.

"Can you give me a little more detail, Mrs. Fratt?"

"Of course," she replied, studying the bronze statue of blind Justice with disinterest. "He was sitting on the bed. I was sitting on the small couch at the foot of the bed. It's a very small apartment, you see, a studio. The bed is in the front room, and there is very little room elsewhere to sit."

"You were wearing a sweatsuit."

"Yes, as I said."

"And your husband, what was he wearing?"

"Poe? He was wearing his pajamas," Louann Fratt replied. "It was, I don't know, two in the morning."

"Uh-huh. Please go on."

"He was sitting next to me, and we were talking, and suddenly he grabbed me by the arm, grabbed me very hard. And he said . . ." She stopped.

"What did he say, Mrs. Fratt?"

"He said . . . 'I'm going to fuck you like you should be fucked.' " There was still no feeling, merely a sense that the subject was vaguely distasteful.

"Uh-huh. And then what happened?"

"Poe pulled me onto the bed and he began tearing at my pants, my sweatpants. And I fought back, I hit him, scratched him."

"Can you remember where you scratched him?"

"In his face. I recall scratching him in his face. But then he hit me in the head, in the side of my head, I believe. And that's when I reached for the knife."

"Now, where was the knife at this time?"

"In the bag, of course."

"And the bag?"

"On the couch. I reached for it. I reached inside and pulled it out. I recall quite clearly yelling at Poe, 'Let go, Poe, I've got a knife.' But he didn't stop. And that's when I stabbed him in the neck."

"Uh-huh."

"I suppose it stunned him," she said without interest. "He

let go, and I jumped up and tried to get around the bed to the front door. But then he must have jumped up, too, because he was standing there, blocking my way to the door. Then he hit me in the face. I think he hit me two or three times." She paused. "Then he said, 'You're not getting out of here alive.' "

"Uh-huh."

"Then, as I've told you, he turned and reached for something, a letter opener, I believe, or a clock. Something on the table, something to hit me with. And while he was turned, I stabbed him."

"In the back."

"Yes. And he turned, and grabbed for the knife in my hand, grabbed the blade. And then he fell down. He just sort of . . . collapsed. And I grabbed the dog, and the bag, and ran out."

"Uh-huh."

"I don't really recall that much after leaving Poe's apartment. The next thing I can remember is being back home. I remember that the sweatsuit was quite bloody, so I changed into a clean one. The pink and blue set. Then I called my son. Poe Junior. I called him at Cornell."

"This was before you called the police?"

"Yes. I told him, I said that I thought I may have killed his father. I said I was going to call the police, and I would call him back. Then I began thinking that perhaps Poe was still alive. So I decided to go back."

"You went back to your husband's apartment?"

"Yes."

"What time was this?"

"I . . . Perhaps three, three-thirty. I'm not certain."

"With the dog?"

"I don't think so."

"And the knife?"

"No, I believe I washed the knife. It was quite bloody."

"And what happened at the apartment?"

"He was lying on the floor. He was dead."

"And then?"

"I left, went back home. I went into the bathroom and washed my hair." She paused. "There was blood in it."

"Uh-huh."

"And then I called the police."

Louann Fratt had just completed describing a slightly unpleasant business transaction.

"Ah, Mrs. Fratt, do you remember what you told the police? What you told them after they arrived?"

"I explained to the officers what had happened."

"But not about the attempted rape."

"No. Then I showed them where the knife was, in the bag."

"You put it back in the bag after washing it."

"Apparently. And then I took them over to Poe's apartment. By that time there were about six officers. And they broke the door in and found Poe."

"Broke it in?"

"It was locked."

"You locked the door after leaving?"

"I don't really recall, Mr. Dowd. In any event, after they found Poe, they arrested me, and read to me about my constitutional rights."

"Uh-huh."

"Although, quite frankly, they read far too quickly to understand."

Dowd continued studying Louann Fratt as she talked on. Had this wealthy socialite come to him expecting to be his next battered wife acquittal? But this did not appear to be a battered wife case. This was not a poor woman from the ghetto who was beaten by her Neanderthal husband on a daily basis. Far from it: This was a pampered member of the privileged class whose idea of abuse was being denied another charge card. Yet ... yet there was something about this woman, something about the cold, unfeeling way she described the rape and stabbing. How could *anyone* be so completely devoid of any emotion? Dowd filed a note in the back of his mind to bounce this off a psychologist.

Louann Fratt's only hope was self-defense. Of course, defending herself against her husband's fists, no matter how big he was, did not legally constitute self-defense. But rape—now that was a different story. The New York statutes on self-defense had been amended to permit the use of deadly force when confronted with *either* deadly force *or rape*. And New York was one of only twenty-two states that legally recognized that a wife could be raped by her husband. True, there was still a statute on the books that defined "woman" for purposes of rape as a female who was not married at the time to the rapist. But that statute had recently been held unconstitutional by an appellate court. If Poe Fratt had, indeed, tried to rape his wife, she would have been legally justified in defending herself with a knife—even to the point of killing him.

Self-defense? Maybe, but there were gaping holes in her story. Holes that made Dowd wonder. Holes that a D.A. would see. Holes that a jury would be gawking through. Why would this woman agree to deliver her estranged husband's mail—at 2:00 in the morning? Why would she go out alone into the streets of New York at that hour? What was the real reason she took a lethal knife with her to visit the man who had abandoned her?

And the rape . . . As any defense lawyer defending an accused rapist routinely tells the jury, rape is an extremely easy charge to make—and a difficult one to disprove. The D.A. would now turn the tables and point out this simple truth for Louann Fratt's jury. And why didn't she tell the police when she made the 911 call? Why didn't she tell the detectives who responded to her home? Why didn't she tell the officers back at the station when she was interrogated? The plain fact was that there was no apparent corroboration of the rape. And she had certainly had plenty of time to fabricate the story.

The thing that bothered Dowd most was Louann Fratt's cold, unfeeling attitude. Was this the reaction of a woman who had been raped? A woman who had stabbed her husband to death? Dowd was neither naive nor an amateur in the criminal field: He was perfectly willing to represent a guilty client. The reality was that over 90 percent of those accused are guilty—and most of them lie even to their own attorneys. No, Dowd's concern about Louann Fratt's attitude was much more pragmatic.

What would a *jury* think of this woman?

CHAPTER 4

The criminal lawyer is a hired gun.

Throughout recorded history, truth and justice have been determined by force of arms. Long before David fought Goliath while their armies watched, men have chosen champions to enter an arena and resolve disputes through combat. America's colorful contribution to this human condition was the gunslinger of the Old West: Conflicts were settled by two hired killers, matched in a "showdown," winner take all.

The Old West is gone—but the method for finding justice is not. True, the method has been refined and formalized, but our system remains essentially intact. Each side hires the most skilled advocate—the "fastest gun"—it can afford; the more money available, the more skilled the lawyer hired. The two combatants then meet in an arena—we now call it a "court of law." Each "gun," whether the prosecutor hired by the state or the defense attorney hired by the accused, has been highly trained for just this kind of showdown. And combat begins, but with very rigid and stylized rules.

Guns have been replaced with words, and juries now determine the victor, but the method is the same: justice through one-on-one combat by professionals.

Dowd was a hired gun. His job was to enter the arena and fight. But did he want to hire out to Louann Fratt?

She hardly seemed a very sympathetic individual. Nor did this privileged member of Park Avenue society appeal to Dowd's weakness for the poor and oppressed. Louann Fratt had killed her husband. She was very possibly a cold-blooded murderer: Dowd had doubts about the truthfulness of her rape story, to say the least. But this was not a major consideration. As with any good defense attorney, the guilt or innocence of the client was not a factor to Dowd in deciding whether to take the case.

There it was again: *the* question. The simple yet so deceptively complex question. The nagging, brooding question that never went away. How many times, at how many cocktail parties, had he patiently tried to answer that question? And after all the pat legal rhetoric, after all the condescending explanations, how many times had he asked himself the same question in the privacy of his own heart?

"How can you defend a guilty person?"

Some of the answers are taught in law school. Theoretical: Our adversary system of justice depends upon the effective presentation of evidence by *both* sides; without the resulting full spectrum of facts and arguments, the jury cannot make an informed decision. Functional: If guilty people cannot have lawyers, how can there be a trial? ("Guilty people shouldn't get trials." But who determines whether they are guilty to begin with?) Constitutional: Even guilty people have rights—and who will safeguard these rights if they have no lawyer? Personal: How can you, the lawyer, ever really *know* that the potential client is guilty? ("Because he *said* he was guilty." Fact: Twenty-eight individuals to date have "confessed" to being Los Angeles's "Hillside Strangler.") Pragmatic: Guilt is only one factor; the vast majority of cases involve a guilty plea, and the lawyer can be effective in seeking a fair and hopefully rehabilitative sentence. Professional: The American Bar Association's Canons of Ethics *tell* lawyers to represent the guilty.

These are valid answers. They satisfy the intellect. But they still leave a gnawing doubt deep in the gut.

Was Louann Fratt guilty of murder? Very possibly, but Dowd once again put this out of his mind as a factor in his decision. Did this woman *need* him? No: She could afford the best of the high-priced guns. Could he *win*—could he come out of the arena the victor? He knew his chances of winning an acquittal for Louann Fratt were slim.

But Michael G. Dowd decided to represent her. He decided to represent Louann Fratt for the oldest and most practical of reasons: money. Fighting lost causes was a pocket-draining pursuit. And the simple fact was that Dowd was nearly broke.

Now it was time to begin the long, tortuous process of getting ready for trial. Dowd began to prepare for battle.

Getting ready for trial means months of laborious, painstaking work—investigating events, locating and interviewing witnesses, discovering prosecution evidence, poring over voluminous reports and records, visiting the crime scene, researching esoteric legal issues, filing pretrial motions, preparing subpoenas, working out strategy and tactics, constructing direct and cross-examinations . . . the list goes on. And all the time carrying on with the pressing needs of other clients as well. The public only sees the criminal lawyer in trial, just as it only sees the boxer in the ring. It does not see the intense labor that precedes the battle. As with the boxer, victory in the arena for the lawyer is usually determined by long, tedious months of preparation.

Debbie Cohen walked into Dowd's office, carrying a slender file. A newly admitted attorney, Cohen was short, well-dressed, and with honey-blond hair cut very much like Louann Fratt's bob. She managed to appear both attractive and all business at the same time. Cohen had been working with Dowd ever since she had graduated from Emory University Law School in Atlanta. She had met him there during one of his periodic visits to teach students the fine points of trial advocacy. And she had known that this was the man she wanted to work for and learn from.

Dowd felt a strong obligation to contribute to the education of the next generation of lawyers. It was for this reason that he made the trips to Atlanta, and it was for this reason also that he accepted students from New York University's law school to work with him on his cases. Students working part time in the law school's Criminal Defense Clinic were farmed out to various prosecutorial agencies and Legal Aid offices, where they hoped to gain experience performing under the supervision of veteran prosecutors or defense attorneys. However, the clinic farmed out very few students to private attorneys, who tended to take advantage of the free labor by assigning the students menial clerical and research work. Dowd was one of the few to whom the clinic entrusted its students.

First things first, Dowd thought to himself. "You got the indictment?"

Cohen pulled a sheet of paper from the file, handed it to him. "Second degree," she said.

Dowd nodded. "Fifteen to twenty-five years." But she had probably already looked up the sentence. Second-degree murder. The intentional killing of a human being. Unlike most other states, New York law did not consider premeditation in determining the type of homicide involved. If the individual *intended* to kill the victim, or if she exhibited a "depraved indifference" toward whether the victim died or not, the charge was second-degree murder. This was raised to first-degree murder under certain limited circumstances, most commonly where the victim was a police officer. On the other hand, the offense was reduced to first-degree manslaughter if the intent was only to cause "great bodily injury"; if the death resulted from reckless conduct, the proper charge was second-degree manslaughter.

It was time to consider possible overall strategies.

"We could go for manslaughter," Dowd suggested.

"Try to show that she wasn't trying to kill her husband? Just trying to wound him?"

"Uh-huh. Might not be too tough. If the jury buys the beating. You got those photos?"

"Sure." Cohen pulled a few 8 × 10 black-and-white photographs from the file, handed them to Dowd.

Dowd studied each photo in turn. They were a series of

facial shots of Louann Fratt, each from a slightly different
perspective. The pictures had been taken by a criminal attorney, John Q. Kelly. Kelly had been called by Louann's son,
Poe Fratt, Jr., while his mother was being booked; he was
replaced by Dowd one week later. Some of the photos had
been taken three days after the incident, some six days later.
The photographs clearly showed a bruise on her right cheek
and another on the side of her head.

"The guy weighed about two twenty," Dowd said, still
looking at the pictures. "Former football player. Still not self-
defense, but a jury would be sympathetic to her. They could
go for intent to injure."

"What about *second*-degree manslaughter?"

"Reckless conduct?" He thought for a moment. "Maybe.
Swinging the knife around recklessly. No intent to kill or
injure, just trying to scare him away. And the knife accidentally . . ." He shook his head, grinning. "She accidentally
stabbed him—twice. In the neck, then in the back."

"I guess that's stretching it, huh?"

"Uh-huh. You reach too far, you lose credibility with the
jury. Then they don't believe you when you ask them to buy
the good stuff."

The young lawyer thought for a moment. "Well," she
asked finally, "what about the attempted rape? What about
self-defense?"

"The bad news is, nobody's going to believe her. First,
there's no corroboration. Second, she never said anything
about a rape to the cops. And third . . . well, she just doesn't
act like her husband tried to rape her."

"God, what's the *good* news?"

"If we present evidence of self-defense, we don't have the
burden of proof. Under New York law, the prosecution has
to *disprove* it—and they have to do it beyond a reasonable
doubt."

"That sounds pretty good."

"Not that good." Dowd leaned back in the green leather
chair. "Truth is, juries pretty much ignore nice legal distinc-
tions like burden of proof. Heck, they have enough trouble
getting presumption of innocence right. Nope, they're going
to expect us to *prove* the attempted rape."

Cohen thought again. "Anything on the husband? I mean, do we have a battered wife here?"

Dowd shook his head. "I don't think so." He thought back to his interview with Louann Fratt. That strange, unfeeling coldness. "Still . . . I think we ought to run her by Julie Blackman."

He punched the intercom button. "Jean?" he said into the speaker. "Would you get me Julie Blackman, please? Thanks."

Dr. Julie Blackman, professor of psychology at Sarah Lawrence College, formerly at Barnard College. The same Dr. Julie Blackman to whom he had been referred when he was struggling to find a way to defend Ann-Marie Brown. The same Dr. Julie Blackman who had been so invaluable in the Karen Straw trial. The same Dr. Julie Blackman who had become such a close friend when both were going through painful marital separations.

Dowd's mind drifted back to the Straw case as he waited to hear the psychologist's voice on the phone. . . .

It had taken Karen Straw three months before she could talk to Michael Dowd.

Karen had been charged with shoving a knife into the heart of her husband. Her trial for murder was scheduled to begin soon in the old courthouse on Sutphin Boulevard in Queens. But she could not talk to her attorney. She was frightened of him. He was a man.

Dowd was able to reconstruct the events that had led up to the killing with the help of a private investigator; the investigator's services were paid for by the Battered Women's Defense Committee in Manhattan. As usual, Dowd had agreed to take the case without a fee. And the facts followed the classic pattern that had by then become so familiar to him.

Karen and her husband, Tony Straw, had been married in 1981 and lived in a welfare apartment in Queens. During the next few years, he repeatedly beat her senseless. On one occasion, Tony grabbed a frozen chicken and smashed it in her face; on another, he loaded a gun and held it to her head, saying, "You're going to die." Karen's repeated calls to the police for help were ignored. She became increasingly fearful for the safety of her two children, aged ten and six.

In July 1986, a police officer found Karen crying on the stairs of her hotel building; her clothes were badly torn and she had been stabbed. He convinced her to file a complaint for assault against her husband. Reduced charges of "harassment" were brought against Tony, and the criminal court judge signed a two-month protective order.

But Tony ignored the order. He kept coming back, beating Karen up, tearing off her clothes, raping her, and then sitting down to smoke some crack. She again tried calling the police, but they would just tell Tony to "cool down" and then they would leave—and she would be beaten again. The system continued to fail Karen: the district attorney's office neglected to get the order extended, neglected to tell her of the expired order, neglected to carry through on the criminal case. And the beatings continued.

During the evening of December 18, 1986, her estranged husband again showed up at the apartment. He smoked crack and abused Karen throughout the night. At one point, Karen tried to escape. Tony caught her, threw her against a wall, and told her he was going to kill her. With a knife pointed at her throat, he told her to take off her clothes. Then, as her two terrified young children watched, he raped her.

During the early morning hours, Tony once again smoked some crack; Karen had fallen asleep on the spot from where he had told her not to move. She awoke, asked if she could leave. He told her he was tired of telling her what to do and began beating her again. He pushed her into the kitchen. A knife was lying on the counter. Frantically, Karen snatched up the knife before he could. He grabbed her, but she broke free and ran out into the hallway. He pulled her back in, but again she broke free. He came after her. And she plunged the knife into his chest.

Before trial, Dowd tried to get Queens District Attorney John Santucci to resubmit the case to the grand jury, offering to produce Karen to testify; this was refused. He then asked for a prison-free plea bargain. Santucci countered: Have Karen Straw testify in a closed hearing; if after reviewing the transcript he believed her, then some deal might be offered. Dowd refused: This would permit the prosecution to prepare for her cross-examination at trial, with no guarantee of a deal.

On the opening day of trial, the courtroom was packed with reporters and observers. Jury selection began—and Assistant D.A. Solomon Landa quickly set the tone of the prosecution with such questions to potential jurors as, "Don't you think there are women who *enjoy* being beaten up? What do you think they have those stores for in Manhattan, with whips and chains?"

It was at this point that Julie Blackman proved so invaluable. She sat next to Dowd during the jury selection process, framing questions for him to ask potential jurors in such a way that hidden biases were brought to the surface—biases that were critical in a case involving a wife who was charged with murdering her own husband.

During a recess in jury selection, Karen wept uncontrollably in the hallway, begging Dowd to let her plead guilty—to *anything*. Dowd was torn. As her attorney, he had to follow her wishes. Yet, he knew that this pathetic woman was incapable of making such a choice. But what if he lost the trial? Did he have a right to gamble with her life?

The trial continued. Witnesses paraded through, one after another, and Landa attacked Karen at every opportunity. At one point, the prosecutor asked a witness if she knew who had fathered one of Karen's children. Judge Lawrence Finnegan stopped the trial and summoned counsel into chambers. With a reporter taking down every word, he called Landa's question "despicable." Landa objected furiously. "It's in the record," the judge retorted. "And I'll say it again: It's despicable that you're conducting yourself in that way in this trial. There's only one thing you should be doing, standing up and dismissing this case in the interest of justice."

It now came time for Karen to take the stand. Dowd was hesitant. After he had finally gotten the woman to talk to him, he had been unable to get her to tell the entire story at one sitting. In trying to prepare her for trial, he had met with her more than a dozen times, and she had never been able to get through without breaking down and fleeing from his office. What would Landa do to her on cross-exam? Dowd hoped he had prepared the jury for this when, in his opening statement, he had told them that she was a timid and frightened little creature, and that the D.A. would destroy her on the stand

—that *he* would do to her exactly what her husband had done to her for years.

Karen took the witness stand. Hesitantly, in a barely audible whisper, the small, shy, fragile-looking woman answered Dowd's questions. She told of the beatings, the threats, the rapes. Landa interrupted throughout her testimony, saying he could not hear her; Judge Finnegan gently kept urging her to speak louder. Finally, Dowd got to the moment when Karen had killed Tony.

She broke down, could not speak. Gently, Dowd asked her to close her eyes, to remember the scene, to describe it. Karen closed her eyes. In a hushed courtroom, she began to stir. Jimmy Breslin later described the moving scene in his newspaper column:

> She was waving her hands to get the husband away from her, to get the knife away from her, to pull back from it all and run from it, from everything, and now her arms thrashed in front of her face and she stood up in the witness box with her head hanging in tears and her arms moving and she swung to the left and kept moving until she was completely turned around and now she tried to run through the wall.
>
> When Karen Straw's face came up against the brown wood wall, she tried to go to the left again, and now she was facing the judge and he had his hand out and he was saying softly, "Almost finished."
>
> Slowly, crying, Karen Straw, a young woman put through torment for no reason, turned to sit down in the witness chair again. . . .

In his closing argument, Landa ridiculed Karen Straw's credibility. Pointing out that she had testified Tony had smoked crack and then removed his pants before raping her, he said, "Here's a cracked-up guy, and here he is methodically taking off his pants." Dowd countered: "Tony Straw smelled like death, looked like death, and promised her only death. All she wanted to do was live."

Jury forewoman Concetta Liotta announced the verdict: "Not guilty." Many in the audience broke into tears; others cheered. Karen Straw stood with Dowd, weeping silently. Dowd asked the judge if she could address the jury. But Karen changed her mind. Reporters crowded in on her. "All I have to say is, I hope this helps other women," she said in a small, soft voice. "I want to go home to my kids now."

Dr. Julie Blackman's voice over the telephone brought Dowd back to the present.

"Michael? Michael?"

"Oh, Julie. Hi. How is everything?"

"Fine, Michael, but you got me in the middle of a meeting. What's up?"

"Look, probably not all that important. Let me call you later."

"No, no, really, what is it?"

"Well, it's a client. Killed her husband. He hits her, she knifes him. He may have tried to rape her, maybe not."

"A battered wife?" she asked.

"I don't think so. Not that kind of history. But . . . well, she seems a bit . . . odd when she talks about the whole thing."

"Odd?"

"Uh-huh, like she doesn't really care. No feeling, you know?"

"No feelings about killing her husband? Sounds like classic denial, repression."

"Anyway, thought it wouldn't hurt to have you check her out, see what you think. Maybe I'm missing something."

"Sure. Send her over."

"Thanks, Julie. Her name's Fratt. Louann Fratt."

"Oh, yes. I think I read about it. Have her give me a call. Got to go."

"Thanks, Julie." Dowd hung up, then looked over to Debbie Cohen. "Okay," he said, "let's get to work."

"The usual?"

"Uh-huh," he said, standing up.

"Anything special in the discovery motion?" Among other things, Cohen was going to prepare a motion requesting the court to order the D.A.'s office to turn over all evidence and material that could prove relevant to a defense in the case.

"Uh, let's see, don't forget the M.E." Dowd was anxious to

see the report of the medical examiner—called a coroner in most states—who had performed the autopsy. The report might tell him a lot about how Poe Fratt had died that night. For example, what was the angle of the knife's entry? This could indicate the positions Louann and her husband were in at the time of the stabbings. And did the corpse have scratch marks on its face?

"Got it."

"And the tapes—I want any tapes of the nine-one-one call our client made. They usually tape those things. And not just transcripts—I want copies of the tape itself, or access to the original." He wanted to know if Louann had possibly mentioned the attempted rape. And he wanted to hear her voice: Had she sounded as calm and unfeeling as she had during their meeting?

"Right."

"I'm late," Dowd said, grabbing for his rumpled coat. "I'm due at Poe Fratt's apartment in half an hour."

CHAPTER 5

$\mathbf{M}$iraculously, Dowd found a parking space on Seventy-eighth Street just off Central Park and pulled his car into the curb.

The car was a cantankerous steel monster that sucked oil by the case and periodically refused to start. Dowd hated fighting the horrendous traffic and parking problems of Manhattan; no New Yorker in his right mind tries to negotiate his way around the island in a car. But there was no easy way to get to and from his home in the middle-class suburb of Queens known as Bayside. So Dowd had to commute by car every day, slipping into traffic on the Clearview Expressway early in the morning. From there, he connected with the Cross Island Parkway, on over to the Whitestone Expressway, then along Grand Central Parkway past La Guardia Airport to the Brooklyn-Queens Expressway. Finally, he crawled over the Williamsburg Bridge and wound his way through the teeming streets of Manhattan toward his office in Soho. Delancey Street to Lafayette, right on Broome, again on Crosby, and finally to Spring. Once safely parked, Dowd abandoned the Detroit nightmare and happily rode the subways. Until evening. Then, usually around 6:30 or 7:00, he began the long, tortuous journey back home.

Home, Dowd realized as he got out of the car and locked the door, was still two hours away. It had been a long day and he was tired, really tired. He was looking forward to the end of the day, to stretching out on the big overstuffed sofa with a can of beer. Of course, friends were coming over for dinner, and Irene would do a slow boil if he was late. But if he hurried, he could take a few notes at the murder scene and still just make it home for dinner. With a little luck. Anyway, it was too late to change plans; Dowd had already arranged for an officer from the Nineteenth Precinct to let him in.

The lawyer walked east on Seventy-eighth toward Madison Avenue. It was a small, pleasant area, lined with carefully manicured trees and sedate brownstone apartment buildings. Like the Seventy-ninth of Louann Fratt's palatial home, it was a quiet, gracious residential enclave, reeking of discreet wealth. It was a world that was alien to Dowd, a world very far removed from the ghettos and tenements that were home to the battered women he defended. In the world of Park Avenue, the women were respected and pampered.

Dowd again thought of his own home as he walked along the gracefully aging brownstones, of the small two-bedroom red brick condo in a middle-class section of Queens. He thought of Irene, home now from a day of keeping a tight lid on a class of rambunctious fifth graders in Flushing. Firm, efficient, no-nonsense Irene. She would be cooking dinner about now, or maybe changing the baby's diaper. Or calmly listening to her eighteen-year-old daughter's latest romantic disaster while trying to fix a leaky faucet.

He had met Irene McCaffrey three years earlier, and had been immediately attracted to the slender thirty-six-year-old woman with the green eyes and shoulder-length ash-blond hair. But he soon learned that this was a very different kind of woman than he had known before, a bright, strong-willed, feisty woman who liked men but did not *need* them. And it was a very different kind of relationship that soon developed, without the fiery, passionate beginning that he had known, a passion that gradually cooled over the years, leaving little in its place. Dowd found that he respected this woman, that he enjoyed her company, and that the passion slowly grew.

They were married later that year. Within months, Irene was pregnant. The pregnancy had been a surprise, but the new baby had brought them even closer together. At forty-six years of age, Michael Dowd had found a new life.

Dowd arrived at Madison Avenue, stood waiting at the traffic light. Was it coincidence? he wondered as he stood there. Was it an accident that he had fallen in love with a strong, emotionally independent person soon after confronting his own attitudes about the oppression of women? No, the battered wife cases had had a tremendous impact. He thought again of Irene's independence, her strength—the things that made her so attractive, so sexy. Ten years ago, he knew, he would have felt threatened by these same traits. He had come a long way, he thought to himself. He had a lot to thank Ann-Marie Brown for.

As he waited for the light to change, Dowd again pictured the likely scene that awaited him at the small red brick condo in Queens: Irene rushing around making last-minute preparations for dinner, frowning at him for being late. His step-daughter loudly sulking over a tragic love. The baby bawling for yet another diaper change. The telephone ringing with worried calls from Dowd's clients.

It was home, and he had never been happier.

Dowd crossed Park Avenue, continued along Seventy-eighth Street. There, on the right, was number 52. Another narrow brownstone, with gray brick walls rising twelve floors high. He walked up the granite steps leading to a concrete Gothic arched doorway. A badly overweight uniformed officer was standing there, eating a candy bar.

"You Dowd?" he asked, bored.

"Uh-huh."

"You got I.D.?"

Dowd pulled out his wallet, showed the officer his state bar card. The officer glanced at the card, took a last bite out of the partially wrapped candy bar, and stuffed it in his pocket. He turned and unlocked the front door. Dowd followed him in.

The officer opened the elevator and the two men got in.

They rode in silence up to the ninth floor. When they stepped out of the elevator, Dowd found himself looking directly across the corridor at the door of an apartment. A police crime scene tape was spread across the door. Apartment 9B. The apartment where Poe Fratt had lived. And died.

The officer pulled the tape down and unlocked the door. He stepped aside. "After you, Counselor."

Dowd walked into the apartment.

The front door opened onto a small studio apartment. To his immediate left was a door leading to the bathroom. In front of him was a modest, spartan kitchen. To the right was a combination living room-bedroom. A round table and a small desk sat against the far wall; books and papers were stacked and strewn along the floor. A bureau stood flush against the near wall, with a couch jutting out next to it. Between these two walls was a third wall, dominated by a large window facing out onto the street. A couch stood against the wall under the window, with a foldout bed extending into the middle of the room. The bed, half covered with a comforter, had not been made up since it had last been used. Spread across the top of the comforter was a large, brownish stain: Poe Fratt's blood.

Directly in front of Dowd, on the carpeted floor between the front door and the kitchen, were more brown stains, but much larger. Drawn across the spreading stains was a white chalked outline of where a body had once lain. The arms were stretched out and above the head, as if desperately reaching for the door. A trail of brownish spots led from the chalked outline back to the bed.

Carefully, Dowd stepped around the outline and walked toward the bed. He looked around the eerily silent apartment. It seemed small for such a wealthy man as Poe Fratt, small and simply furnished. The plain, functional furniture, probably supplied by the landlord, was a sharp contrast to the elegant furnishings of the co-op on Seventy-ninth. And the apartment seemed almost claustrophobic compared to the open spaces of Poe Fratt's former home.

What bothered Dowd was that the apartment appeared fairly neat. Except for the books and papers on the floor, everything seemed normal and in place. It did not look like the scene of a violent fight, of an attempted rape and a multiple stabbing. Why weren't chairs knocked over? Why weren't objects lying all over the place?

Dowd walked into the kitchen. A bachelor's kitchen —clean, fairly orderly, unused. The bottle of wine that Louann had mentioned still sat on the counter: a 1986 Clos du Bois. The sides of the bottle were dusted with white powder. The fingerprint boys had been busy.

Dowd left the kitchen, poked his head into the plain, functional bathroom. Comb, toothbrush, toothpaste, shampoo, razor, soiled towel—it looked as if the occupant had just stepped out and would be back in a few minutes.

Dowd returned to the front room. It seemed so odd. Like the bathroom, as if everything had suddenly stopped, frozen in time, preserved forever in a crystal-clear aspic.

Why had Poe Fratt ended the marriage? Why had he abandoned his wife after thirty years? Was there another woman? Why had Louann Fratt come to this apartment so late that night? Had she really brought the eight-inch knife to defend herself against muggers on the streets—or against Poe Fratt? Or was the knife brought here for a very different reason than protection? How had she felt about being dumped after thirty years of marriage? Had Poe Fratt really tried to rape his own wife that night? If so, why had she never mentioned it to the police? How could such a small, frail, older woman manage to stab to death a 220-pound former football player? And why did Louann Fratt seem so . . . indifferent in recalling the rape and murder?

"About done here, Counselor?" the officer asked impatiently, standing just inside the doorway. He was again chewing on the candy bar.

"Uh-huh," Dowd replied. He took one last look around the front room.

What had happened in this empty, silent room that night? What had taken place between this man and this woman who had shared their lives for thirty years? A man and a woman who had once loved one another? Who had given birth to three children, had been a family? What had gone so wrong, so terribly, tragically, violently wrong?

Only two people knew. And one was dead.

CHAPTER 6

Dowd climbed the first set of dirty concrete steps leading up from the noisy, harshly lit caverns of the subway. He felt the familiar edge of claustrophobia as he followed the flow of the mob up the stairs and then down a narrow corridor lined with torn posters and spray-painted graffiti. A thunderous sound in the distance began to echo through the corridor, growing quickly into an almost deafening roar, then suddenly subsiding.

He continued along with the stream of humanity, unable to move any faster or slower. He almost stumbled over a figure lying on the ground; the man was dressed in filthy rags, curled up on his side and apparently asleep. Or dead. Dowd could glance only for a moment before being pushed along the hurrying crowd toward a second series of trash-strewn steps. Such sights were common in Manhattan, of course, but Dowd never quite got used to them. He always felt a sharp ache of sorrow. And guilt.

He finally emerged onto Canal Street. Like other New Yorkers, he had become inured to the discomfort and dangers of subway travel. But there was still the sense of relief, of escape, that came with surfacing into the open air.

Canal Street. The open vein of Chinatown. A teeming mass of Oriental humanity packed into a warren of crowded tenements and frantic commerce. Canal Street, lined with hundreds of tiny storefronts, their windows jammed with designer luggage, crisply roasted ducks hanging from hooks, stacks of Calvin Klein jeans, boxes of Chanel No. 5, slippery rows of strange-looking fish. Sidewalks filled with crowds milling around folding tables spilling over with high-tech toys, fake and stolen Rolexes, Asian vegetables. Hawkers yelling out their wares. Cars honking. Always the crowd moving, pushing, flowing. Ordered chaos.

Walk along Canal through Chinatown for two more blocks and you cross Mulberry Street. Turn left there and you suddenly leave the Orient and find yourself in Little Italy, an enclave of Italian restaurants and businesses slowly being pushed farther north by the crush of the Chinese. Two or three more blocks and you hit the Bowery.

But Dowd turned right on Centre Street, then walked two blocks to the towering, darkly ominous granite monolith that was so familiar to him. He stopped. There was a foreboding, slightly malevolent aura to the towering old building. The cold, massive blocks of gray granite, pitted and blackened by half a century of pollution, rose ominously from narrow, dirty streets high into the downtown skyline. Below, lying at the foot of this grim structure, were two large entrances, each recessed deeply into the surrounding stone in a way that gave the approaching visitor a feeling of being swallowed.

It was here, in this cheerless monument, where society opened its eyes to the violence men do. It was here where the torn and the violated came to relive their pain publicly. It was here where the predators were accused, paraded, and finally damned.

This was Manhattan's Criminal Courts Building.

It was here where Louann Fratt would be tried for murder.

Dowd walked over to a hot dog cart in front of the building, ordered a hot potato knish. He was late and he had missed lunch. The vendor reached into the steaming box on wheels and handed the knish to the lawyer. Dowd paid, then began wolfing down the Jewish version of the Irish national food.

He looked up the broad steps leading to the twin arched entrances. Chiseled into the dark stone, above the little people filing meekly into the building's inner sanctum, were somber warnings: "Be just and fear not"; "Where law ends there tyranny begins"; "Every place is safe to him who lives in justice." The old building had always reminded Dowd of the "Ministry of Justice" in George Orwell's *1984*.

If you continued on down Centre, past the Criminal Courts Building, bearing to the left, you would enter the gothic wealth of Wall Street. The heart of the world's financial body. Chinatown on a grander, more dignified scale. Bear to the right off Centre instead, past the old City Hall, across the shabby reach of Broadway, and a much more modern world of commerce opens up. At its heart, with the largest shopping mall in New York City buried in the ground beneath it, were the twin slabs of glass known as the World Trade Center.

Chinatown, Little Italy, the Bowery, Wall Street, Broadway. The Criminal Courts Building stood in the center of these strange neighbors, towering over them like a dark threat.

However, Dowd's business today was not in the Criminal Courts Building. It was in the next structure on Centre Street, the old New York State Office Building. Separating these two towering behemoths and sandwiched tightly between them, almost hidden from notice in their shadows, was a tiny street—more an alley—called Hogan Place, named after a onetime district attorney. To the left was a small side door leading into the Criminal Courts Building. This was a private entrance, leading to separate elevators up to the district attorney's office. But the D.A.'s office had grown too large: Crime was a growth industry. So the offices had spilled over into leased space in the state building. And it was there where Dowd's business lay. It was there where he would meet the man who would prosecute Louann Fratt.

Dowd walked across the street to the state building, up the steps and into the high-ceilinged lobby. He rushed to an open elevator and squeezed himself into the crowd just as the doors closed.

When they opened again, he found himself on a floor filled with a maze of cubicles. Each office was separated by smoked-glass partitions that rose halfway to the high ceiling. A small table stood directly in front of him. Behind it, a short, muscular young man in a white shirt and tie sat reading a book. Dowd walked up to the table.

The man continued reading the book.

"Excuse me," Dowd said.

"Yeah?" the young man said finally, looking up. "Waddya want?"

"Assistant D.A. Daniel Brownell," Dowd said. The man returned to his book. "Down the hall, to your left," he said, once again oblivious to the lawyer.

Dowd grinned, then walked down a corridor between two rows of partitions, his shoes echoing along the highly polished floor. There were two nameplates on the third door. One of them read "D. Brownell, ADA." Dowd knocked.

"Come in," a voice said.

Dowd opened the door and stepped inside. It was a small office, with two desks. One of the desks was empty. Behind the other one was a young man in a dark blue suit. The man looked up, studied the lawyer for a brief moment.

"Michael Dowd," the big Irishman said.

The man rose from his desk. "Daniel Brownell," he said very seriously, shaking Dowd's hand. "Please," he said, indicating an empty chair in front of the desk.

"Thanks." Dowd sat down.

It was that awkward time when you first met your opponent. The politeness, the formalities, the feeling out. Very civilized. Very professional. But behind it, two hired guns coldly assessing each other for a coming showdown. Who was this man? How fast was he on the draw? How good a shot? What were his nerves like? Could he be bluffed? Was he battle-weary? Where were the weaknesses?

"Let's see," Brownell said, looking around his desk in vain, "I can't seem to find the judge's order."

"Here," Dowd said, handing him a copy of the discovery order. *No, I do not come unprepared. You cannot rely upon that in our battle to come.*

"Yeah, thanks," Brownell said, taking the order. Debbie Cohen had filed a motion in court, asking the judge to order the D.A. to turn over potential evidence. The judge had granted most of these requests and issued an order. Brownell now leaned back in his chair, pretending to review once again the list of items in the order.

Daniel Brownell was a tall, slender, strikingly handsome young man with dark, sharply angular features, jet black hair, and piercing olive-green eyes. The brooding intensity of his face was matched by a deadly seriousness, almost a lack of any sense of humor. He had graduated from Fordham Law School and, like Dowd an idealist at heart, became a Legal Aid lawyer. But reality soon set in. Tired of defending the refuse of New York on an unending series of drug charges, he switched sides and began prosecuting his former clients. The true hired gun.

"You thought about a plea?" Brownell asked casually, still pretending to read the order.

"Sure."

"Yeah?" He looked up at Dowd.

"Disturbing the peace. I think she'd go for that."

A wry smile from Brownell.

"What'd you have in mind?" Dowd countered.

Brownell shrugged. "Plead straight up. Go easy at sentence."

"Hell of a deal," Dowd said, grinning. The opening offer was no offer at all: The D.A. would remain silent when it came time to pass sentence, leaving the matter entirely up to the judge. Of course, if their case was as strong as it looked, that might be the best they would offer.

"So . . . what's your client looking for?" Brownell asked with feigned disinterest.

"Hadn't really thought about it," Dowd lied.

"Yeah."

"Manslaughter two. Maybe. I'd have to run it by her, of course."

Brownell laughed. "Manslaughter two. Right. And a pat on the butt."

The two men continued to spar like that, feeling each other out as they casually discussed the fate of a human being much like they would the price of a used car. This was the evil known as "plea bargaining." Born of necessity—of the simple, unavoidable truth that the criminal courts could no longer handle the tidal wave of crime. The answer: justice through barter. Let's make a deal. Two rapes for the price of one.

In this case, however, neither man had any expectation of reaching an agreement on a plea. And both knew it. The D.A.'s case was too strong to give up very much. And it was a high-profile case: The newspapers would be closely monitoring any developments. Finally, Dowd had won too many highly publicized murder cases; the Fratt case was the perfect vehicle for evening the score. It was unlikely, then, that Brownell's superiors would authorize any worthwhile offers.

Louann Fratt would go to trial.

"Well," Brownell continued, "bounce it off your client, Mr. Dowd. She might want to think about it."

"I'll do that."

"She's facing a lot of time. At her age . . . probably the rest of her life."

That sobering thought had already occurred to Dowd. But this was no time to show weakness. "Or an acquittal," he countered.

"She carries a butcher knife over to the guy's apartment . . . at two in the morning . . . stabs him three times. Then spills her guts to the police. Fingerprints all over the knife . . . bloody footprints in the apartment." A slight smile crossed his face. "I don't see an acquittal."

Three times? Louann had stabbed her husband *three* times? "You never know," Dowd said, his eyes twinkling but his brain processing the new fact. Bluff. Probe for weaknesses. Lay smoke. Fish for information.

Dowd was beginning to get an uncomfortable feeling. He had asked around about Brownell, of course. The word was that he was not very experienced—maybe a dozen felony trials, give or take. But he had done well in them. Well prepared, thorough, a plodder—but an effective plodder. Honest, ethical. Now, seeing him in person, he could sense in Brownell a calm, low-keyed, sincere manner. This added to Dowd's worries. He would much rather go up against the flashy, aggressive, ambitious, fire-breathing type of prosecutor commonly found in the D.A.'s office. Contrary to Hollywood wisdom, juries are swayed more by sincerity than cleverness. Brownell was deceptive. He would be tough.

The young assistant D.A. was studying his opponent as well. He had heard about Michael G. Dowd. His string of "battered woman" victories was common knowledge in the office. But just as common was knowledge of a darker side of Dowd. And it was this darker side that Brownell was recalling now as front-page headlines in *The New York Times* drifted back from the past, announcing that Queens Borough President Donald R. Manes had committed suicide, stabbing himself in the heart with a kitchen knife. . . .

It was 1979, and Dowd and his law partner, Albert Pennisi, occupied offices over a corner drugstore in Kew Gardens, across from the Queens Criminal Court Building. The two men were putting in long hours, handling everything from drafting wills to defending murderers, slowly building up their practice to the point where Dowd could finally afford to buy a small house for his family in Queens. He had recently returned to his wife after a painful separation, determined to make the marriage succeed for the sake of their fourteen-year-old daughter.

One day Pennisi came to Dowd with a business proposition that had been presented to him. A man named Pat Miranda owned a small collection agency called Computrace, Inc. Although the business had been only marginally profitable, the city of New York was giving out lucrative contracts to collect on millions of dollars in unpaid parking tickets. A contract could mean hundreds of thousands of dollars in commissions, and Miranda was confident he could win one. His proposition: In exchange for their providing him with office space, Miranda would give the two men stock in the small company.

Dowd and Pennisi talked it over. Dowd was a terrible businessman, and he knew it. And their fledgling law firm was just beginning to get on its feet. Still, there was plenty of space above the drugstore for a small office. And if Miranda was successful in getting one of the contracts, the shares would prove a good investment; if he was not, the only loss would be a temporary inconvenience. The two men agreed to the deal.

Miranda soon made good on his word: Computrace was

the smallest of eleven companies to land a contract with New York City's Parking Violations Bureau. Despite the contract, however, Miranda began to lose money. The sudden increase in business meant a big increase in overhead; employees had to be hired, computer systems installed. Yet, the long delays in getting paid commissions from the city created a cash-flow problem—and mounting debts.

Miranda went to Dowd and Pennisi with another proposition: In exchange for their covering the debts, he would give them still more stock in the company. The two lawyers talked it over. Dowd was beginning to get a vaguely uncomfortable feeling; he had a family to support, a mortgage to meet, and the overhead of the law office to cover. However, Miranda did have the contract with the city, and it seemed merely a matter of time before the commissions began rolling in. It was an investment, he decided finally, and probably a pretty safe one. Eventually, they agreed to the deal.

Dowd's sense of discomfort soon turned to outright nervousness as his savings were quickly eaten up by Miranda's company. And the cash-flow problem continued. He and his partner were soon faced with a tough decision: personally co-sign a bank loan for Computrace to keep it afloat—or watch the company go bankrupt and lose all the money they had invested. Agonizing for days, Dowd finally chose along with Pennisi to co-sign, guaranteeing the loan with his family's new house as collateral.

Over the next two years, the two men continued to co-sign loans and sink the law firm's profits into Computrace until finally each held 41 percent of the company's stock. By this time they were no longer just passive investors; as majority stockholders, they had become increasingly liable for the agency's debts. The "investment" was rapidly turning into a pit of quicksand. Still, the city contract offered the hope of eventual profits.

The turnaround finally came late in 1981: Computrace was at last beginning to operate in the black. Dowd began to breathe a little easier.

Then, in the spring of 1982, Dowd had lunch with an old friend, Sheldon Chevlowe. Chevlowe was a Queens bail bondsman who had been appointed a city marshal and then assigned to the Parking Violations Bureau. Obviously embarrassed, Chevlowe suddenly told Dowd that if he wanted to continue getting the city's business, he'd "have to take care of some people"—to the tune of 5 percent of gross traffic ticket collections. "Look, Mike," he continued, "it's not me. But either you do it or you're out of business."

Dowd was stunned. He thought about it over the next few days, thought about the financial situation he was in. All of his savings had been poured into keeping Computrace afloat. The agency was finally beginning to make a profit. Without the city contract, however, the business would quickly fail—and Dowd and his partner would be left with huge debts to pay. His office furniture would be seized and the house that had been promised as collateral would be lost. He and his family would be out on the street.

Dowd anguished for days, then finally decided with Pennisi to pay the price of doing business with city government. It was a decision that was later to cost him dearly.

After that, Chevlowe would visit Dowd at his office, receiving envelopes filled with cash. Dowd did not yet know to whom the payments were going.

In May of 1983, Chevlowe died of cancer. At his funeral, Dowd was approached for the first time by Donald Manes, one of the most powerful men in New York City politics. Manes quietly told him that Geoffrey "Jeff" Lindenauer would be taking Chevlowe's place; Lindenauer was deputy director of the Parking Violations Bureau. One week later, Lindenauer met with Dowd and, over the next year and a half, collected payments totaling more than $30,000.

Dowd became increasingly uncomfortable with the payoffs. As he later told his friend author Peter Maas, "I didn't want a foot on my throat for the rest of my life; I couldn't stomach it anymore."

In January 1985, Dowd stopped paying Lindenauer and refused to take his calls. He met with Manes and told him he wasn't going to pay anymore. Manes tried to get him to change his mind on a number of occasions over the next few months, but Dowd was firm.

In December 1985, Lindenauer came to Dowd and tried again to squeeze him, telling him that the city was terminating

Computrace's contract if he did not make payments. Dowd refused.

At about this time, the U.S. attorney for Manhattan, Rudolph Giuliani, began an investigation into various corrupt practices in New York City government. Then, on January 11, 1986, the front pages of New York newspapers carried a strange story: Manes had been found by police in his car near Shea Stadium at 1:50 A.M.—with his wrist slashed. Manes claimed at the time that he had been kidnapped and wounded; eleven days later, he admitted to a suicide attempt.

Four days after the attempted suicide, Lindenauer was arrested on charges that he had extorted $5,000 in bribes from a large collection agency, Citisource, Inc. Citisource's director and one of its major stockholders was Stanley M. Friedman, the reigning Democratic power broker in the Bronx.

Dowd was advised by friends to stay out of it. There was nothing to indicate that either Manes or Dowd was under investigation. Accusing Manes would be dangerous: He was a powerful man with many influential friends, including Mayor Ed Koch. And Dowd had no evidence other than his own word.

Dowd agonized. Then he made his decision. On January 22, he went to Giuliani and told him everything—the first evidence linking Manes to the extortion. The story broke two days later; Dowd found his picture on the front page of *The New York Times*. On February 10, Dowd testified before a federal grand jury; Manes resigned as borough president the next day.

Lindenauer was indicted on the strength of Dowd's testimony. Giuliani began pressuring Lindenauer to testify against Manes in exchange for a deal; he badly needed corroboration for Dowd's unsupported testimony. On March 11, Lindenauer finally agreed to testify. Two days later, Manes killed himself.

The investigation continued—leading, eventually, to the Wedtech scandal. Friedman, along with three others, was indicted. The trial was moved to New Haven, where Giuliani prepared to try his first case since he had taken office three years earlier. His first witness: Michael G. Dowd. On November 25, Friedman and the others were convicted under the RICO statute of racketeering and conspiracy.

Giuliani praised Dowd for his courage in stepping forward. Jimmy Breslin wrote in his column: "Only Mike Dowd stepped up and shook his city." But Dowd was still scarred by the experience—the threats, the accusations, the fear, the long, sleepless nights. It is difficult to appreciate the danger of a grizzly bear once it lies dead at your feet: Manes had been a powerful man—no one knew just how powerful. If that power had reached into the U.S. attorney's office, Dowd would have been destroyed.

The experience has changed him. In a 1988 newspaper profile, a reporter commented: "Almost three years after he gave federal prosecutors the evidence that helped expose the scandal, Dowd has remade his life as the legal defender of women accused of domestic violence." However, attorney Brian O'Dwyer scoffed at that suggestion: "Mike Dowd doesn't need redemption from anything. He's a hell of a lawyer who's spent a good portion of his life giving his time to activist causes." In that same profile, Dowd gave his own view of the change: "Twelve years ago I wanted to be famous. Now all I care about is trying my cases and being with my wife and family."

As events were later to prove, however, the power brokers of New York were not going to forget Michael G. Dowd.

Brownell continued studying the big Irishman. "I really don't see it, Mr. Dowd. Self-defense?" He shook his head. "You're going to need more than those bruises on her head."

So the police reports *did* mention the presence of bruises. Or maybe Brownell even had photos, taken soon after the arrest—not days later, as with John Kelly's pictures.

"I don't see a jury buying it," Brownell continued. Was this prosecutor trying to argue for a plea? Or was he just trying to undermine Dowd's confidence? "Not when she takes the knife over there with her. And the bruises just indicate she got hit with a fist. He could have been defending himself against the knife attack. Anyway, you know there has to be deadly force. And there's nothing to show the victim used any deadly force against her."

Dowd continued smiling, as if he knew a great secret. Keep smiling. Don't let him know you're drowning.

Brownell stared at him in silence. "Battered wife syndrome," he said simply.

Dowd winked at him.

Brownell shook his head in disgust. "You can go to the well just so many times."

The young prosecutor reached down, pulled out a thick file from his desk drawer, set it on the desk. He muttered to himself as he began rifling through the file. "Let's see. Autopsy, yeah . . . police reports, yeah . . . field notes . . ."

Dowd watched Brownell as he sorted through the file, looking for the items he had been ordered to turn over. If he could get this D.A. to think that this was yet another of Dowd's battered wife cases . . . If he could get him to concentrate his efforts on preparing for a nonexistent defense . . .

"You know," Brownell continued, still looking through the file, "I've already talked with the kids. Your client's children." He looked up, met Dowd's gaze. "Louann Fratt was no battered wife. No way."

Dowd just continued his knowing grin. But he knew he was not the only one hiding his cards. What was the *motive* in this case? What did Brownell intend to prove was the *reason* Louann murdered her husband? Money? Abandonment? Technically, of course, motive was irrelevant. To get a conviction for murder, the prosecutor only had to prove two things: a killing and an intent to kill. Motive was not an element of the "corpus delicti"—the "body," or technical elements, of the crime. But the simple reality was that few juries would convict without proof of motive.

What was the D.A.'s evidence of *why* Louann killed her husband? It was a question that was to haunt Dowd. It was a question that would not be answered until halfway through the trial.

"Well," Brownell said, "I'll expect notice." The prosecutor was referring to a New York law requiring attorneys to give advance written notice to their opponents if they intended to offer any psychiatric or psychological expert witnesses. This was intended to give the opponent a chance to prepare for cross-examination and to find expert witnesses of his own. Certainly, if Dowd intended to present a battered-wife-syndrome defense, it would have to rely heavily upon such expert testimony—and he would have to give formal notice to the D.A. The sanction for failing to give notice was that the expert testimony simply could not be used in trial. When the deadline for notice came and passed, Brownell would know that the defense would not be battered wife syndrome. Until then, however, maybe Dowd could lure Brownell into sniffing along false trails.

"Here," Brownell said, pushing a stack of documents across the desk. "I think that's all of it."

"Photos?"

"Yeah, they're in there. Oh . . ." Brownell stood, walked across the room to a table. On top of the table was a small tape recorder. "The nine-one-one call . . ."

Louann Fratt's phone call to the police. As Dowd suspected, it had been taped. And now he would hear it. He would hear his client confess to murder. "Can I get a transcript later?"

"Yeah," Brownell said, threading the tape into the machine, "I'll have one of the secretaries transcribe it."

Dowd tried not to appear too interested. But the simple fact was that the tape was critical evidence. Brownell was not expecting a self-defense case. Since he apparently knew nothing of an attempted rape, Louann had been correct in telling him that she had not mentioned it during the call. What was critical, however, was *how her voice sounded* on the tape. The jury would be listening to this same recording, probably at a dramatic moment during the trial. Would she sound like a terrified woman—a woman who had just been forced to stab her own husband to death to defend herself against a brutal rape? Or would she sound like a cold, calculating, uncaring murderer—as she had in Dowd's office?

The voice on the tape would be the jury's window into Louann Fratt's heart.

Brownell finished making adjustments to the tape recorder. "Ready?" he asked.

"Uh-huh," Dowd replied, sounding bored.

Brownell turned on the machine, then stood there as the tape played. He was carefully watching the expression on Dowd's face.

Dowd tried to look only vaguely interested as the woman's

voice came out of the speaker. But he could feel his heart beginning to pound faster, harder.

"Police?" the voice said. "I've stabbed my husband. I believe he's dead. . . ."

The voice of Louann Fratt. The calm, cool, unemotional voice of Louann Fratt.

CHAPTER 7

T he tall, dark-haired woman was waiting for Dowd when he got back to his office.

Dowd stepped out of the elevator and spotted Dr. Julie Blackman seated in the reception area. "Oh, my God!" he said, slamming his forehead with the palm of his hand.

The woman rose from her chair, smiling. "One of these days you really should get organized, Michael," she said gently.

"Oh, my God!" he repeated. "I'm sorry, Julie. I am so sorry. I . . ." He looked down helplessly at the stack of papers under his arm. "I got tied up at the D.A.'s office, getting this stuff, and I . . . I just forgot!"

"It's all right," she said, still smiling in amusement. "It's really all right. I needed the break."

Dowd dropped the papers on the receptionist's desk, then met Blackman's eyes for a long moment. They stepped toward each other, arms out, and hugged in a warm embrace.

"How are you, Michael?" Blackman asked finally.

Dowd smiled, nodded. "Fine, Julie. You?"

She nodded also, the smile spreading into a happy grin.

"C'mon," he said, waving toward his office. "Let's talk."

Blackman picked up a slim burgundy leather briefcase and walked into Dowd's office. Dowd turned to the young receptionist. "Any messages?"

The woman handed him a stack of message slips. Without reading them, Dowd stuffed the slips into a coat pocket and followed the psychologist into his office.

Blackman grinned again. "Married life suits you, Michael."

"Irene keeps me in line." Dowd dumped the stack of papers on the desk, then took off his coat and threw it in a pile on a chair. He lighted up a cigarette, sat down, and looked across the desk at his close friend.

Dr. Julie Blackman was very tall and very slender, with long, dark brown hair that hung straight down below her shoulders. She wore plain-rimmed glasses and a drab blue and white print challis dress. She was in her early thirties, but her height, thin, angular features, and plain clothes gave the impression of a gangly, somewhat homely schoolgirl. Sadly, though, the schoolgirl look was marred by a grotesque hunching in her left shoulder, the result of an unknown disease that had attacked the nerves in her neck eight years earlier. Despite this deformity, Julie Blackman was a woman who radiated warmth and gentleness. It was Julie Blackman who had gotten Dowd through the pain of his separation and eventual divorce from his first wife. Later, Dowd had been able to return the kindness when the psychologist had entered a painful period in her own life.

"How does it look?" she asked.

Dowd shrugged. "The D.A.'s got a pretty solid case. A midnight visit, a dead body, a murder weapon, prints everywhere—all nicely wrapped up with a confession." He paused. "Only thing . . ."

"Yes?"

"The motive. I can't figure out what the D.A.'s going to come up with for a motive. A woman scorned, maybe—revenge for leaving her after thirty years? Money? There was a life insurance policy, a couple hundred grand. And the property they were fighting over was worth a few million. But I can't see that . . ." He looked at Blackman. "You've seen Louann Fratt three times now, right?"

"Yes."

"Okay, why *did* she kill her husband?"

"She says her husband was trying to rape her, Michael."

"Do you believe her?"

Blackman thought for a moment. "Yes, I do."

"You know there's no corroboration."

She nodded.

"And she never told the police—never told anyone until she saw me a week later."

"So you've said."

"And . . ." He shook his head slowly. "I mean . . . She doesn't *sound* like she . . . like her husband had been trying to rape her. God, when she talks about the incident, the stabbing and all, she sounds like she's ordering a ham and cheese to go."

"What's she supposed to sound like, Michael?" the psychologist asked softly.

"Well, I guess I expect her to sound a little . . . *upset* when she's reliving the incident. Someone who's stabbed her husband to death after he beat her up and tried to rape her—well, I think I'd expect a little emotion."

"You've never been raped."

"No. No, and I've never killed anyone, either. But I have clients who have, and they usually show a little feeling when they talk about it."

"Michael, let me make a suggestion."

"Sure."

"I've only seen Louann for evaluation purposes, but it seemed to me that she needed help. I think she was repressing the whole incident. And . . . there's something else going on deep inside her. I don't exactly know what. Anyway, I referred her for therapy to another psychologist. A Dr. Marsha Rosen, on the staff at St. Luke's. Louann's already started seeing her."

"Dr. Marsha Rosen," Dowd repeated, writing the name down. "St. Luke's."

"She has a small office on the Upper East Side. You might want to give her a call. She'll have a much better picture of what's going on inside of Louann."

"Uh-huh."

Blackman grinned. "Keep an open mind, Michael."

"I just hope the *jury* will keep an open mind." He thought for a moment. "I'll tell you, Julie . . . If Louann Fratt takes the stand and tells those twelve people sitting in that box . . . if she tells them about the rape and the killing the same way she told me . . ."

"Yes, I see. What about keeping her off the stand? She doesn't have to testify, does she?"

"No," Dowd said pensively. "No, she doesn't have to testify. She has a Fifth Amendment right. And the judge will instruct the jury that they can't infer anything from her not testifying."

"So?"

"So the jury will ignore the judge."

"But why would the jury—"

"Julie, no matter what the judge says, the jurors are going to be thinking, 'If she's innocent, why's she afraid to testify? What's she trying to hide?' And no legal niceties like the Fifth Amendment are going to change that simple fact."

"I see."

"Louann has to take the stand. She has to tell the jury what happened that night." Dowd paused. "Anyway, she's the only witness. There's no other way of getting in evidence about the attempted rape."

"You've got a problem."

"Even if she didn't testify, the D.A. has a tape recording of her calling the police. And she sounds just as flat and unemotional on the tape as she would if she took the stand."

Blackman thought about this for a moment. "This taped phone call, it was right after the attempted rape?"

"Uh-huh. And she never mentioned the attempted rape then, either."

"Have you ever heard of 'rape trauma syndrome'?"

"My God," Dowd said, shaking his head, "where do you shrinks come up with all these syndromes?"

Blackman smiled. "It's a very real phenomenon, Michael. It's difficult for a man to understand what it's like to be . . . raped. It's difficult to understand what goes on in the mind."

"So what's this 'syndrome'?"

"Look, this isn't really my area. I've read about it. I can tell you it involves a cluster of common reactions to being raped, subconscious reactions. Repression, for example. Denial."

"Uh-huh."

"Michael, let me refer you to someone who's an expert on rape trauma syndrome. I really think it might help."

"This expert's going to explain why my client talked to the police about killing her husband like you and I would about buying a loaf of bread?"

"Maybe."

"And why she never mentioned any attempted rape?"

"Maybe."

Dowd sighed. "Okay, Julie. I'll give it a try."

"Dr. Lois Veronen. Probably the foremost authority in the country today on the psychological consequences of rape."

"Uh-huh."

"She's a professor at some southern college. I'll have to get the number for you."

"Uh-huh."

"Don't be such a chauvinist, Michael."

Dowd grinned. "Thanks," he said. "Now . . . what about *your* area of expertise?"

"She's not a battered wife," Blackman said simply.

Dowd nodded glumly.

"At least, not *physically* battered," she added.

Dowd looked up, the question on his face.

"I mean Louann Fratt doesn't fit the characteristics of the battered wife syndrome. There's no history of beatings, no cycles of repeated violence. No sense of helplessness. Oh, her husband was no angel. She says he struck her on three or four occasions. But over thirty years, this hardly qualifies."

"So we're out of luck there. Well, I pretty much figured." He looked out over the downtown skyline, watched the traffic inching its way over the Brooklyn Bridge.

"The odd thing is . . ."

"Yeah?"

"Well, Louann exhibits many of the *symptoms* of battered wife syndrome."

"What do you mean?" Dowd asked, turning back to the psychologist.

"I mean, based purely on her symptoms, I might be

tempted to diagnose the presence of the syndrome. It's just that the syndrome, as we presently understand it, is caused by repeated physical violence."

"I don't get it."

"Look, there's no history of cycles of violence. And although she may have felt helpless in the marriage, she *could* perceive options—such as divorce. The true battered wife is incapable of perceiving options. She kills because she believes that it is the only way out, that she will be killed otherwise."

"Uh-huh."

"So I can't diagnose battered wife syndrome. But . . . Louann exhibits many of the symptoms. The destruction of self-esteem and the 'learned helplessness,' the feeling that she is worthless, stupid, unable to survive without her husband."

"Uh-huh. So what are you saying?"

"Louann wasn't physically abused. But I think she may have been *emotionally* abused."

"Emotionally abused . . ."

"Yes. An emotionally battered wife, if you want."

"Uh-huh. And where does that leave us?"

"Probably nowhere," Blackman sighed. "I can't testify that she was suffering from battered wife syndrome. I can't testify that she killed out of desperation, out of a sense that it was the only way to survive."

"So . . . back to the drawing board," Dowd said, again looking out at the panoramic view.

"Not exactly." Blackman paused. "When you asked me to see her, you said one of the things you wanted to find out was why she would walk over to her husband's apartment so late at night."

"Uh-huh. Other than to stab him in his sleep."

"Of course, she told me the same thing she told you. She went over there because her husband asked her to. He wanted his mail."

"Right. And no jury is going to buy that."

"No, it seems pretty unreasonable," Blackman agreed. "No woman is going to walk the streets of New York alone at two in the morning, just because a husband who's divorcing her wants his mail."

"Uh-huh."

"Unless the woman were exhibiting symptoms of the battered wife syndrome."

Dowd turned away from the window, looked at the psychologist. "You just got through saying this wasn't a syndrome case."

"I also said she was showing some of the symptoms. Why, I'm not sure. The loss of self-esteem, the sense of complete dependence on the husband, the subversion of ego . . ."

"In English, Julie."

"I mean, something's going on inside Louann, something that alters her perceptions of the world. Something that would make her go out into the night to deliver mail to a man who left her."

"And something that would make her talk about rape and murder like it were a church social?"

"Maybe."

"Uh-huh, so what is it?" Dowd asked doubtfully. "What's the magic key?"

"I think you need to talk with Dr. Rosen."

CHAPTER 8

The man's body was lying face down. He was wearing pajamas, and his arms were stretched out above his head. Spread across his back was a large stain. Blood.

Dowd turned the photograph over, set it down on his desk. He looked at the next one. Again, the large man's bloodstained body, this time from a different angle.

Quickly, methodically, he laid this 8 × 10 down over the previous one and studied the next one. A shot of the living room, showing the foldout bed with the bloodstains across the comforter. Then another black-and-white of the living room, this one from an angle that showed the trail of stains leading from the bed. A shot of the kitchen, the bottle of wine clearly visible. A close-up of the carpet, showing a small dark stain.

Dowd leaned back in his chair, continued sorting through the D.A.'s photographs. A snapshot of the knife. Then a series of close-up glossies of Poe Fratt's body with the pajamas removed. The stab wound in the back. Then the neck, showing a thin, dark puncture. Then the chest, the third stab wound—the one Louann hadn't mentioned. A shot of one of his hands, showing cuts on the fingers. Where he had grabbed at the knife Louann was swinging. Then a close-up of the man's face.

Dowd stared at the face for a long time. Charles Kennedy Poe Fratt. College football hero. Senior vice president of Peat Marwick. National Democratic party kingpin. Millionaire. Husband. Father of three grown children . . . but who *was* he? Why had he left his wife after thirty years? Had he raped her on the loveseat of their home, as Louann claimed? Why does a man rape his wife? Sex? Violence? Control? Had Poe Fratt tried to rape her again the night he died? Was this man the attacker that night—or the victim?

Dowd continued staring at the expressionless face. At fifty-seven years of age, Fratt was semibald with a slightly fleshy face. The eyes were closed, the lips set slightly apart. A prominent nose, large ears, and a strong jawline hinted at the size and power of the man. But it was a lifeless face now. An empty face. Dead.

Dowd reached into a file lying on the floor, shuffled through its contents, and finally pulled out a newspaper. It was the *Cornell Daily Sun*. The headline on the front page read EX-TRUSTEE KILLED IN NYC APARTMENT. Underneath the headline was a picture of a handsome young man in a suit and tie; the caption read "C. K. Poe Fratt, 1953 Football M.V.P." The story briefly told of the murder, then reminisced about the man. ". . . Although Fratt will always be honored as one of Cornell's top players, several of his former teammates said they remembered his sense of humor more than his football achievements. . . . The star football player, who was nicknamed 'Floppy' by football coach Lefty James because of the way his legs kicked out when he ran, was also a member of Phi Gamma Delta fraternity. . . . He always had a smile on his face. . . . His clowning around helped alleviate a lot of the tension among the players. . . ."

Dowd studied the handsome face of the confident young man in the suit again, then replaced the article in the file. He turned back to the stark black-and-white photograph of the much older man's lifeless face.

Who *was* Poe Fratt?

Dowd turned the glossy photo over and set it on top of

the others on his desk. He turned to the next one. A man's naked body, stretched out on its back on a stainless steel gurney. Poe Fratt's body. At the autopsy. More photos of the naked body. Close-ups of the knife wounds. The body face down on the cold steel. Cold. Dead. Obscene.

The next photographs were a series of close-ups of Louann Fratt. The time and date on the first 8 × 10 indicated that they had been taken at 8:30 on the morning of November 22—a few hours after the killing. Louann stared into the police camera without expression, her eyes seeming to be without sight, her face as lifeless as that of her dead husband. Her left cheek appeared slightly swollen, and there was a discoloration on her forehead. Another shot of her face, from the side. Still another snapshot, a profile from the other side. No expression, no life.

With a sigh, Dowd turned the last of the photographs over and placed it on the stack on his desk. He turned to the pile of papers, pulled the top one off, and began to read the photocopied sheet. It was the criminal complaint. He scanned the document briefly. "People of the State of New York vs. Louann Fratt (F 55) . . . Det. Robert Tiburcio, shield #00354 of the 19th PDS, being duly sworn . . . On November 22, 1988, at about 0230 hours at 52 East 78th Street apt 9B in the County of . . . committed the offense of PL 125.25(1) Murder in the 2nd degree . . . with intent to cause the death of another person did cause the death of such person . . ."

Dowd placed this in a new pile, then reached for the next document. A prisoner's property form—a receipt for items taken from his client during booking. The list was pathetically short. Shoelaces, removed so she wouldn't try to hang herself. A comb. Lipstick. Nothing else—no money, no credit cards, no identification, no address book. Louann Fratt had prepared herself for jail, as she probably had for life, with a comb and a tube of lipstick.

On the line reading "Signature—prisoner," there was the barely legible handwriting of Dowd's client. The hand had been shaking badly; the signature looked as if it had been made by a first grader. Maybe Louann hadn't been so calm and unemotional after all, Dowd thought to himself.

The next document was a copy of an affidavit for a search

warrant. "Det. Robert Tiburcio of the Police Department of the City of New York, being duly sworn . . . Mrs. Fratt stated, in substance, to Sgt. Nevins that she had stabbed . . . I am further informed by Sgt. Nevins that he also observed a nightgown with drops of blood on it in Mrs. Fratt's apartment, which he seized. . . ."

Dowd stopped. A *nightgown*? With blood on it? Louann hadn't mentioned any nightgown. What had she been doing with a nightgown? And how had blood gotten on it? Dowd was beginning to experience a sinking feeling.

". . . further informed by Sgt. Nevins that Mrs. Fratt stated, in substance, that she had returned to . . . Based upon the foregoing . . . probable cause to believe that further articles of clothing worn by Mrs. Fratt when she stabbed her husband and materials used by her to wash blood from herself, are located at 151 East . . . Wherefore, I respectfully request that the Court issue a warrant and Order of Seizure. . . ."

Had Louann been wearing a *nightgown* when she stabbed her husband?

Dowd threw the affidavit on the desk, then began looking through the stack of documents for the "return" on the warrant—the formal report of what was found during the search. He found the warrant itself, issued at 3:45 P.M. on November 22: "Proof by affidavit having been made . . . probable cause to believe that certain property, to wit, blood samples, clothing and other materials containing blood . . . You are therefore commanded, between the hours of 6:00 A.M. and 9:00 P.M., to make an immediate search of 151 East 79th Street, fifth floor. . . ."

Finally, he found the return. "On 11/22/88 at about 1720 hrs. the undersigned along with Sgt. Fornabaio and ADA Brownell made a visit to 151 E. 79th st. NYC apt. 5th floor. At which time an execution of search warrant was conducted. . . . The execution of the above search warrant resulted in negative findings. . . ."

A nightgown! A bloody nightgown! What had Louann been doing in Poe's apartment at 2:00 in the morning with a nightgown? And what did that do to her claim of attempted rape?

Dowd played with the different possibilities as he put the

warrant and the return on the desk. He would confront Louann with the nightgown. Demand the truth. Threaten to withdraw if she didn't come clean.

He grabbed the next document, a property clerk's invoice. It was a list of the evidence seized from Poe Fratt's apartment. "1 bed quilt . . . 2 bed sheets . . . possible blood sample from phone receiver . . . possible blood sample on sheet paper." Then another invoice, this one from Louann's co-op. "1 kitchen knife . . . possible blood from handle . . . possible blood from blade . . . 1 brown bag containing 1 brown handbag, 1 left Reebok shoe, 1 right Reebok shoe, 1 Christian Dior lingerie . . ."

"1 Christian Dior lingerie." The nightgown had been found inside Louann's brown and yellow Louis Vuitton bag—the bag in which she had taken the mail and knife to her husband's apartment. Presumably, she had delivered the mail. And the knife had been turned over to the police. What were the sneakers doing in the bag? And the nightgown. The damned nightgown . . .

The next photocopied sheet was a police laboratory examination request form. Listed under the items for blood analysis were the knife, the nightgown, the sneakers, the quilt, the sheets, and the samples from the phone and the paper. Nothing indicating any results yet. But this was not critical evidence, Dowd realized: The defense was ready to admit the blood was Poe Fratt's. Still, it showed there was blood on the sneakers. She must have worn them in her husband's apartment, stepped in the blood. But why had she put them in the bag? She wouldn't have had any reason to do this back at her co-op, so she must have done it at the apartment. But why? And what had she worn to walk home? And where had she gotten a second pair of shoes? Nothing was making sense.

Next, a fingerprint report. Dowd's eyes quickly scanned for the wine bottle and glass. If the print man had found Louann's fingerprints on one of these, it would tend to corroborate her story—or, at least, eliminate the possibility that she had entered the apartment while her estranged husband slept and then stabbed him in the dark. But the fingerprint report was "inconclusive"—the prints were too smudged to identify.

Dowd turned to a series of officer's investigative reports.

Report of Detective D. Marousek, Crime Scene Unit: Inventory of evidence taken at Poe Fratt's apartment . . . list of photographs . . . diagrams of Poe Fratt's body and the wounds . . . diagram of the apartment . . . latent fingerprint record.

Report of Detective J. Farrell: "On this date at 0430 hrs. the undersigned along with Det. Rosario responded to the location. . . . The victim was found lying face down in the small foyer with his head against the front door to the apartment. The victim was dressed in yellow PJs which were covered with blood both on the shirt and the pants. . . . There was blood on the sheets of the sofabed which was opened as if someone was in bed. . . ."

Why had someone been in the bed? Dowd thought to himself. Poe Fratt wouldn't have gone to bed if he knew Louann was coming over. Had he been asleep when she arrived? Or had he been in bed with Louann—Louann in her nightgown?

". . . On the kitchen countertop was a bottle of Clos du Bois 1986 wine that was opened and not capped. . . . There was a telephone answering machine that Sgt. Nevins 19th Pct states has telephone messages from a male asking to speak to his mother and identifying himself as Poe Fratt Jr. Sgt. Nevins states that these calls came into the machine while he was waiting for the undersigned to arrive. . . ."

Poe Fratt, Jr. Louann had called her youngest son at Cornell just before calling the police, Dowd thought. She had told him that she had stabbed his father, maybe killed him. Poe Jr. must have been frantic, helpless so far away, desperately calling his father's number, listening to his father's voice on the machine. His dead father's voice.

Dowd picked up a photocopy of an officer's field notes, handwritten at the scene. These belonged to Sergeant Nevins. The handwriting was difficult to read. ". . . Upon arrival met on 5th floor by F/W/50s"—a white female in her fifties—"who states, 'I've stabbed my husband I think I killed him'. . . .

SGT.: where?
F/W/50s: 52 E. 78 St.
SGT.: are you sure he's dead?
F/W/50s: I think so.

SGT.: where's the knife?
F/w/50s: over there in the bag.
   [Knife & bloody clothes recovered at this time.]
SGT.: how come there's no blood on you?
F/w/50s: I washed it off.
SGT.: why?
F/w/50s: We're getting a divorce—we had a fight."

Dowd put the notes down. No mention of an attempted rape. Nothing about having been beaten by her husband. Just "we had a fight."

He put the notes away, then took the next document from the pile. Another handwritten set of notes, these from an Officer Walter Lapinski.

> . . . 0345—responding to 151 East 79 on a family dispute—man stabbed by wife.
> 0350—woman states that she stabbed her husband at his apartment at 52 East 78 and that she does not know if he is alive or dead. Woman stated that her husband had called her and asked her to come to his apartment to talk about their pending divorce. She said after she stabbed him she came home, washed up and put the knife and other things in a brown bag that was lying on the apartment floor.

She put the knife, shoes, and nightgown in the bag *after* getting back to her co-op? It would explain the shoes, Dowd thought silently, but it didn't make a whole lot of sense. Was Louann Fratt neatly gathering all of the evidence for the arrival of the police?

> 0355—en route to 52 east 78 st. . . .
> 0405—door to apt kicked in due to nobody answering the door.
> 0408—male found lying face down with head toward the apt door. . . .

More handwritten field notes, these belonging to an Officer Schlesinger. ". . . 0418 hrs Miranda given . . . I stabbed my husband. I think he's dead. They were going through a divorce. I want to call my son."

Dowd plowed on through the thick stack of paperwork. This was the tedious part of preparing for trial—the hours of sifting through piles of reports, documents, notes, receipts, photos. But hidden here and there, waiting to be dug out, were the little gems that an entire case could hang on. And the only way to find them was to dig, and keep digging.

A report from Detective Rosario, describing an interview with the doorman at Louann's co-op, Pedro Sanchez: ". . . At approximately 0230 hours he observed Mrs. Fratt leave the building with her dog. He added that approximately 20 minutes later she returned. He claimed that she did not appear nervous or excited and that he did not notice any blood on her clothing. . . ."

Dowd shook his head. There it was again: ". . . she did not appear nervous or excited." Brownell not only had a tape recording of Louann's casual attitude, he had an eyewitness to it.

". . . He added that she usually walks her dog at this time. He further informed me that at approximately 0320 hours he observed her leaving the building again. This time she did not have the dog. . . ."

Louann had returned to her husband's apartment, as she had told Dowd. But she had not told the police about this. Why was so much of what she had told them inaccurate? Dowd wondered. Why wash her hair? Why wash the knife? Why pack the evidence neatly into her bag before calling the police? Dowd was beginning to think that below Louann's calm, unemotional surface might lie a brain that was short-circuiting.

". . . He claimed that she did not appear intoxicated, which was unusual, he claimed that she was usually intoxicated. . . ."

Was Louann Fratt a heavy drinker? Dowd pondered. Had she gotten drunk that night and gone to her husband's apartment and—No, the doorman said she did *not* appear intoxicated that night. Dowd made a mental note to make sure to ask the trial judge to suppress any testimony by the doorman about Louann being habitually intoxicated. It was not relevant to what happened that night, and it would prejudice the jury.

". . . he further informed me that he observed her walking south on Lexington ave from 79th street and that approximately 30 minutes later she returned home. . . ."

Dowd considered the doorman's time estimates. How could the first trip have taken only twenty minutes? And the second—where Louann simply checked to see if her husband was dead—how could it have taken ten minutes longer? Dowd suspected that the doorman, like most witnesses, recalled events with considerable inaccuracy, particularly when it came to time estimates. Either that, or . . .

Dowd continued reading the officer's report. ". . . He claimed that she seemed to be in good spirits. . . ."

God, Dowd thought, the jury would hang her for that alone.

". . . He did not notice any injuries or blood on her clothing. . . ."

Dowd thought of the photographs he had just viewed, showing the bruising and swelling on Louann's face. How could the doorman not have noticed this? Maybe he could put a dent in this witness's credibility with Brownell's own photos.

With a deep sigh, Dowd threw this report on the growing stack on his desk. He read through seven or eight other police reports of no particular consequence. Then came a series of reports from the medical examiner's office. The first was a "Personal Identification of Body," signed by Charles Kennedy Poe Fratt, Jr., the day after his father's death. The second was a certification of cause of death, signed by a Dr. Waglae Charlot and establishing that cause to be "homicide." Finally, the autopsy report.

Dowd studied the report carefully. It was here that he might find some vital clues to what had happened at the apartment. But the report was difficult to read. The same Dr. Charlot had conducted the autopsy, but her handwriting was nearly illegible. Still, Dowd could make out the gist of the findings. The autopsy had been conducted on November 23, the day after the killing. There were, in fact, three stab wounds. A wound to the right side of the neck was not lethal, just missing the carotid artery and jugular vein. A second wound to the back was also not lethal, the knife entering to a depth of only 1 3/4 inches. Death had been caused by the third wound—the thrust into the chest that Louann had not recalled. The knife had entered the left side of the chest, at the fifth intercostal space; this meant between the ribs, below the nipple. It had pierced the right ventricle of the heart, passed on through the diaphragm, and finally come to rest in the liver. Death would have occurred within seconds.

One heck of a wound from a small fifty-five-year-old woman, Dowd thought to himself. He noticed that all three wounds had been downward thrusts. Brownell could argue that this was consistent with stabbing Poe Fratt while he lay in bed. But it was also consistent with two people standing, one stabbing downward with overhead thrusts.

What bothered Dowd more than the angles of entry was the placing of the three wounds. He would expect a woman defending herself against attack to swing the knife wildly. The result should be randomly placed wounds—on the assailant's arms, shoulders, legs, head, as well as to various parts of the abdomen. But the three wounds Poe Fratt received were all potentially lethal. Each of the three knife thrusts had been to a critical part of the body—to the carotid and jugular of the neck, into the back and the lungs, and into the chest and heart.

Dowd leaned back in his chair and pondered the meaning of the report. Had the placing of the knife wounds been coincidental? Was it just dumb luck that each had been potentially deadly? Or had the thrusts been carefully planned and executed?

Feeling very tired now, Dowd continued reading Dr. Charlot's findings. Lots of medical terminology meaning nothing. Normal, healthy organs. Scars. He studied the diagrams of the body again. Then he noticed a set of tiny marks around the chin. He read the scrawled notes next to it. Small, curving lacerations, the notes said, freshly made—and consistent with fingernail scratches!

Dowd felt a surge of energy. Someone had raked Poe Fratt's face with their fingernails. And that someone had been Louann. Had she attacked him in a fury, and finished the job with the knife? Or had she been defending herself—possibly against rape? If you are planning to kill someone, Dowd thought to himself, you don't start by clawing his face. No, these were the marks of a woman defending herself.

Dowd set the autopsy report down on the desk and reached once again for the bottomless pile of paperwork. He found another report, this one from a Dr. Stajic of the medical examiner's toxicology laboratory. Parts of Poe Fratt's body had been forwarded from the autopsy to the laboratory for routine analysis to detect the possible presence of drugs or alcohol. No drugs had been found in either the blood, brain, or urine, Dowd noted. But something else *had* been found. And as Dowd read the word that stared up at him, that magic word, he felt a sense of elation. For he knew that that one word could change the whole picture. That one lovely word could go a long way toward saving his client.

Ethanol.

Also known as alcohol. Drinking alcohol. Poe Fratt had 0.11 percent ethanol in his blood—enough to make him legally intoxicated under New York's drunk driving statute.

Poe Fratt had been drunk when Louann had come over that night.

Maybe he *had* tried to rape her.

CHAPTER 9

"Yes, I was with Louann the day . . . the day that unfortunate incident took place."

"What time was this, Mrs. Keating?" Dowd asked.

"Well, let me see . . ." The woman looked up at the ceiling, then closed her eyes. She sat there in silence for a moment, pulling gently at the loose, slightly wrinkled skin of her neck.

Dowd studied the small woman in the plain but elegant navy blue wool dress and matching pumps. Peggy Keating. Bright, lively, attractive. In her fifties. Neatly coiffed reddish brown hair. Simple, plain-framed eyeglasses. A smile always on her face, yet seemingly sincere. Pleasant, gracious, refined. She and Louann had known each other for nine years.

The woman fingered her pearl necklace slowly, her eyes still closed in concentration. "I believe . . . yes, I believe I first met Louann that day at . . . Yes, it must have been two-thirty. It was." She opened her eyes again, looked back at Dowd. "It was two-thirty. Yes, I recall quite clearly now."

"Two-thirty in the afternoon."

"Yes. I'm quite sure."

"November twenty-first."

"If that was the date when Louann . . . well, went over to Poe's apartment later that evening. Yes."

"Uh-huh. How do you remember that day so well, Mrs. Keating?" Dowd asked casually. The last thing he needed was Louann Fratt's best friend covering for her—a friend who would fall apart under Brownell's cross-examination.

"The lighting ceremonies," she said with a smile.

"The lighting ceremonies."

"Yes. The *origami* exhibit. At the Metropolitan Museum of Natural History."

"Uh-huh."

"You haven't heard of it," she said with disappointment.

"I'm sorry."

"Oh, it's really quite lovely. No matter," she said with a wave of the hand. "Well, you see, Christmas was coming, and there are the traditional lighting ceremonies—lighting the Christmas trees?"

"Yes."

"Only this . . . this was quite different. You *are* familiar with *origami*?"

"The paper birds?"

"Birds, yes, and many other objects. It's an art, really, a very clever Japanese art."

"Uh-huh."

"Well, the museum has a huge *origami* tree, you see. A tree made of these beautiful works of art."

"Uh-huh."

"And on that day—November twenty-first?—Louann and I attended the lighting ceremony."

"I see. You met her at the museum?"

"No. No, I met Louann at her apartment. At two-thirty, as I said. I believe we had coffee, or some such thing. And *then* we went to the museum." She looked at the cup in Dowd's lap. "Oh, dear," she said, rising from her chair. "Let me get you some more coffee, Mr. Dowd."

"That would be lovely, Mrs. Keating. Thank you."

The woman took the gilded china cup and saucer from Dowd, then walked over to a mahogany table. She began pouring coffee from a polished silver pot sitting on a silver serving tray. Dowd looked around the huge, beautifully furnished living room. The place reeked of money; Peggy Keating was married to the senior partner of a large admiralty law firm. Yet, the room was restrained, tasteful. Another world, Dowd thought to himself. Maybe the address said it all: 935 Park Avenue.

"Where were we, Mr. Dowd?" the woman said as she handed him the filled cup and saucer.

"Thank you. Uh, the museum. The lighting ceremony? How long were the two of you there, Mrs. Keating?"

"Oh, it was about an hour, I'd say," she replied, sitting down. "Yes, an hour."

"And what did you do after the ceremony?"

"We went back to Louann's apartment."

"Uh-huh."

"Yes."

"What did you do there?"

Mrs. Keating smiled happily. "This is really quite like a trial, isn't it? I mean, the questions and all."

"I'm sorry, Mrs. Keating," Dowd said grinning. "Just force of habit."

"No, no, don't apologize. I find it quite . . . interesting." She paused, then leaned forward conspiratorially. "Will I be testifying at the trial?"

"Well, I guess that's what I'm trying to figure out right now."

She nodded. "Well, anything I can do to help poor Louann." She shook her head sadly. "It's all so . . ."

"Yes. It is."

Peggy Keating lifted her chin valiantly. "What more would you like to know, Mr. Dowd?"

"Uh, you returned to Mrs. Fratt's apartment about when, Mrs. Keating?"

"It would have been . . . Let's see . . . two-thirty, coffee, the museum, an hour. I'd say about four. Perhaps four-thirty."

"And what did you do then?"

"Oh, we chatted for a bit. And then I left. I remembered I had wanted to borrow a bowl from Louann, a crystal bowl. For the holidays, you know. So I took the bowl with me when I left."

"And when was this, that you left?"

"Soon after. Five perhaps."

"You went home."

"Yes."

"And that was the last time you saw Mrs. Fratt."

"The last time before . . . yes."

"So this was approximately eight hours before she went to her husband's apartment."

The woman looked down at her lap, nodded slowly.

"Uh-huh." Dowd raised the china cup from its saucer and sipped at the coffee. "Now, this is very important, Mrs. Keating . . ."

She looked up, attentive.

"You were the last person to see Mrs. Fratt before . . . the incident."

"Yes," she said, considering the idea carefully. "I suppose I was."

"Can you tell me how she seemed to you that afternoon?"

"Seemed?"

"Was she depressed? Angry?"

"No," Peggy Keating replied, thinking about it. "No, quite the contrary. Louann was really in a very good mood. We were laughing and joking and just having a very good time."

"She seemed happy to you."

"Yes. Quite happy."

"Did she talk about her husband?" Dowd asked.

"Poe?" she repeated, again reflecting. "No, no, I don't believe so. No, I don't believe she mentioned him at all."

"Did she say anything about visiting him later that evening?"

"No. No, I'm quite sure she mentioned nothing like that."

"Then . . . you would say nothing seemed to be bothering Louann that afternoon?"

"Nothing that I could see, Mr. Dowd."

"She seemed to be in good spirits?"

"Yes, quite good spirits."

"And she had no plans to see her husband?"

"Not that I'm aware of."

Dowd nodded, reflecting on this.

"I suppose this would all be fascinating," Peggy Keating said finally, "if it weren't so . . . sad."

"Yes, I suppose so."

"You're fortunate to have such an . . . interesting line of work, Mr. Dowd."

Dowd smiled. "I guess I am."

"And I understand you're quite good."

"Thank you," he replied uncomfortably. "I've been pretty lucky lately."

"Luck? I hardly think so. I hardly think luck had anything to do with that trial—last month was it? . . . the poor woman."

Ann Green. Her face came drifting back to him now. Her face, and the bodies . . . the tiny, helpless little bodies.

"It was a difficult case," Dowd said. Yes, difficult, he thought to himself.

"The poor woman," Peggy Keating repeated. "But the *Times* said you were brilliant, really brilliant."

The tiny little bodies . . .

The first "incident" had taken place at 2:30 in the morning. Dowd recalled the simply furnished one-bedroom apartment. Once again, he saw the rather plain-looking woman in her mid-thirties seated in a chair, nursing a newborn baby. She was talking softly to the baby, lovingly. The baby started to cry. The woman covered her breast, stood up, and began slowly pacing the room with the baby cradled gently in her arms. She was tenderly rocking it and singing a lullaby. When the baby finally stopped crying, she carefully placed it in a pink crib. She leaned down and kissed the baby, watched as it fell to sleep. Then she walked into the bathroom, closed the door. She started crying, softly at first, then in heaving sobs.

When she finished, she came back out and lay down on her bed.

After a few minutes, the woman got back up and walked over to the crib. She stood there, silently staring at the baby. Then, slowly and without any apparent emotion, the woman picked up a pillow and calmly placed it over the baby's face. The baby began to kick. The woman pressed down firmly as the baby weakly flailed its arms and legs. The woman's face was still empty of feeling. Gradually, the tiny limbs grew weaker, then finally stopped. . . .

Dowd remembered the day seven years later, on December 10, 1987, when he first met Ann Green in his office. She was shy, quiet; she seemed fragile, almost childlike. Her husband, Larry, was with her; he was blind. She had been a pediatric nurse at New York Hospital-Cornell Medical Center for thirteen years. She was devoted to children. And she was charged with murdering two of her own babies and attempting to murder the third.

Dowd had read of the case in the newspapers. Within hours of taking her first baby home from the hospital where she worked, Ann Green smothered it with a pillow; the medical finding was "crib death." Two years later, she brought her second newborn baby home from the same hospital. Hours later, she ran back to the hospital with the baby, now turned blue; he was placed on a life-support system. Three weeks later, the system was disconnected; he died in Ann's arms as she gently rocked him. The official conclusion was again "crib death."

In 1985, Ann Green brought home a third baby. At 4:15 A.M., she ran next door to her neighbor, screaming, "Please help me! I think my baby is dead!" As the neighbor gave the unconscious infant mouth-to-mouth resuscitation, Ann kept repeating over and over, "It's happening again, it's happening again." This time, the infant lived.

Seven months later Ann was arrested and charged with two counts of murder and one count of attempted murder. The case had been stalled in the court system for two years, waiting for the assigned judge to finish the Bernhard Goetz trial.

Dowd recalled Ann telling him what she remembered—the deep desire for children, visits to the fertility clinic, the elation of pregnancy, the joy of birth. Then the terrible depression, crying for no reason, a feeling of failure and inadequacy. She recalled the babies' deaths, recalled watching herself as if she were another person place the pillows over their little faces. Each time she could not recall anything about the incidents for about thirty days; she only remembered the babies crying, and then they were turning blue. After thirty days, she would begin to feel a vague sense of having done something wrong—guilt, confusion. She knew that she had killed them, and yet it had not been her: "I loved them—I could never have hurt them."

Dowd learned that one month after trying to kill her third baby—half a year before being arrested—Ann had voluntarily committed herself to N.Y.U. Medical Center for psychiatric evaluation and treatment; she was released two months later. Shortly thereafter, she underwent surgical sterilization.

When Ann left, Dowd considered the case. He was convinced she had killed her babies. But *why*? She was clearly a sweet, gentle, loving woman—why would she murder the infants she wanted and loved so much? It didn't make sense.

Dowd remembered the long process he went through to learn about women who kill their babies. Julie Blackman mentioned the possibility of something called "postpartum depression." Dowd turned to the catalog of mental illnesses recognized by psychiatry and the law; nowhere did it list such a condition.

Dowd then met with a noted psychiatrist in the field, Dr. Stuart Asch at New York Hospital. For ten hours, Dr. Asch patiently lectured him on the little-known area of postpartum depression. Prior to childbirth, levels of progesterone and estrogen in the mother are as much as fifty times higher than normal; within hours of giving birth, the amounts of these hormones fall to below normal levels. Although the exact effects of such drastic hormonal changes are not understood, it is known that low levels cause depression and erratic mood swings.

Dr. Asch explained that reactions to these changes differ among women. Somewhere between 50 per cent and 70 per cent of all women experience what is called "baby blues"—a relatively mild depression that usually involves unexplained mood swings and crying jags; it normally lasts for only a few days. A smaller number of women—perhaps 10 per cent—experience a more serious reaction known as "postpartum depression," possibly a severe version of "baby blues." This will last much longer and, in some cases, may result in a "bonding disorder" in which the mother experiences indifferent, hostile, or even murderous feelings toward her baby.

Finally, a third and even more serious condition can occur: "postpartum psychosis." Afflicting only one or two women out of a thousand, this is a severely disabling illness. A woman suffering from this condition becomes confused and disoriented; although she may appear quite normal one moment, in the next she may completely lose touch with all reality. She may become self-destructive; because she may be unable to differentiate between the baby and her "self," suicide may take the form of murdering the infant.

Infanticide that occurs because of postpartum depression or psychosis is more prevalent than commonly realized: Asch estimated that 10 per cent to 20 per cent of the twenty to thirty thousand infants who succumb every year to "crib death" were actually murdered by their mothers.

Dowd remembered leaving Asch's office and suddenly recalling his own wife, Irene, telling him how she had been so deeply and unaccountably depressed after her first childbirth. Now she was pregnant again—and due to deliver about the time he would be in trial on the Ann Green case.

On the eve of the Green trial, Dowd was unable to sleep. . . . After a long meeting with Ann's psychologist during her commitment, the celebrated Dr. Murray Alpert, Dowd had been convinced she was suffering from postpartum psychosis. Accordingly, he had changed her plea to "not guilty by reason of insanity"—in the face of violent objections from her husband and her wealthy parents, who continued to insist that Ann had simply not killed the babies. But would a jury buy such a novel psychiatric theory? The simple fact was that there was no precedent for a "baby blues" defense—the American Psychiatric Society did not recognize postpartum depression or psychosis, and Dowd's research had disclosed that there had never been a jury verdict in which the defendant had been found insane on such grounds.

As Dowd tossed in his bed, he kept seeing Ann in his mind, so fragile, so completely entrusting her life to him. Had he violated that trust? Why had he ever decided on this foolish "baby blues" strategy? He had no right to gamble this woman's life on such a half-baked defense. But it was too late now.

Dowd remembered looking over at Irene, stirring in her sleep. He recalled the horror stories she had told him about her depression after her first baby. Would it be like that again?

Could it be worse? In his mind the scene of Ann calmly, coldly holding the pillow over the tiny, weakly struggling little body replayed itself over and over. And then it was Irene's face he saw. . . .

After prosecutor Mary Beth Richroathe rested her case, Dowd called his first witness: Ann Green. He had decided to gamble, believing that she would be the best evidence of her own illness. And he had doubled his bet by calling her first—before his experts could prepare the jury for her. Let the jury see the fragile, naive, childlike woman so devoted to children, so overjoyed at her own pregnancy. Why would she murder her babies? It didn't make sense. And that was the key. Let the experts put their labels on it. All Dowd knew was that mothers who love their babies don't kill them—not *sane* mothers.

Dowd led Ann through the story of her efforts to become pregnant, the joy of childbirth, then the unexplainable depression. He asked her simple questions, leading her along like the childlike person she was, until it finally came time to describe the first killing:

> I remember lying down . . . and I got up, and then I saw myself standing over her, and I felt like a part of me wasn't there, that another part of me was there, doing something to my baby, and I couldn't believe this was happening. . . .

Ann began to cry. Dowd tenderly:

And did something happen to this child?
I was seeing myself or part of my hands. . . . They were hands, were trying—trying to hurt this baby and I don't know why.
How, Ann? What did you see the hands doing?
They were trying to suffocate the baby with a pillow and I felt there was another person there.
Ann, Ann, how could you do this to your child?
(Sobbing) *I didn't want to do it to my baby. I never wanted it to happen.*
Did you want to hurt your baby?

I wanted my own baby to love. I tried so hard to have my own baby and something happened.
    What happened, Ann?
    (Head rolling, tears flowing) *I don't know, I don't know.*

Dowd sat down.

Finally, it was time for closing arguments to the jury. And Dowd delivered an impassioned plea:

> . . . We all know that there are evil people who do evil things in this world. But there are also people who are ill, and a measure of us as a society is our ability to distinguish between the two. It is our ability to walk out of the darkness of ignorance and fear and into the light of reason and decency. . . .
>
> I ask you to judge this woman, this unique human being. You are not judging a disease. You are not judging anything except this one human being. I suggest to you that to be led to the conclusion offered by the prosecution is to be led back into the darkness—darkness created by ignorance, fear, and prejudice.

The jury returned with identical verdicts as to each count: "Not responsible, by virtue of mental disease or defect."

Judge Crane thanked Dowd, announcing to the packed courtroom: "This case brought about public scrutiny, and great introspection and scientific examination, of a phenomenon that has been swept under the rug for too long."

Two days after the verdict, Michael Dowd's wife gave birth to a healthy baby girl. She experienced no postpartum depression.

Under New York law, Ann Green underwent evaluation by court-appointed psychiatrists. If she was found to be a danger to society, she would have to be committed; if not, she would become a free woman. Soon after the verdict, Larry Green died of lung cancer; he had sat behind Ann throughout the trial, suffering in silence. Judge Crane eventually found that Ann was not a continuing danger; however, he recommended that custody of the surviving baby be taken from her and that visits be supervised.

"... really don't recall, Mr. Dowd."

Dowd blinked, his mind returning to the Park Avenue apartment and the woman seated across from him. "Uh, how often did you, uh, you and Mrs. Fratt see one another, Mrs. Keating?"

"Oh, Louann and I ... I'd say every two or three days."

"When was the last time before November twenty-first?"

Peggy Keating again looked to the ceiling, her eyes closed, her fingers playing with the pearls. "Five days," she said finally, looking back at Dowd.

"And where was this?"

"At a patrons' dinner. At the Metropolitan Museum of Art."

"A patrons' dinner."

"Yes. You see, Louann and I are both patrons of the museum. It was an annual event."

"And nothing unusual in her ... in how she seemed to you that night?"

The woman shook her head slowly, thinking. "No, no, she was just ... Louann."

"Was Mrs. Fratt with anyone at the dinner?"

"I believe she was attending with Bob ... Bob Ault."

"Bob Ault."

"Yes. Well, I assumed you knew. . . ."

"Knew?"

"I mean, Louann and Bob were ... They had been seeing each other. After the separation, of course. After Poe left."

"Uh-huh." Bob Ault. The boyfriend. Had Louann been seeing him *before* her husband moved out? Was that why he had left her? Dowd made a mental note to add this to the list of things he had to discuss with his client when she got back from visiting her daughter in San Francisco.

"Goodness, I hope I haven't said anything to—"

"No, no, you've been a great help, Mrs. Keating," Dowd said, rising and putting the cup and saucer on the coffee table. "Thanks very much for the coffee." He added, smiling, "And the company."

She would make a good witness, Dowd thought. A pleasant and intelligent older woman. The jury would like her. More important they would *believe* her. Of course, her testimony wasn't exactly earthshaking, but it could be helpful. Brownell would probably be trying to prove that Louann Fratt went to her husband's apartment that night with the knife intending to kill him. He would try to show that she *planned* the murder. But Peggy Keating would testify that she seemed happy that afternoon, with not a care in the world—hardly the attitude of someone who was planning to murder her husband a few hours later.

Peggy Keating recovered Dowd's tan trench coat from the closet, handed it to him at the door.

"Please," she said, "I want to help in any way I can."

"You're very kind, Mrs. Keating. And I'll probably be taking you up on that."

"I hope so, Mr. Dowd."

A nice lady, Dowd thought to himself as he shook her hand. A good witness. But his mind would not let go of the name Bob Ault.

Dowd kept thinking about it as he rode the elevator down and walked out into sunlight and the crisp, fresh air of Park Avenue. It was a beautiful autumn day, and the leaves of the trees were turning color all along the avenue.

Evidence of a boyfriend at the time of the killing might not hurt, he thought—might even help: A woman happily involved with a boyfriend is less likely to kill a husband who left her.

Or was there more to it? Would Brownell be calling Ault as a witness? Was he the key to the motive?

What *was* the motive?

CHAPTER 10

"Information," the bored voice on the telephone said. "What city, please?"

"Aberdeen, operator," Dowd said. "Aberdeen, Washington."

"Yes, may I help you?"

"Uh, the number of . . ." There couldn't have been more than one small high school in that town, at least back in the fifties. What would it have been called? ". . . Aberdeen High School." What the hell.

"One moment, please."

Dowd leaned back in the green leather chair. He looked out the window into the twilight. A brilliant sea of lights was slowly being born, spreading now across Manhattan like an incoming phosphorescent tide. Beautiful. But it was late, and he was tired. Still, the puzzle would not stop nagging at him.

"Sir? I don't find an Aberdeen High School listed."

"Uh-huh, well . . ."

"The only high school listed in Aberdeen is a *Weatherwax* High School."

"Weatherwax," Dowd repeated. "Yes, that's it."

"One moment, please."

The next sound he heard was an automated voice giving

him the phone number. He hurriedly shuffled through the piles of paper on his desk, found a yellow legal pad, and scribbled down the number. Then he hung up. A long shot, he thought, and probably another dead end. But he had to solve the puzzle. And he had to do it with little help from his client.

It would be about 4:00 in Washington State. He quickly dialed the number. An elderly woman's voice answered.

"Weatherwax High School."

"Uh, yes, may I have the registrar's office, please?"

"I'm sorry, everyone's gone," she said. "I'm pretty much holding down the fort."

"I see. Well . . ."

"Is there something I can help you with?" There was a cheerful friendliness in her voice, something Dowd wasn't used to in New York.

"Well . . . I'm trying to locate some classmates of a woman who graduated from Weatherwax. She would have graduated sometime in the early fifties."

"Why don't you give me her name? I've got the records right here."

"That'd be great, thanks. Louann Johnson," Dowd said, giving her the maiden name.

"Just a minute."

Dowd searched his pockets for a cigarette, found none. He dug through the pile of papers, files, and books that covered his desk, all the time trying to balance the receiver between his shoulder and ear. Nothing. He began opening drawers, each stuffed with more disorganized piles of paperwork. A bottle of Irish whiskey stood wedged among a stack of files in one drawer. In another, a framed award rested atop a jungle of documents and office supplies. A third drawer held a strange combination of books, papers, a can of shaving cream, a crumpled tie . . . and a smashed, half-empty pack of Salem cigarettes.

Dowd grabbed the pack and quickly pulled out a cigarette. It was broken in half. He threw it back in the drawer, then pulled another one from the pack. This one was badly bent, but he stuck it in his mouth and lighted up.

"Hello?"

"Yes, ma'am," Dowd said, coughing from the smoke.

"Louann Christine Johnson," the voice said triumphantly. "Class of fifty-one."

"That's great, thanks. What I'm trying to do, I'm trying to find some classmates who knew her."

"That wouldn't be too difficult. They were pretty small classes back in those days. Everybody knew everybody." She laughed. "To tell the truth, things haven't changed all that much."

"Can you give me some names and addresses?"

"Well, I don't have any addresses but, let's see . . ." There was a moment of silence. "You know what? The person for you to talk to is Richard Rasanen."

"Richard Rasanen," Dowd repeated, writing the name down on the legal pad.

"R-A-S-A-N-E-N. Class of fifty-one. He was in here the other day, talking about a class reunion—a fortieth reunion in a couple of years. Yep, he'd be the one to talk to. He's sort of an organizer around town, keeps track of everybody."

"And how can I get hold of Mr. Rasanen?"

"*Doctor* Rasanen," she said. "He's a dentist here in town. Just a second, I'll check the directory for you."

"Many thanks."

Dowd leaned back in his chair again, blowing a stream of smoke at the ceiling. Calling a high school three thousand miles away where his client graduated forty years ago was a pretty good indication of how desperate he had become, Dowd thought to himself. Lord knows how many other futile calls he had made in the last few weeks—he and Debbie Cohen. But the trial date was drawing ominously near. And the puzzle remained—a puzzle that his client could not help him with.

Who *was* Louann Fratt?

"Yep, here it is." The voice rattled off a phone number.

Dowd took down the number. "Many thanks, ma'am. I sure appreciate the help."

"You give him a call. He'll know your Louann Christine Johnson."

"Thanks again. You're very kind."

"Not at all," she said cheerfully. "Good luck, young man."

Dowd hung up, then immediately dialed the number the woman had given him.

"Dr. Rasanen's office," a much younger woman's voice said.

"Uh, may I speak with Dr. Rasanen?"

"May I say who's calling?"

"Sure. Michael Dowd. From New York."

"Please hold."

Dowd blew more smoke at the ceiling, then coughed. Miserable habit, he thought, then took another drag. What am I doing at 7:00 at night, in a deserted office, trying to get hold of some small-town dentist in Washington?

Dowd took another deep drag off of the bent cigarette, then flicked the ashes at the ashtray. He missed.

"Hello?"

"Uh, Dr. Rasanen?"

"Yes?"

"My name is Michael Dowd. I'm an attorney in New York, and I'm representing a client charged with murder." He paused. "I believe you may have gone to school with her."

"Louann Johnson," the voice said quietly.

"Yes," Dowd said, surprised. "Her name's Louann Fratt now."

"We read about it in the newspaper here. I mean, her being a local girl."

"Uh-huh, well, the thing is, I'm trying to locate some classmates of hers from high school, some people who might have known her fairly closely. Can you recall any of her close friends?"

"Can I recall. . . ?" Dr. Rasanen chuckled. "Say, I figured you called me because you *knew*."

"Knew?"

"Well, I mean, Louann and I . . . well, we were about as close as it gets."

"You were—"

"Boyfriend, girlfriend . . . you know, going together? Heck, Louann and I started going together long before high school."

Bull's-eye.

"Uh-huh. Well, it seems I found the right person."

"I'd say." The voice seemed cheerful, friendly, like the woman at the high school. Was it something they all ate out there? "What would you like to know?"

"What can you tell me about her? What was she like? What kind of family? That kind of thing."

"Louann Johnson . . ." Dr. Rasanen repeated to himself. "That was a long, long time ago, you know."

"I know."

"Well, let's see. . . . Her dad was Gus Johnson. Owned the lumber company here. He was a big guy, tough. Real quiet, kept to himself. Straitlaced. Ran the family pretty strict. Did a lot of drinking, they say. Anyway, they were pretty well off, at least for Aberdeen. Lived in a house in the Bel Air section, up on Broadway Hill. Had the first TV in town, I remember that."

"What about her mother."

"Iva Lee Tikka, her name was. Came from a farming family near here. Finnish. They still live outside Aberdeen. Anyway, she was real quiet, too. Quiet, timid, reserved. Stayed to herself. And there were, let's see . . . two boys—no, three. And a girl. The two older boys, Dirk, I think, and Don, they were a lot older than Louann. They became loggers, like their dad. One of them died in a fire, down in Gold Beach. And the other boy, John, he wasn't born until Louann was in high school. He's a dentist now, in Seattle. So none of them were anywhere near close to Louann's age. I guess that's why she was never very close to them."

"And the sister?"

"Suzie. She was only a couple of years younger than Louann. But they weren't very close, either. Didn't really care a whole lot for each other. Fact is, Suzie and Louann were as different as night and day."

"How do you mean?"

"Well, Suzie was quiet, like her mom. And always very proper, you know? Appearances meant a whole lot. Straitlaced and all. Very religious, too. Ended up marrying a minister."

"What about Louann?"

"A whole different thing. Louann was real warm, outgoing, sociable. Real popular, you know? One of the most popular girls at Weatherwax."

"Uh-huh." Warm, Dowd thought to himself. Outgoing. Sociable. Was this man describing the same woman Dowd had met in his office?

"And she was about the prettiest thing in Aberdeen. She had every guy in town after her. But the thing is, Louann'd ask *them* out. I mean, this was way back before woman's lib. She wasn't bashful at all. If she liked a boy, why, she just went up and asked him out. That was pretty unusual in those days. But then Louann was like that."

"Uh-huh."

"Oh, don't get me wrong. I don't mean she was loose, or anything like that. Fact is, she belonged to some Presbyterian youth group. Christian Endeavor, I think it was called."

Dowd kept scribbling notes on the legal pad, the receiver squeezed between his shoulder and ear.

"You say Louann wasn't very close to her brothers or her sister."

"Yeah."

"What about her parents?"

"Well, you know, she wasn't very close to her mother, either. There just wasn't a lot there, I don't know why. But her dad, now, that was a different story. Louann really thought a lot of her dad."

"Uh-huh."

"Mr. . . . Dodd, was it?" Dr. Rasanen asked.

"Dowd."

"Mr. Dowd, I'm really sorry. I've got a patient waiting."

"I understand. Is there a better time—"

"Tell you what. The person you should talk with is Ann Scroggs."

"Ann Scroggs," Dowd repeated, writing the name down.

"Louann's best friend. All the way through high school and then at the university."

"That sounds great. Do you happen to have her phone number?"

"She lives right here in town. Give me a second . . . Scroggs . . . Scroggs. . . . Yep, here it is."

Dowd took down the number, then thanked the dentist and hung up. He dialed the new number.

This was what being a criminal lawyer was really all about—unending hours and hours and hours of phone calls and interviews. Sticking your nose uninvited into the lives of others, digging, probing, bothering people, asking for favors, for information, for secrets. It was tiring. It was degrading. And most of the time it was fruitless.

Many lawyers simply hired investigators to do the tedious footwork. But Dowd believed in doing most of it himself. It gave him a better feel for the case. It was like the race car driver who liked to work on the engine himself, or the marksman who made his own ammunition. And Dowd knew the hard work paid off in trial. How many times had he been able to react instantly during a cross-examination because he knew—really *knew*—the heart of the case? How many trials had he won because he could *feel* rather than think?

The simple fact was that the lawyer who could act on "instinct"—an instinct born of total immersion into the case —would defeat the lawyer who had to think. Put another way, the trial lawyer who relied upon others to prepare him for battle was lost.

Dowd had learned the secret of his trade—a secret very few trial lawyers ever learned. That secret was simply that *a trial was a living thing*! It was not a seemingly cold series of technical procedures and formalities. It was not a logical system for determining truth and justice; it was not even conceptual or inanimate. Each trial was, in fact, a constantly changing organism with a life of its own, each unique, each a living plasma of lawyers, judges, jurors, defendants, witnesses, facts, emotions, tactics, skills, weaknesses, secrets, hatreds, fears, truths, half-truths, deceptions, motives, biases. . . . And in understanding that secret, Dowd knew the key to winning at trial was simple—simple but demanding: preparation. You had to *understand* that living thing, understand what it was made of, understand the *flow* of the trial animal, understand and become a part of it.

The Zen swordsman *feels* his opponent's movements.

"Hello?" It was a woman's voice.

"May I speak with Ann Scroggs, please?"

"This is Ann Scroggs."

"Uh, Mrs. Scroggs, my name is Michael Dowd. I'm an attorney from New York, and I'm representing a former friend of yours, Louann Johnson?"

"Oh, yes."

"You've heard about the case?"

"I've read about it, yes."

"I'm trying to contact her friends, to find out about her

background, her family, school, and so on. I understand you and Louann were best friends."

"Who are you again?"

"Michael Dowd, ma'am. I'm Louann Johnson's attorney. I'm defending her on the murder charge."

"I see. And what do you want?"

"I'm trying to learn about her earlier years, about her family and friends, what she was like."

"I see. Well, I don't know. . . ."

This was what Dowd hated. Selling used cars to people who didn't want to buy one.

"It could be very helpful to Louann's case."

"Well, I just don't know. . . ."

"Dr. Rasanen tells me she was a very popular girl at Weatherwax."

Steer her toward the car.

"You've talked with Richard?"

"Yes," Dowd said. "He was very cooperative."

"I see."

"He thought you probably knew Louann better than anyone."

"Yes, I suppose so. But . . ."

"It could be very helpful to Louann, Mrs. Scroggs."

Ease her in behind the wheel.

"I really don't see how I could help."

"You could help me understand what happened when Louann killed her husband, why it happened."

"She really did it, then?"

"I think she had good reasons, Mrs. Scroggs. I think she was defending herself."

"Defending herself. . . . Well, I just don't know."

"Is it true that you and Louann were best friends in high school and college?"

"Yes, that's true."

"I guess you knew her pretty well, then?"

"Yes."

"What was she like back in high school?"

Hand her the keys.

"Well . . ." A deep sigh. "Louann was . . . well, she was friendly, outgoing."

"Uh-huh."

"She was a very attractive young lady. Pretty, and she had a very nice figure. I remember she used to do modeling. She was a very popular girl."

"Uh-huh."

Take it out for a spin.

"And very ambitious."

"Ambitious."

"Yes. She always wanted the best, I remember that very clearly. She always knew what she wanted and she went after it."

"Uh-huh."

"Her family wasn't really like that. They had money, but there were no social aspirations. But Louann, she was different. She wasn't about to stay in Aberdeen. She was going to get out of this town and get what she wanted."

"And what was it that she wanted?" Dowd asked.

"Well, back in those days, a woman looked for a man and got married. Louann was no different. It's just that she wanted the best. She wanted to find the right kind of man."

"The right kind of man."

"Yes. I suppose you could say Louann was a social climber."

"Uh-huh."

"Louann always knew exactly what she wanted and she always went after it." The woman paused for a moment. "And she usually got it." Another brief pause as she thought back to another time. "She wasn't very shy, you know. If she liked a boy, she went up to him and asked him out. Simple as that."

The woman was warming to the subject, Dowd thought. She seemed to be unusually frank. Or was that a touch of resentment, maybe jealousy?

"The thing I remember about Louann . . . she was always very definitely in command of the situation." A pause. "In those days, I think we called them designing women."

A designing woman, Dowd thought to himself. Always in control of the situation. Knew what she wanted and went after it. Was this the same woman Julie Blackman thought was lacking in self-esteem and completely dependent upon her husband?

"You and Louann both went to college together, I understand," Dowd said.

"Yes, the university."

"The University of Washington," Dowd guessed.

"Yes," she said. Of course.

"Did you belong to a sorority?"

"I joined the Kappas. Kappa Kappa Gamma. Louann joined the Thetas. Kappa Alpha Theta." Another pause. "Louann would only join the best. She always belonged to the right organizations. It was all part of her plan."

"Her plan?"

"Yes. To meet the right people, find the right man, live in the right place, wear the right clothes." She paused again before continuing. "You know, when I heard that Louann was living off Park Avenue, married to a big executive, I wasn't surprised. I mean, that's just exactly what she had been planning for all along, wasn't it?"

"Uh-huh."

The woman paused once more. "I always thought Louann had it all," she said finally. Another moment of silence. "I wonder what went wrong."

"I don't know," Dowd said.

CHAPTER 11

"Why did Louann kill her husband?"

Dr. Marsha Rosen studied Dowd for a moment, then leaned back slightly in the Scandinavian modern brown leather chair. "Because her husband was trying to rape her," she replied.

"You believe that, then?" Dowd asked.

The psychologist nodded slowly. "Yes, I believe it. I can't be certain, of course, but I believe she's telling the truth."

"You're aware of certain . . . problems in her story?"

"You mean the fact that she went to her husband's apartment late at night?"

"Just because he asked her to."

"Yes, I'm aware of that."

"And her attitude, Doctor," Dowd said. "A doorman saw her minutes after she killed him. Then she was tape-recorded when she called the police an hour or so after the killing. And she was interrogated shortly after that. Each time, Louann showed absolutely no feeling. And she still feels nothing."

"*Feels* nothing?" Dr. Rosen asked. "Or *shows* nothing?"

She ground out her cigarette in an ashtray on a small

table next to her chair. She immediately pulled out another one, lighted it, and quickly blew a stream of smoke at the ceiling. She uncrossed her long legs, then recrossed them. Dr. Marsha Rosen was in her late forties, but she had the trim, athletic figure of a much younger woman. She had dark eyes that were perfectly made up, stylish eyeglasses, and dark brown hair that hung straight to her shoulders. She wore a form-fitting red gabardine Anne Klein suit, with a black print silk scarf wrapped around the neck, and black high-heeled shoes on gracefully tapering legs. She was an attractive woman.

The psychologist suddenly stood up and walked over to a bookcase that completely covered one wall of the small office. She found a file, then returned to the chair and began reading some notes inside the file.

"A moment," she said.

Dowd lit up a cigarette of his own, then looked around the office. It was small, and simply furnished. But tastefully, expensively. The Scandinavian chair. The very comfortable easy chair in which Dowd sat. A brown leather divan where patients could lie down while they talked. And the small table next to Dr. Rosen, holding nothing but an ashtray and a telephone. No desk. No filing cabinets. This was a room designed for intimate conversation.

The office was actually part of a co-op apartment located off Madison Avenue, near the Metropolitan Museum of Art. Patients of the psychologist took an elevator up to the fifth floor. Upon entering the apartment, visitors proceeded to a small anteroom off to the right where they could sit and wait; a door in the anteroom led into the office. The rest of the apartment was where Dr. Rosen and her husband, a technical writer, lived.

The psychologist glanced at a few more pages of notes in the file, then leaned back in her chair. Calmly, patiently, she began the summary for the lawyer.

"Louann Fratt was raised in a small town in Washington State. A lumber town. Family fairly well-to-do. Conservative, religious upbringing. Four siblings, though little bonding noted. Traditional patriarchal family structure."

"Uh-huh," Dowd said.

"The mother appears to have been rather submissive, quiet, reclusive. Again, little bonding between Louann and her mother. The father was the traditional dominant male figure. A physically large and strong person. Also reclusive, uncommunicative. Here, however, we have a stronger relationship with the father."

"Uh-huh."

"Within the family, there appears to have been very little physical or verbal expression of affection. Or of any other feelings for that matter." The psychologist paused, glancing again at her notes. She looked back up at Dowd. "I believe this is important."

"That they weren't affectionate."

"In other words, Mr. Dowd, emotion was not freely expressed. To the contrary, expression of emotion—whether anger, love, pain, or whatever—was strongly discouraged in the Johnson household. Showing your feelings was considered . . . inappropriate."

"So you're saying Louann was raised to keep her feelings to herself."

"Yes. And I believe this is relevant to understanding her apparently unemotional attitude in relating the . . . death of her husband. And the rape."

"Wait a minute," Dowd said. "You're not telling me she feels nothing about an attempted rape and a stabbing just because she's *stoic*."

Dr. Rosen sighed. "Her stoicism, as you put it, is not the reason she displays no feeling. That's just a mechanism she was taught as a child, a mechanism that proved very useful in her marriage to her husband."

"Then what *is* the reason?"

"Denial."

"Denial," Dowd repeated doubtfully.

"Louann Fratt has been denying—repressing—a very deep and painful reality in her life for a very long time now."

"And what is that?"

"The emptiness of her existence, Mr. Dowd."

Dowd just stared at the psychologist. Somewhere, deep inside, there was a sick feeling of something collapsing in on itself. My God, he thought, I'm supposed to convince a jury to acquit her because she's denying the emptiness of her existence!

"Let me go back," Dr. Rosen continued. "To appreciate Louann's perceptions of her own role in her marriage, I think it's important to understand the influence of the two role models in her formative years. These were, of course, her father and her mother."

"Uh-huh." The emptiness of her existence, Dowd kept thinking to himself. The jury would love that as a defense.

"Her father gave her the model of a husband: a big, physically powerful man, ambitious, competitive, materially successful, dominating . . . a tower of silent strength. In other words, the traditional ideal of the male in American society."

"So you're saying this is what she was looking for in a husband—a clone of her father."

"More or less. And notice the type of man she did, in fact, marry." Dr. Rosen glanced again at her notes, then back at Dowd. "Poe Fratt. A physically big man—a star football player, in fact. Aggressive, competitive. Business graduate of an Ivy League university, master's from Stanford—obviously a man headed for material success in the business world, like Louann's father. A traditional man, with traditional views of male-female relationships. And a dominating personality."

"So she married her dad."

"In a way," Dr. Rosen replied. "Now let's take a look at the role model for a wife—the role Louann observed and learned. Her mother was a very quiet, dutiful woman, completely subservient to her husband. She produced five children, raised them, maintained the household and, essentially, followed orders and kept her complaints to herself. Once again, the traditional ideal of the female in our society."

"Louann married her dad, and became her mom." Dowd glanced absently at his watch.

"Simplistic, of course, but essentially correct. At least in terms of viewing the respective roles in the marital relationship." Dr. Rosen took off her glasses, began wiping them clean with a small piece of blue cloth. "That's not unusual, you

understand. Those *were* the traditional roles. Even to a considerable extent today, these are the respected role models that
are played out by the parents and learned by the offspring."

"I guess I don't see how that explains—"

Dr. Rosen held her hand up. "I'm getting to that, Mr.
Dowd. Please bear with me."

"Sorry."

"When Louann met her future husband, she was a stewardess with United Airlines—a subservient role, not coinci-
dentally. Poe Fratt was just out of college and, at the time, an
army officer—a role of power and authority. He was big,
strong, dominating, successful. He met her needs and expecta-
tions. And the attractive, shapely, submissive Louann met Poe
Fratt's need for a dutiful wife who would be an asset in his
climb to the top of the corporate ladder."

"Uh-huh."

"Louann married Poe Fratt. As you said, she married her
father, and became her mother. Poe was the dominant head
of the household, in complete control, Louann the submissive
support system. Within five years, she had given birth to three
children. And for the thirty years of their marriage, she was
the faithful executive's wife—raising the children, providing
a home for her husband, entertaining his business associates,
attending social functions, belonging to the right organizations, moving whenever his career dictated . . ."

"That sounds like a lot of women."

"Yes," Dr. Rosen replied thoughtfully, almost sadly.

"So how was Louann different?"

"Not different. The process was just much more intense."

"I don't get it."

"Look at the family finances," she said. "Poe Fratt made
all of the decisions. All of the investments were in his name,
the stocks, the bonds, the real estate—even the car and the co-
op on Seventy-ninth. He had nine credit cards and unlimited
funds; she had one card and a limited expense account to pay
household bills."

"Uh-huh."

"Look, let me give you an example." Dr. Rosen leaned
forward slightly, her eyes still intently on Dowd. "During one
of my sessions with Louann, she mentioned something about

borrowing the keys from her husband so she could use the car. I asked her why she hadn't had a second set of keys made. Do you know what she said? She said, 'Oh, Poe would never permit that!' "

Dowd nodded slowly.

"Do you see? She couldn't even perceive that she had a *right* to use the car."

"Yeah." But he didn't see. You can't kill your husband just because he's domineering—at least, not in New York.

"This gives you some idea of how completely Poe controlled their marriage," the psychologist continued. "And, of course, all of this fit in with the role Louann had learned."

"So he dominated Louann," Dowd repeated to himself, trying to understand the significance of the fact.

"Completely. So much so that, in time, Louann Fratt began to lose her own identity."

Dowd just stared at the woman seated across the desk without comprehension.

"You see," Dr. Rosen said, "Louann discarded her own life. She became an appendage of Poe Fratt. She existed only in terms of him—his career, his needs, his desires, his commands. In other words, she ceased to be Louann Fratt and became, instead, a part of her husband."

Dowd once more just nodded slowly.

"We have a name for this," she said. "Dependent personality disorder."

"Dependent personality disorder," Dowd repeated.

"Yes. An individual's personality becomes subservient to that of another individual. In effect, that individual's personality simply disappears as a separate entity."

"Uh-huh."

"Let me put it another way. If Louann Fratt were walking on the beach with her husband, I would bet anything that she would be very careful to step in his footprints."

Dowd envisioned the scene, the couple walking on the beach, Louann trailing her husband, carefully placing her feet in the large footprints.

"Okay. I think I get the picture. But how does that help me defend her in trial?"

Dr. Rosen was silent for a moment. She blew another

stream of smoke at the ceiling. "Her master's voice," she said
finally.

"What?"

"Her master's voice," she repeated. "Look, you said that a
jury wouldn't believe she went over to Poe Fratt's apartment
in the middle of the night just because he asked her to bring
his mail."

"That's a fact."

"Well, Louann went for a simple reason: The master called
and she obeyed."

Dowd thought for a moment. "Her master's voice," he
repeated to himself. "Dependent personality disorder . . ."

"Yes."

Dowd frowned, shook his head. "But they'd been separated for half a year. He wasn't the master anymore."

"That didn't change who she was, who she had become.
Six months wouldn't have changed thirty years of indoctrina-
tion, of brainwashing, if you will."

"Her master's voice," Dowd said again quietly. The phrase
had a nice sound to it, the kind that would echo in a juror's
mind during those long hours of deliberations. The kind of
sound that resulted in acquittals. Louann Fratt had come to
the apartment that night because, quite simply, her master
had commanded it.

"Her master's voice," Dr. Rosen repeated.

Dowd continued to wrestle with these new concepts, trying to understand where they fit in the slowly emerging picture
of what had happened on the night his client had killed her
husband—what had happened, and why.

Just before Louann Fratt had stabbed her husband to
death, she had walked to his apartment in the middle of the
night. Alone, on the deserted streets of New York. With a knife.
To deliver his mail. No jury in the world would buy that.

Dowd studied Dr. Rosen as she continued to explain the
reasons for her patient's strange behavior. Would the jury
listen to this woman? he wondered. Would the jury accept her
explanation—theory?—that the defendant had gone simply
because her estranged husband told her to?

He knew that juries inherently distrusted psychologists
and psychiatrists. He knew that the average juror would not

let an "expert" tell him why people acted the way they did; the average juror believed he *knew*. And Dowd knew that jurors, deep inside, could not accept the concept that a person may not be accountable for his actions. This was the real reason the public had been so outraged at the John Hinckley decision—despite not being familiar with any of the evidence. And despite such occasional aberrations as the Hinckley verdict, Dowd knew that more than 90 percent of insanity defenses failed—usually because jurors simply rejected psychiatric testimony.

Of course, there was good reason for jurors' mistrust of psychiatric witnesses. What were they *supposed* to think when each side produced doctors who testified to opposing "truths"? It was common knowledge in the legal community that "experts" were available to testify to anything a lawyer wanted. These witnesses were referred to, appropriately, as "medical whores." And there was no shortage of them. Want to convince a jury that your client didn't know what he was doing when he molested and then murdered a little boy? There was a list of fifteen highly qualified doctors in the Manhattan area alone who would swear to it—for the right price. Want to prosecute a retarded and mentally incompetent fifteen-year-old for beating his mother to death? There were twenty-two respected members of the medical profession who were willing to testify that he was as fit to stand trial as you or I—for the right price.

But Dr. Marsha Rosen was another matter. She didn't sell her testimony. She wasn't on any list. In fact, she had never been in court in her life. Her practice was limited to helping people who needed her.

Dowd continued looking at the psychologist. She would be a good witness, he thought. Calm, articulate, professional, sincere. And, for all their shortcomings, Dowd had faith in juries. He knew they had an innate sense of what was right and what was wrong, what was true and what was not. Jurors would respect Dr. Rosen, trust her. And, he hoped, believe her.

". . . incapable of conceiving alternatives," the psychologist was saying.

Dowd came back to earth. "Uh, how does all this explain why Louann is so . . . unfeeling about the whole thing?"

"It doesn't—by itself. We have to look further. And this is where the denial, the repression, comes in."

"Uh-huh."

"Look, it's one thing to devote your entire life to your husband, to lose your very identity to him. It's quite another to then be betrayed by that husband."

"Betrayed?"

"Yes. A wife could exist—millions do—if that devotion is repaid with affection or, at least, respect. But Poe Fratt had little but contempt for his wife. He ridiculed her in front of friends, he constantly called her 'stupid,' he knocked her to the ground on a few occasions, he doled out money as he saw fit, he had affairs with other women . . . Louann was an *emotionally* battered woman, Mr. Dowd—a woman who suffered from some of the same symptoms of helplessness, dependency, and low self-esteem as physically battered women."

Dr. Rosen waited for a moment, letting it sink in. Then she continued. "Quite simply, Louann's husband considered her as chattel—a possession to be used."

"Chattel."

"Yes. Poe Fratt dominated Louann, owned her, controlled her, used her. And when finally he tired of his property after thirty years, he discarded her." Dr. Rosen's professional voice had developed a hint of anger.

Again, Dowd's mind was processing the new information, adding the pieces to the jigsaw puzzle, trying to make out the emerging picture. Processing the information—and weighing it for its effect in trial. Chattel . . . a possession . . . used, then discarded . . .

"Imagine what it must be like, Mr. Dowd," the psychologist continued. "Imagine devoting your entire life to another person, and in the process becoming completely dependent upon that person. Imagine, then, when you are old and your usefulness is diminished, that person simply abandoning you." She paused. "How would you feel?"

Dowd thought for a moment. He tried to put himself in that position, tried to understand what it felt like. But he could not. "I don't know," he said finally, "I really don't."

Would a juror be able to feel it? Could a female juror? Would it take an older married woman to understand —feel—what Louann went through?

"Well," Dr. Rosen continued, "Louann dealt with it by using a classical mechanism—a mechanism she learned in her childhood: repression. She simply denies, or represses, the painful reality. She represses her own feelings. It is too costly, emotionally too costly, to admit to herself the valueless role she has played for thirty years. It is too costly to admit the emotional betrayal by her husband. Too costly to deal with being raped by your own husband."

Denial, Dowd thought to himself. Repression. Emotional betrayal.

"And," the psychologist continued, "ultimately, too costly to confront the emotional reality of stabbing your husband to death."

Dowd worked on this for a moment. "So . . . she shows no feelings," he said hesitantly, "when she talks about the killing . . . because those feelings would be too painful . . . and so she represses them, denies them . . . like she did as a child."

"Yes. In effect, she becomes a spectator."

"A spectator."

"On the sidelines, talking about events in her own life. An unemotional, uninvolved observer."

Dowd played with the concept. An observer. The voice on the 911 tape sounded like an observer's. The woman who was interrogated by the police was an observer. And the woman who told Dowd about rape and murder was certainly nothing more than an observer.

"I would expect," Dr. Rosen said, "that Louann Fratt recounted the murder to you as if she were describing a slightly distasteful encounter with a store clerk."

Dowd nodded slowly. "That's about what it sounded like."

He suddenly felt that familiar electric charge surge through his body, that first faint, exciting scent of a distant victory. The pieces were falling into place. A picture was beginning to emerge, a hazy window into the soul of Louann Fratt. And with it, hope.

Dowd found himself thinking about one of the hundreds

of tactical decisions he had to make before trial. It involved a seemingly unimportant procedural matter: Should he send notice to the district attorney that he intended to use psychiatric testimony? The New York statutes required the attorney for either side to notify his opponent of his intention to offer testimony of a psychiatric nature. The purpose of the requirement was, first, to help eliminate the element of surprise from criminal trials and, second, to give the opposing counsel a chance to produce opposing evidence so that the jury would get both sides of an issue. It was one of dozens of procedural requirements that had to be complied with before trial. And it did not appear to have any particularly critical strategic importance.

Dowd could not know that this decision was later to prove nearly fatal to his client.

Should he send notice? The statutory deadline for giving notice was fast approaching, as was the trial date. Certainly, Daniel Brownell was expecting the notice—but he was anticipating testimony very different than that of Dr. Rosen. Brownell was expecting Dowd to produce experts to testify that Louann Fratt had been suffering from battered wife syndrome. Of course, Dowd had no intention of presenting a syndrome defense: His case was based upon simple, old-fashioned self-defense.

Dowd knew that the longer he could keep Brownell preparing to counter a nonexistent defense, the better chance Louann Fratt would have for an acquittal. When the deadline for sending notice came and went, however, the young prosecutor would immediately realize that there was no battered wife defense. He would also realize that Dowd's only other possible position had to be self-defense.

If Dowd did not send notice, he would not be permitted at trial to produce any testimony of a psychiatric nature: Dr. Rosen could not testify. And Brownell would point his investigators in a new direction—gathering evidence to disprove self-defense. If Dowd *did* send notice, Dr. Rosen could testify—and Brownell would continue to believe that the psychiatric testimony to be produced related to battered wife syndrome.

An easy decision.

Dowd decided to send the notice of psychiatric testimony to Brownell. First thing tomorrow.

Dr. Rosen's voice returned. ". . . not eliminated, of course. The trauma is simply repressed, buried."

She would be a terrific witness, Dowd thought again to himself as he listened to the psychologist. Her testimony would be critical in explaining why Louann Fratt had gone to her husband's apartment late that night. No less important, it would explain her seemingly uncaring attitude when she testified about the killing.

But there was still a nagging doubt in his mind. There was this irritating little fact that would not go away.

"Doctor," Dowd said, "I can understand how this . . . repression could make Louann sound unemotional when she was talking to me a few days after the killing. And it could explain how she may sound that way on the witness stand during trial, months after it happened."

"Yes?"

"Still . . . wouldn't she show feelings right after the killing? I mean, repressing feelings about things that have happened in the past is one thing. But . . . stabbing your husband to death after he tries to rape you—how do you repress feelings *right now?*"

Dr. Rosen nodded her head slowly. "Her denial mechanism may not be effective in dealing with immediate trauma."

There were pieces still missing from the puzzle.

"Then we're right back to trying to explain why she appeared so calm and unaffected to the doorman minutes after the killing," Dowd said, "and to the cops shortly after that. And the voice on the nine-one-one tape . . ."

"It had to be some kind of reaction to the trauma."

"Uh-huh."

"It's my guess that her system just shut down, emotionally. An overload, if you will."

Dowd considered this, again weighing it for fit and feel.

"Have you ever heard of 'rape trauma syndrome,' Mr. Dowd?"

"Yeah. Julie Blackman mentioned that."

"Well, it's not my field, but you might want to look into it."

Dowd thought for a moment. "You know, Louann wasn't actually *raped*, Doctor. Her husband just grabbed her, *tried* to rape her."

"I know. But I think it would be helpful to talk with an expert."

Dowd nodded, considering this. "Julie gave me the name of an expert," he said.

"Dr. Veronen?"

"I think that's it."

Dr. Rosen nodded approvingly, then became silent.

"Well . . ." Dowd said, rising from the chair.

Dr. Rosen stood also, smiling now. She quickly smoothed a few wrinkles from her skirt, then extended her hand.

"Many thanks," Dowd said, taking the offered hand. "You've been a great help. You really have." He paused. "I hope I can count on your testimony." It was a question.

"Of course. Anything I can do."

Dowd turned to leave.

"It's strange," Dr. Rosen said quietly, almost to herself.

Dowd turned back. "What did you say?"

She stared down at the file on her desk. "The world saw Louann Fratt as a wealthy, influential socialite, the privileged wife of a top executive." She paused. "Every woman's dream." She looked up at Dowd. "The simple fact is that she led an empty, meaningless life, ridiculed and betrayed by her husband."

Dowd said nothing.

The psychologist was silent again for a moment, then smiled sadly. "The woman who had everything . . . had nothing."

Dowd stood there for a moment, looking at Dr. Rosen. Then he turned and walked out of the office.

CHAPTER 12

This was the courtroom where Louann Fratt would soon be tried for murder.

Dowd sat in the front row of wooden pews, his battered leather satchel on his lap. He only half listened as a young black female prosecutor in a conservative gray wool suit explained to the judge why a motion by the defense to postpone the trial for two months should not be granted. The defense lawyer, a hugely obese man in a beige polyester leisure suit, stood silently next to his client, a tall black man in black jeans and a black leather jacket. The lawyer appeared intensely bored.

". . . the third time he's asked for a continuance, Your Honor," the prosecutor was saying. "The People of the State of New York have a right to speedy trial, too."

The judge looked at the defense lawyer. "Counselor?" he growled.

Judge Budd Goodman was a short, high-strung, irritable man in his fifties, with piercing black eyes and large black eyebrows that seemed permanently furrowed into a scowl. A contrasting salt-and-pepper beard and a semibald head accentuated his dark brows and eyes, giving them an even more forbidding appearance. His large, square, tortoiseshell-rimmed glasses seemed strangely out of place. Oddly, the judge did not sit behind the bench, but rather stood and paced nervously back and forth behind the bench as the two attorneys argued.

The fat lawyer shrugged. "What can I do, Your Honor? I mean, we're talking a key witness. We're talking a key witness. Mr. Henderson here"—he nodded at his client—"he's, I mean, he's got a right to due process. He's got a right."

Dowd smiled to himself. Every lawyer in the room knew who the missing witness was: the ubiquitous "Mr. Green." The client hadn't paid the fat man all of his fee yet. So the lawyer was asking for a continuance, stalling the case until more money was forthcoming.

Due process.

Dowd looked around the courtroom again, familiarizing himself with the lay of the land. Located on the sixteenth floor of the Criminal Courts Building, this room was officially known as Part 62 of the Supreme Court of New York. This was to be the battleground. This was where Dowd and Brownell would meet in combat. This was where the fate of Louann Fratt would be decided.

But not today. The Fratt trial was still weeks away. Today, the judge to whom the case had been assigned had scheduled a routine pretrial hearing. Dowd and Brownell would present any last-minute motions or bring up any possible problems that needed resolving before the day of trial.

Dowd continued studying the courtroom, much as a general might study the terrain on the eve of battle. It was a large room, divided in half by a three-foot-high wooden partition that separated the audience pews from the working area; a swinging gate in the center of the partition permitted access between the two halves of the room. A badly peeling sign on the partition read FRONT ROW ATTORNEYS AND POLICE OFFICERS ONLY.

The light brown linoleum floor was cracking and, in two or three places, beginning to curl. The rear and side walls were painted an odd fleshlike color, while the front wall was wallpapered to give a beige rattan effect; large clusters of lumps and bubbles attested to a civil service papering job.

Backed up against the front wall, and commanding the

entire room, was the massive, raised wooden bench of the judge. On the bench was a brass gavel and a plaque reading HON. BUDD G. GOODMAN. On the wall behind the bench, spread out across the rattan wallpaper, were large brass letters spelling out the words IN GOD WE TRUST.

Directly in front of and below the bench was a small table and an empty chair. During trial, a court reporter with a stenotype machine would sit at the table and take down everything that was said. To the left of the bench was a simple wooden chair on a raised platform: the witness chair. Behind the empty chair was a U.S. flag on a tall pole. To the right of the bench, against the wall, was a coatrack loaded with coats and a metal filing cabinet. This wall was covered with a confusion of pinned-up notices, memoranda, directories, and a large, heavily marked Municipal Credit Union calendar.

The jury box was flush against the left wall, encased in another three-foot-high wooden partition. Two rows of swivel chairs, empty now, were lined up along two successively higher platforms, parallel to the wall and facing across the room.

On the right side of the courtroom were two large old oak desks, belonging to the court clerk and the bailiff. The desks were arranged side by side so that they faced back across the room at the jury box. At the clerk's desk, a harried-looking man in a white shirt with rolled-up sleeves and a paisley tie was frantically shuffling through papers while whispering into a telephone receiver balanced on his shoulder. Two bailiffs sat on the edge of the other desk, appearing terminally bored; they wore white shirts with gold badges, black ties, dark blue trousers, and black leather belts loaded down with holsters, guns, ammunition holders, and keychains.

In the center of the room were two large wooden tables, each with two wooden chairs, facing the judge's bench. These were the counsel tables. By tradition, the table closest to the jury was for the prosecutor; the second chair was for any legal assistant or investigating officer. The table to the right was for the defendant and his attorney.

Behind the counsel tables was the wooden partition beyond which was the audience area—a dozen or so rows of wooden pews separated by an aisle that ran down the center from the entrance door to the swinging gate. The pews were almost all empty now, save for a few attorneys and a defendant or two. Taking up the far right side of the audience area was an eight-foot-high partition. This was "the pen," a narrow, enclosed area where shackled prisoners were led in through a hidden door and held until their case was called.

The room, like most courtrooms, was laid out like an arena or a boxing ring, with judge, jury, officials, and audience lined up along the four sides. Directly in the center were the two combatants.

". . . plead to count three, we dismiss one and two." The prosecutor's voice droned on as Dowd's mind drifted.

He looked out two large windows on the right side of the room, out over the jungle of Lower East Side rooftops far below. The skies were cold and dark with the threat of rain, the darkness accentuated by the harsh glare of the fluorescent lighting inside the courtroom. The contrast was heightened by the suffocating heat in the room.

". . . no way my client does three years. No way, Your Honor. Not for a lousy two ounces."

Dowd again looked around the courtroom for some relief from the boredom. Seated to his right on the wooden bench were two younger lawyers. One was immaculately dressed in a three-piece pin-striped suit. The other wore fashionably baggy trousers, an open-necked silk shirt under a white sport coat, a gold chain necklace, and one pierced earring. Identical burgundy leather briefcases rested on the floor between them.

To Dowd's left was an older lawyer in a plain brown suit, leaning back with his legs crossed and reading one of the New York tabloids. Dowd knew him slightly as a "runner"—a lawyer hungry enough for money to appear for other, busier lawyers on such unimportant but time-consuming matters as arraignments and motions to continue. A dozen years ago this man had been a gifted prosecutor with a nearly unbroken string of convictions. Then came the alcohol. And the cocaine.

Dowd knew a lot of men like this one. Good, competent attorneys. But they cracked. They fell apart. Battle fatigue was part of it, shell shock—the constant strain of being in trial day after day, year after year, in a war seemingly without end. And, of course, there were the effects of dealing with the darkest side of human nature, of living in a dehumanizing world of senseless violence and mangled victims, of drug addiction and mutilated children. And there were the lies—the rampant, corrupting, suffocating lying by witnesses, cops, lawyers, judges—so pervasive that truth became no longer recognizable or even relevant.

Burnout.

Dowd found himself once again wondering if it would happen to him. And if it did, then what? What does a worn-out, middle-aged criminal lawyer do? How does he support a family?

Dowd glanced again at the older lawyer reading his paper.

What Dowd did not realize was that he would never crack, never fall apart. What saved him, what protected him from the ravages of battle and darkness, was his passion and his idealism. Dowd believed in what he was doing and believed it was right and good. As long as he believed that, he would be safe.

Dowd's mind came back to reality as Daniel Brownell walked down the aisle and quietly sat down in the front pew on the other side of the room. He nodded toward Dowd. Dowd smiled, nodded back.

The enemy.

". . . time off for good behavior, do two years, no more," the prosecutor was saying.

"Now look, goddamn it!" Judge Goodman said, suddenly stopping his pacing behind the bench. "You two get out of here and you sit down and talk, you hear me?"

"Judge—" the prosecutor began.

"I don't want to hear it!" the judge interrupted her. "You two work it out. We got no time for cases like this! We got a busy calendar." He leaned forward, staring intently at the prosecutor. "You work a deal. You got that?"

"Yes, Your Honor," she sighed resignedly.

The fat lawyer smiled slightly as he reached down for his Samsonite attaché. The case was a complete loser, but he had won a victory. The client had paid him $7,500 of the $10,000 fee; the lawyer would probably never see the rest. Since the scumbag client would never have agreed to plead "straight up," the case would have gone to trial. That meant three or four days of hard work. Now, because of a congested court docket, the case would be plea-bargained. It was simple: $7,500 for a couple of hours setting up a plea versus $7,500 for three or four days of hard work in trial. A victory.

"Well, Mr. Brownell!" Judge Goodman said, looking down at the young prosecutor in the audience. "How kind of you to grace my courtroom."

"Good morning, Your Honor," Brownell replied politely, ignoring the sarcasm. He rose to his feet.

"When I say calendar call goes at nine thirty, I don't mean nine forty-five."

"I apologize, Your Honor," the prosecutor said, stepping forward. "I was tied up in another court."

"Next time, you better bring your toothbrush."

"I understand, Your Honor."

The clerk walked to the bench with a file, handed it to the judge.

"People versus . . .", Goodman said, glancing at the file name. "Fratt, Louann Fratt." He looked up. "Mr. Dowd?"

"Right here, Your Honor," Dowd said, standing up. He and Brownell stepped forward through the swinging door as the fat lawyer and his client walked out, the female prosecutor following. She looked at Brownell for a moment as they passed, shaking her head slightly in disgust.

Dowd set his briefcase down on the counsel table and remained standing. Brownell stood behind the other table.

"Your reputation precedes you, Mr. Dowd," the judge said. "Are we going to have another of your tea and crumpets defenses?"

It was going to be a long day, Dowd thought to himself. And a long trial.

"All right," Goodman growled, stepping down from behind the bench and walking over to the counsel tables. He unsnapped his black robe so that it was completely open in front and sat down on Dowd's table. "We're here for pretrial. Any problems? Any motions? What have you two got?"

Dowd had heard about Judge Budd Goodman. When the Fratt case had been assigned to Part 62, Dowd had asked around about him. The good news was that he was honest, hardworking, and independent. In 1975, he had testified against an attorney who had tried to bribe him; Goodman had reported the matter and had agreed to being wired at a later meeting with the lawyer. He was also one of only two judges in the state designated by the governor to handle cases involving corruption within the legal system. And, unlike many judges, he was totally oblivious of the political power of the district attorney's office: Prosecutors received no favorable treatment in his courtroom.

The bad news was that Goodman had a reputation among some female lawyers as an ill-tempered tyrant and a sexist. He was also reportedly going through a bitter divorce from his wife at the time. This last fact was particularly troublesome to Dowd. Louann Fratt's case involved a wife who killed her estranged husband during a divorce. Could Goodman handle the case without any personal prejudice? And would his chauvinist views preclude him from being fair about the psychological issues involved in the case?

The "tea and crumpets" comment did not ease any of Dowd's concerns.

Dowd was beginning to get an uncomfortably familiar feeling, a feeling he had during the Ciervo case. . . .

Doris Ciervo lived in the middle-class neighborhood of Ozone Park in Queens. And she was married to a man who beat and tortured her.

On one occasion, for example, Louis Ciervo beat her so badly with a fireplace poker that she spent five days in the hospital. On other occasions he cut her with a knife, pistol-whipped her in the shower with his gun, and repeatedly put out cigarettes on her leg. And, to "loosen her up" sexually, he forced her to take illegal drugs. Louis also repeatedly told Doris that if she tried to leave him, he would kill her and the two children.

Their eight-year-old daughter Jennifer was a terrified witness to these beatings. She noticed a pattern: Her father would beat her mother for a while, then go into the kitchen for a break; after a time, he would come back out and resume hitting her. At night Jennifer would hear crying and screams from her parents' bedroom. In the mornings she would find her mother lying on bloody sheets, her face and body cut and bruised.

Jennifer became almost like a mother to her own mother, soothing her and cleaning her wounds and changing the sheets. Inevitably, Jennifer became an object of abuse herself: On one occasion she lost a week of school recovering from a "punishment" administered by her father for calling the police during a particularly violent episode with her mother.

At about 5:00 one morning, Louis began hitting Jennifer's head against the back of a dining room chair, accusing her of always taking her mother's side. At this point, Doris was awakened by the screaming and came into the dining room. After pausing for a beer, Louis then grabbed their young son and, calling him a "faggot," began banging his head against the dining table.

After that Louis followed his familiar pattern, going into the kitchen for a break before resuming the violence. Doris was now frightened for her children's lives: Her husband "had a funny look in his eyes—he looked crazy." She went into the bedroom, got Louis's gun, walked into the kitchen, and shot him in the head.

As he had done so often before, Dowd decided to represent the woman without charge.

In September 1984, trial began in the Supreme Court of Queens. From the beginning the trial was a farce, presided over by a blatantly sexist seventy-five-year-old judge who had earlier been censured for his comments in two rape cases. Interestingly, the prosecutor opposing Dowd was a woman; in a tactic that was to become familiar to Dowd, the D.A.'s office had decided to "fight fire with fire."

The judge repeatedly kept Dowd from offering evidence of Louis's violence, while permitting the prosecutor to show that any beatings were—incredibly—*justified*! Thus, for example, the judge refused to permit defense witnesses to testify to Doris's periodic battered appearance for the two years preceding the killing. Yet, when Doris took the stand, the judge permitted a freewheeling character assassination during cross-examination. Over Dowd's violent objections, the prosecutor established that the children stayed up later at night with

Doris than they did with their grandparents, that there was a lock on the children's bedroom door, and that after her arrest they had stayed with a girlfriend of hers rather than with Doris herself. All of this was permitted by the judge on the grounds that it was relevant to whether Doris had been a poor mother—and, so, whether Louis had been reasonably provoked to beat her!

The judge then permitted evidence that Doris had had an affair with a man—again as evidence that Louis was "justified" in beating her. Amazingly, the prosecutor even offered to prove that Doris had been involved in two car accidents, running a red light in one of them; the judge ruled that the evidence was admissible only if the prosecutor could show that these were acts that provoked Louis to beat his wife.

The prosecutor was permitted to ask Doris if she had used drugs—once again, to prove that Louis had reasonable grounds for beating her. Yet, in perhaps the most amazing ruling of the trial, the judge then refused to permit Dowd to offer evidence that Louis was a drug dealer and had forced her to take the drugs!

Two experts testified. Dowd called Dr. Julie Doron, a psychology professor at Barnard College. She characterized Doris Ciervo as a classic "battered woman." She explained that "people who have the most power over us are those who can move us through the broadest emotional ranges; battered women remain in relationships where these ranges are extreme, running from grave despair to times of peace and tremendous relief." Noting that Doris had "admitted" during cross-examination that many of her beatings had been "reasonable," she pointed out that women suffering from the syndrome typically believe they deserve the abuse they receive.

The prosecutor called Dr. Debra Kaiser in rebuttal: In Dr. Kaiser's opinion, Doris was simply not a "battered woman."

As he always did, Dowd spent the first ten minutes of cross-examination asking unimportant questions designed to "train" the witness, control her, and finally dominate her. "You have to get them to answer yes or no, teach them not to argue, to understand who's the boss," Dowd would explain. "Once you've got them, *then* you get into the important questions."

And Dowd destroyed the prosecution's "expert": Under his intense questioning, Dr. Kaiser admitted that she had never done any research on battered wives—in fact, had never even *read* anything on the subject until asked to do so by the prosecutor.

Despite the travesty of a trial, the jury remained deadlocked for days. They finally returned with a verdict: guilty of manslaughter in the first degree and of possession of (Louis's) weapon. The judge sentenced Doris Ciervo to five to ten years in prison.

Dowd immediately filed an appeal. For two years Dowd fought her conviction in the appellate courts.

In November 1986, his long struggle was rewarded: The conviction was reversed and the case remanded for a new trial. Emotionally unable to face a second trial, Doris agreed to the D.A.'s offer of a reduced charge with a guarantee of no time in custody.

Although Dowd succeeded in keeping Doris out of prison (he had gotten her out on bail during the appeal), he felt no joy. Doris had lost forty pounds and most of her hair, and had become addicted to crack.

"You never really win these cases," he says. "These women are never the same again."

Judge Goodman looked at Brownell and Dowd. "Any motions to suppress?"

"No, Your Honor," Dowd said. "There was a search warrant, but nothing came of it."

"Any problems with discovery?"

"A few things left," Dowd said, "but we're working on them."

"Well, well," the judge said, "it looks like the decks are cleared."

"One thing, Your Honor," Brownell said quietly.

"Yeah?"

"Ah . . . counsel has forwarded notice of psychiatric testimony."

Goodman looked at Dowd with undisguised disgust. Tea and crumpets. "So?" he said to Brownell.

"Well, it was just a blanket notice. I think we're entitled to specifics."

"Specifics?" Dowd asked. What did he mean, "specifics"?

"Go on," Goodman said to the prosecutor.

"Well, he hasn't given me the *names* of the witnesses."

"The *names*!" Dowd repeated incredulously.

"Or their C.V.s. Or the nature of their testimony."

"What!" Dowd almost yelled.

"Calm down!" Goodman said to Dowd. Then, to Brownell: "Go on."

Brownell shrugged. "Under the statute, we're entitled to know who the experts are, what their training and experience is, what they're going to testify to."

"The *hell* you are!" Dowd roared.

The judge glared at Dowd. "This is *my* courtroom, Mr. Dowd!" He thought for a moment. Then, to the prosecutor, "What's the cite?"

Brownell opened his briefcase, shuffled through some notes. "Crim. Procedure," he said finally. "Section 250.10c."

Goodman turned to the clerk. "Criminal Procedure," he yelled. The clerk immediately put down a file he was reviewing and brought over a book.

Goodman fingered through some pages, then stopped and read in silence. Finally, he looked up at Dowd. "Well?"

"He's asking to see our cards," Dowd said angrily. "The prosecution's never had the right to anything but notice that testimony of a psychiatric nature will be offered."

"This is a recently revised statute," Brownell said.

"Yeah, it's revised, but it doesn't say anything about having to tell you who our witnesses are and what they're going to say."

Goodman read again, then looked back up at Dowd. "It says you have to advise them of evidence relating to a psychiatric-type defense."

"And I *did*. I advised them I would be offering that kind of evidence."

"That's not what the statute means," Brownell injected. "You have to tell us what the evidence *is*, not just that it exists."

"The *hell* I do!" Dowd roared.

Goodman glared at Dowd. Then he looked back in the book, read again.

Dowd couldn't believe that the judge was even considering Brownell's suggestion. An adverse ruling here would be a big blow strategically. Dowd would have to tell Brownell about Dr. Rosen and what she would testify to. And about Dr. Veronen, too, if she had anything to offer. It would not only let Brownell know that there was no battered wife syndrome evidence, it would give him a close look at Louann's entire defense. As it stood, the prosecutor was still in the dark. He would have to wait until the evidence was offered in trial; he would have to hurriedly prepare cross-examination and then scramble for witnesses of his own for his rebuttal. If Goodman accepted Brownell's interpretation of the statute, however, the young prosecutor would be ready with detailed cross-examination before trial, probably prepared with the help of experts. More important, he would take the wind out of Dowd's sails by producing experts to discredit the defense theory—before Dowd even had a chance to call Dr. Rosen.

Goodman looked up at the two lawyers. "Do either of you have any cases?"

The judge was asking if there were any appellate court decisions that interpreted what the words of the statute meant.

Brownell shook his head. "It was just revised. There haven't been any decisions yet."

Goodman nodded. "Well," he said cheerfully, "then *this* will be the one." He looked at Dowd. "You will give notice to the prosecution of the names of any witnesses—"

"But—" Dowd protested.

"—along with their résumés, and the subject matter of their testimony."

"Your Honor—"

"That is the court's ruling," Goodman said with finality.

"Damn it, that's not what the statute says!" Dowd exploded. "And no court has ever held it says that!"

Goodman glared at Dowd again in silence. Goodman was known to throw lawyers in jail for contempt, and Dowd was now on the ragged edge of doing some time.

"Anything else?" the judge said ominously.

Dowd took a deep breath, gritted his teeth, then let his breath out. He said nothing.

Goodman looked to Brownell.

"No, sir," the prosecutor said.

"Very well," Judge Goodman said. Then, smiling slightly at Dowd, "I'll see you in trial."

CHAPTER 13

Charles Kennedy Poe Fratt, Jr., looked like a heavyweight boxer trying to pass as a Wall Street broker.

Dowd could see the father in Poe Jr.'s solidly built linebacker's body, in the broad cheekbones, the heavy eyebrows, and the massive jaw. But the mother was in his fine, straight blond hair and, most noticeably, in his eyes—the deep green eyes set in narrow slits that were a trademark of all three Fratt kids. From no one in particular, Poe Jr. had also acquired a scarred left eyebrow and a damaged right eyeball. At twenty-eight years of age, the ruggedly handsome Poe Fratt, Jr., looked like he had lost more than his share of fights.

Yet, the scarred, swollen-eyed, muscular young man was dressed in a conservative pin-striped dark blue suit, immaculate white shirt, silk burgundy tie, and black wing-tip shoes. And when he spoke, it was in a soft voice, at times almost inaudible, but always polite, respectful. What appeared to be a punch-drunk street fighter was, in reality, a sensitive, intelligent, and well-mannered young man.

"What time was it when she called?" Dowd asked.

"About three," Poe Jr. said. "Maybe three-thirty."

Dowd wrote something down on a yellow legal pad lying on his desk. "And you were in Ithaca. Cornell."

"Yes, sir."

Following in his father's footsteps, Dowd thought to himself. An M.B.A. from the old alma mater, then on into the business world, maybe a giant accounting firm like Peat Marwick. Looking at the young man seated across the desk from him, Dowd had the strange feeling that he was talking to a clone of the elder Poe Fratt. Except for the eyes. It was Louann's narrow green eyes that looked back at him. He wondered how much of his mother was in this young man.

"You were asleep when she called?"

"Yes, sir."

"Please tell me again what she said."

Poe Jr. took a deep breath, let it out. "She . . . My mother . . . called, and she said, 'I think I've killed your father.' "

"Uh-huh."

"And then she said that she wasn't sure, and she was going to call Emergency Services. She said she'd call back as soon as she found out if he was alive or not."

"Uh-huh," Dowd said, still studying Louann Fratt's son. What had it been like? What was it like to have your mother call in the middle of the night and tell you that she's just stabbed your father to death?

"Did she say anything else?"

"Just . . . that she was going to call the police, and she'd call back."

"But she never did call back."

"No, sir."

"Tell me, Poe, what did your mother *sound* like when she was talking to you on the phone?"

"Sound like?"

"Yes, you know, did she sound hysterical? Was she crying?"

The young man thought back for a moment, then shook his head slowly. "No, no, she sounded pretty much like she always does."

"Like she always does."

"Yes, sir."

"Uh-huh. Did you say anything, ask her anything?"

"I don't think so. I guess I was pretty sleepy."

"How long did this conversation take?"

"Oh . . . maybe a minute, maybe two. No more than that."

Dowd leaned back in the green leather chair, continuing to watch the handsome young man across the desk. What was going on in his mind as he talked to a stranger about the murder of his father by his mother? It was hard to tell; like the mother, the son kept his feelings to himself.

Dowd grabbed a crumpled pack of cigarettes from among the pile of papers, pulled one out. "You mind?" he asked, holding the cigarette up.

Poe Jr. shook his head.

Dowd lit up, took a deep drag. "What did you do after that?"

"Well, I made some calls. Then I got dressed and I drove to Manhattan, to the police station."

"Who did you call?"

"First, I tried to call my father. But all I got was his answering machine."

"Uh-huh."

"I called there five or six times, I guess. Trying to get him. Then trying to get my mother. I mean, she said she was going over there."

Dowd wrote down something.

"And I tried calling my mother at home. I couldn't get her either. I remember I also called a friend. To get the name of a good criminal lawyer. I got a name, and I called the guy. You know, John Kelly. I told him what happened, and he said he'd meet me at the police station."

"And you drove to the station and met him there?"

"Yes, sir. Well, she was at the police station for a few minutes, then she was taken to the hospital for an hour or two." Poe Jr. looked down at the hands folded in his lap. "She had some bruises on her face, some cuts on her hands," he added quietly.

Dowd nodded. After a moment, he asked, "Then you went back to the police station?"

"Yes, sir," he said, looking back up, his chin higher than before. "They brought her back after the doctor saw her."

"And you saw your mother."

"Yes, sir."

"How did she seem to you?"

"Seem?"

"Depressed? Crying?"

Poe Jr. shrugged. "Quiet. Tired. Pretty unhappy, I guess."

"Uh-huh."

"After that, we left the station. I mean, they booked her, and put her in . . . they put her in jail." Dowd could see the slight twitching of his jaw muscles. "The lawyer, Kelly, he talked with her. We couldn't get bail, but Kelly said he'd try another court or something. Anyway, we left."

"Uh-huh."

"I called my brother and my sister, they're in California." He shrugged.

Dowd made a few more notes on the legal pad. The young man would make a credible witness, but he didn't have a whole lot to contribute yet.

"Poe, when was the last time you saw your father?"

"I . . . identified him in the morgue."

Oh, Jesus. "I'm sorry. I meant when was the last time you saw him alive?"

"Oh. Well, uh, that would have been . . . the Saturday before that."

"Four days earlier."

"I guess so. The Cornell-Penn game."

"Uh-huh."

"My father came up for the game, like he usually does."

"You were with him at the game?"

"Well, no. He was with some . . . friends. We got together for a few minutes at halftime, that was all. Then my father had to leave right after the game."

Dowd again studied his client's son in silence. Well, he thought to himself, it was time to start asking the tough questions.

"Okay . . . uh, Poe, how would you characterize your parents' marriage?"

"It seemed okay to me." The young man shrugged slightly. "I don't know. They seemed . . . happy." He looked away from Dowd, began studying the bronze statue of Justice intently. "I guess they weren't."

"Did they . . ." Dowd hesitated. "Poe, I know this is tough. But I've got to—"

"I understand, Mr. Dowd."

"Did your folks ever, well, have fights? I mean, physical fights?"

Poe Jr. shook his head. "No, sir. Never."

"Was your father . . . was he seeing another woman, Poe?"

The young man looked away, again gazing at the bronze statue. "I don't know." Flat, distant this time.

"And your mother?"

"I don't know."

Was he telling the truth? Or was he protecting someone? His mother? The memory of his father?

"Poe, you understand I *have* to know the truth. If I'm going to defend your mother, I have to know what happened. Even if it's bad. If I know, I can be ready for it. But if it comes at me in the middle of trial . . ."

Poe Jr. nodded.

Dowd took another drag from the cigarette, then ground it into the overflowing ashtray. "Can you think of any reason why your father decided to . . . leave?"

"No, sir," he said, shaking his head again slowly. "We were all pretty surprised. We . . . it was . . . a surprise."

"Uh-huh."

The intercom light started flashing on the telephone.

"Excuse me a second," Dowd said to the young man, picking up the receiver. Then, into the receiver, "Yeah? . . . Uh-huh . . . Yeah, uh, I'll be right out." He hung up, then stood. "I'll be right back, Poe."

"Sure."

Dowd walked out of the office, closing the door behind him. He crossed the reception area to the woman sitting behind the desk. She held the receiver out to Dowd, then pushed a flashing red button.

Dowd took the receiver. "Mr. Ault?" he asked.

"Yes," the voice replied tentatively.

"Thank you for returning my call." Six or seven calls, Dowd thought to himself. "I assume you know why I called?"

"Louann," the voice said simply.

"That's right. I'm representing Mrs. Fratt on the . . . murder charge."

Silence.

"You're familiar with the facts?" Dowd asked finally.

"Yes."

"Uh-huh. Well, I understand that you and Mrs. Fratt were . . . seeing each other in the months preceding the death."

Silence.

"Mr. Dowd," the voice said finally, "I really don't know anything about any of this. I don't think I can be of any help to you."

"Well, there were just a few questions . . ."

"I really don't know anything about any of this."

"Uh-huh. Well, I just wanted to—"

"I'm married now."

"What?"

"I'm married now," the voice repeated.

"Uh-huh. Well, if I could just ask you a few questions . . ."

Silence.

After a moment, Dowd continued. "Uh . . . Let's see, you live in Greenwich? Connecticut?"

Pause. Then, reluctantly, "Yes."

"You're an engineer, and your office is in Westchester?"

Another pause. "Yes."

"Uh, now, you and Louann *were* seeing each other, toward the end of 1988?"

A long pause. "We were . . . seeing each other, yes."

"Would you characterize it as a *serious* relationship?"

"Mr. Dowd . . . I don't know what it is you're looking for, but I repeat, I know nothing about any of this."

"Mr. Ault, I'm defending Mrs. Fratt on a murder charge. The prosecutor may try to show that the reason she killed her husband was revenge, or anger at being left, or another woman."

"I still don't see—"

"Mr. Ault, if she were . . . *involved* with another man at the time, it makes it less likely that she would kill her ex-husband out of anger, or revenge, or jealousy, doesn't it?"

More silence. Then, coldly, "I suppose so."

"Well, that's why your relationship with Mrs. Fratt may be relevant to this case."

"There was no . . . relationship, Mr. Dowd. We weren't *that* involved."

"That's not what Mrs. Fratt says."

"Well, I'm sorry. But we weren't."

"You stayed overnight at Mrs. Fratt's apartment on a number of occasions, didn't you?"

The line was silent for ten or fifteen seconds.

"Mr. Ault?"

"Yes."

Time to get tough. "We can do this one of two ways. You can talk to me now . . . or I can serve you with a subpoena and you can talk to a jury."

Silence.

"We didn't actually . . . *sleep* together."

"You didn't—"

"We didn't sleep together," the voice repeated.

"Uh-huh."

"I know you don't believe me, Mr. Dowd, but Louann and I didn't ever sleep together. We . . . felt it wouldn't be right. I mean, she wasn't divorced yet."

"Uh-huh."

"I . . . we slept in separate bedrooms."

"In separate bedrooms."

"Yes."

It was just strange enough to be the truth, Dowd thought to himself.

"But you *were* seeing each other . . . exclusively."

"I think Louann took the relationship more seriously than it was."

"You were seeing each other exclusively?" Dowd repeated doggedly.

"I suppose so."

"How did you meet her, Mr. Ault?"

After another long pause, "I . . . met her through Poe."

"Through her husband?"

"Poe and I were friends. From Cornell. I knew her through him."

"And after the separation, you asked her out?"

Silence.

"Mr. Ault?" Dowd prompted.

"Yes. Yes, I asked her out."

"Okay. And when did the two of you—you and Mrs. Fratt—finally break up?"

Pause. "After . . . after the . . . After Poe died."

"And you got married a few months after that?"

"Yes." Then, after another pause, "Look, Mr. Dowd, I'm late for an appointment. I really have to leave now."

"Uh-huh. Well—"

"I'm sorry, but I really have to leave now."

"Okay. Maybe we can—"

"Mr. Dowd, I really don't think you want to call me as a witness."

"Uh-huh."

"I really don't."

"Well—"

"Goodbye." A click, and a dial tone.

Dowd just stared at the receptionist for a moment, then handed her the receiver. He turned, walked back to his office.

Bob Ault's testimony could be helpful, he thought to himself. Or could it? He still didn't know what motive Brownell would present to the jury. Maybe the motive was money. Or maybe Ault was the "other man." Of course, the fact that she was seeing a man did not mean that she could not harbor anger or jealousy toward Poe, if that was the motive. Worse, Ault could prove more damaging than helpful; certainly, he would be a very reluctant and possibly even antagonistic witness. Would he say something during his testimony to hurt Louann? Dowd recalled the cardinal principle when examining a witness before a jury: *Never* ask a question when you are not sure of the answer. And the simple fact was that he could not be sure what Ault would say on the stand. He certainly did not need his own witness to blurt out to the jury that, for example, his client was an alcoholic or had a violent temper.

Another tough decision.

Poe Jr. was still sitting in the chair, staring vacantly at the wall, when Dowd reentered the office.

"Sorry," Dowd said, sitting down.

"No problem."

"Uh . . . Let's see, where were we?"

"The divorce," Poe Jr. replied quietly.

Dowd nodded. "Poe, do you understand that you might be testifying at the trial?"

"I assumed so."

"We may need you to tell the jury about your mother's phone call, how she looked at the police station—that kind of thing."

"All right."

That's a lie, Dowd thought to himself. Louann's youngest son didn't really have much to say that could help his mother. The value of Poe Fratt, Jr., as a witness in trial was in his very *existence*: It was important that the jury be aware that Louann Fratt *had* three children—that there were sons and daughters who loved their mother, who would suffer if she were convicted of murdering their father, who would miss her if she were sent to prison. A juror—particularly one who was a mother—would be less likely to vote for conviction if that meant orphaning three children.

Of course, the testimony of the children was legally not relevant: Presenting Poe Jr. as a witness was nothing more than an appeal to the emotions and sympathies of the jury. And it was technically a violation of the canons of ethics knowingly to offer evidence for an inadmissible purpose. But appealing to emotions was routine in the no-holds-barred world of trial. Dowd knew, for example, that the prosecutor would offer gruesome close-up photographs of Poe's corpse—not to prove the indisputable fact that Poe was dead, but to horrify and disgust the jury.

Dowd had once wondered whether that justified his actions—whether two wrongs made a right. But he had long since stopped wondering. He had come to realize that he simply could not afford the luxury of such nice ethical gymnastics. Or, more accurately, his clients could not afford them, since it was they who ultimately paid the price. Just as a doctor had to decide for himself whether to perform an abortion, Dowd had slowly developed his own sense of what was right and what was wrong, what was ethical and what was not.

"Are Laura and William still in California?" Dowd asked.

"Laura's here now," Poe Jr. replied. "Bill's still in San Francisco."

"It's important they're here for the trial." Dowd paused. "We may need their testimony, too."

Another lie. But Dowd knew the value of having the three children sitting together in the audience from the beginning of the trial to the end. Let the jury see them sitting there, day after day. Let them see the kids bringing their mother to court every morning, and leaving with her after the evening adjournment. Let them see Louann desperately embracing her children during recesses. Let them know that they would have to face those three children when the verdict was finally read.

Sure, this was dirty ball, Dowd realized. But how many times had prosecutors made sure that the alleged victim in a rape case sat in the front row throughout the trial?

"I understand," Poe Jr. said.

"Even if they don't testify, your mother will need all the support she can get." At least that was true.

"They'll be here."

"Good."

The room was suddenly quiet.

"Mr. Dowd?"

"Yeah?"

"What's going to happen to my mother?"

Dowd looked at the young man without saying anything for a moment.

"I don't know, Poe," he said finally. "I'm going to do everything I can for her, but . . . I can't tell you how it's all going to come out."

Poe Jr. looked down at his hands and nodded silently. After a moment, he said softly, "I loved my father."

Dowd said nothing.

The young man looked up at the lawyer. "I don't understand what happened, Mr. Dowd," he said. "But I love my mother, too."

Dowd nodded slightly.

"Please help her."

CHAPTER 14

"And then you shoved the knife into his neck, didn't you?"

"I stabbed him, yes."

"You were going for the jugular vein."

"No, of course not."

"Oh? You were going for the windpipe?"

"No. No, I . . . I just stabbed *at* him, and it hit his neck, the knife hit his neck."

"The knife just *happened* to hit his neck."

"Yes."

"It just *happened* to barely miss the jugular, the carotid artery, and the windpipe?"

"I suppose so."

"But you weren't trying to kill your husband, were you, Mrs. Fratt?"

"No, I was not."

"Of course not. And the second blow, you stabbed him in the back?"

"Yes, when he turned."

"He turned? Or he was lying face down in bed, asleep, when you stabbed him?"

"No, that's ridiculous. He turned, he turned to reach for something, a letter opener, a clock, something."

"Why did he need a letter opener or a clock to defend himself against you, Mrs. Fratt? Didn't you say he weighed twice as much as you?"

"I don't know."

"You don't know if you said that?"

"No, no, I don't know why he reached for the clock."

"Or the letter opener."

"Yes."

"So you stabbed him in the back."

"Yes."

"Were you going for the lungs this time? Or the heart?"

"I . . . I wasn't going . . . I was simply trying to get out, to get out of the apartment. I was frightened."

"I see. So rather than run for the door when he turned away from you, you stabbed him again?"

"He was in the way. He was between me and the door."

"So the knife just *happened* to go into your husband's body at another lethal spot?"

"I don't know, I wasn't thinking of that."

"It was just coincidence—both blows being potentially deadly?"

"I suppose so."

"And the third time you stabbed Poe Fratt, this was straight into the heart, wasn't it?"

"I don't remember that."

"You don't recall shoving that eight-inch knife deep into your husband's heart, Mrs. Fratt?"

"No."

"You remember the first two blows, but not the one that killed him?"

"That's correct."

"Do you think someone else did it?"

"No, no, I'm quite sure it was me."

"Tell me, Mrs. Fratt, how was it that you were able to deliver three lethal blows to a man who was twice as big as you?"

"I . . . I—"

"He was a former football player, wasn't he?"

"He . . . yes, he . . ."

"But you overpowered him, didn't you?"

"I didn't . . . overpower him. . . ."

"Don't you think it odd that there were no knife wounds anywhere else on his body?"

"I don't understand."

"Well, you claim he was swinging at you, hitting you with his fists."

"Yes, he was."

"And you were swinging the knife around wildly."

"Yes."

"Yet there were no cuts on his upper or lower arms, were there?"

"I can't say."

"Would you like to see the medical examiner's report?"

"No."

"And there were no wounds to the legs, or the shoulders—or any other nonlethal part of the body."

"I suppose not."

"Only three wounds—all carefully delivered to lethal points."

"I didn't—"

"All delivered with deadly precision—while you were supposedly being raped and beaten by a former football player."

"I *was* being beaten."

"The fact is, Mrs. Fratt, your husband was lying down in bed when you attacked him, wasn't he?"

"No. That's not true."

"He was asleep."

"No, he was not. He was not. He was trying to . . ."

Dowd leaned back in the black leather chair and watched with a sinking feeling as the cross-examination continued.

Louann Fratt, tastefully dressed in a beige wool suit, black silk blouse, and pearl necklace, was sitting primly in a chair to the left of Dowd, at one end of a large mahogany conference table. The table took up most of the floor space in the law library Dowd shared with his two associates. With six of the leather chairs ringing it, there was barely enough space to walk around the table and along the four walls lined almost to the ceiling with hundreds of ornately bound law books. A large coffeepot and five coffee mugs in assorted sizes and colors sat on a large tray in the middle of the table. Two tall green plants in large ceramic pots stood in opposite corners of the library.

Dowd was sitting along one side of the table, a legal pad lying in front of him. A thin column of smoke from a burning cigarette rose from an ashtray next to the pad. Across from him was seated Julie Blackman, also with a legal pad. She was intently studying Louann Fratt as Louann "testified," assessing her performance, looking for facial expressions, body language, and other telltale signs that would subconsciously communicate messages to a jury. So far, all she had seen was a woman calmly recalling the murder of her husband with absolutely no sign of caring or emotion.

To Dowd's right, at the end of the conference table opposite Louann, a man stood and paced back and forth as he fired one stinging question after another with mind-numbing speed at Dowd's miserable client.

He was a tall man, maybe six feet in height, and in his late forties. He had a black moustache and black hair that curled almost uncontrollably beyond a receding hairline. More than anything else, he looked like a flag-burning radical from the sixties. And, in this man's case, appearances were accurate: He had, in fact, been a political activist—and still was. In the years since the antiwar period, the man had become a criminal lawyer and had defended Black Panthers, I.R.A. terrorists, Hell's Angels, and prisoners in the Attica prison riots. In a few more months, he would be appointed a judge of the New York Superior Court.

William "Billy" Mogulescu was also the best cross-examiner Dowd had ever seen.

As a favor to his friend, Mogulescu had agreed to expose Louann to a taste of cross-examination—to give her a "baptism of fire." This would serve two purposes. First, the questioning would, Dowd hoped, prepare her *emotionally* for Brownell's cross-examination. Very few witnesses are ready for the traumatic experience of an effective "cross"; some become rattled and fall apart on the stand. Louann would have only one shot at testifying before the jury, and Dowd would be able to do little to protect her. Hopefully, undergoing this ordeal now would steel her for the real thing.

The second purpose for Mogulescu's questions was to expose weaknesses in her testimony that could possibly be addressed and remedied before trial. This did not mean making up false answers. The simple fact was that most witnesses are caught unaware during cross; they do not recall all of the details, have not thought out the possible implications, have not considered reasons and explanations. The three stab wounds, for example: Louann would not have time to *think* during a rapid-fire cross. Now, she would think about it during the few days left before trial. She would go back over the incident, try harder to recall the details, try to remember exactly what happened, why she stabbed him here, why there, what he was doing to her. But the answers had to come from her. Dowd would not patch up her testimony for her.

". . . can't recall that."

"Your husband was in his pajamas when he was found dead, was he not?"

"Yes."

"And the bed—it had been slept in?"

"I don't know."

"It was unmade, wasn't it? Sheets and comforter pulled back?"

"Yes, I believe so."

"But you claim he *wasn't* asleep when you stabbed him to death."

"He wasn't."

"You claim he wasn't even in the bed."

"He . . . I . . . He was in bed, on the bed, when I stabbed him the first time, in the neck."

"Were you in bed with him, Mrs. Fratt?"

"What?"

"I said, were you in bed with him?"

"I don't understand."

"Come now, Mrs. Fratt, the police found the nightgown in your bag."

"The nightgown . . ."

"Yes, the nightgown. With blood on it. Your husband's blood."

"I don't—"

"You were in bed with Poe Fratt when you stabbed him to death, weren't you?"

"No, I was not. I was not."

"You waited until he fell asleep, and then you murdered him."

"No, that's not true."

"He made love to you, and he fell asleep, and you stabbed him to death—that's what happened, wasn't it!"

"No. That's . . . that never happened. That's . . . just not true."

"How do you explain the nightgown, then, and the blood?"

"I . . . The nightgown was hanging up in my bathroom. I had blood on my hands, my hair . . . I touched it and . . ."

"And how did it get into the bag?"

"It was never in the bag."

"The police are lying?"

"No. I don't know. The nightgown was in my bathroom."

Mogulescu was using the "scatter-gun" technique of cross-examination. Rather than leading the witness through her story in a chronological, orderly manner, attacking each part of the testimony in turn, he was skipping back and forth, from one part to another, with no apparent design. This method tended to confuse the witness, since she was never able to mentally orient herself to the new subject matter and never knew what was coming next. It was a difficult technique to master, requiring an exceptionally nimble mind, but effective in keeping the witness constantly off-balance.

"Now, let me see if I understand this, Mrs. Fratt. You went over to your husband's apartment that night . . . because he *asked* you to?"

"Yes. That, and there were some things we had to discuss about an investment, an oil company."

"You could not discuss the investment over the phone?"

"I . . . suppose we could have."

"He wanted his mail, is that right?"

"Yes, he was leaving on a trip the next day."

"And this was after one o'clock in the morning?"

"About that, yes."

"And so you walked out into the streets of New York at one o'clock in the morning."

"Yes."

"Alone."

"Yes."

"To deliver mail."

"Yes."

"Because the man who had abandoned you and was divorcing you *asked* you to."

"I . . . Yes."

"And you expect the jury to *believe* that."

Louann closed her eyes, sighed almost imperceptibly. She raised one hand to her eyes, massaged them for a moment in silence. It was the closest she had come to appearing human.

"It's what happened," she said finally, looking back up at the tall, dark-haired man pacing at the other end of the table.

"I see. But you had more than mail in the mailbag, didn't you?"

"Yes."

"You had brought along an eight-inch knife."

"Yes."

"The knife you were going to use to murder your husband."

"No, of course not. I was carrying it for protection. I always do."

"How old are you, Mrs. Fratt?"

"I'm . . . fifty-six."

"And you expect the jury to believe that a fifty-six-year-old woman was going to overpower muggers and street gangs with a kitchen knife?"

"It's better than nothing."

"How much did you have to drink that night, Mrs. Fratt?"

"What?"

"How much did you have to drink?"

"I . . . well, I had some wine at home. . . ."

"*Some* wine?"

"A glass. Two glasses, perhaps. Yes, I think I had two glasses."

"This was just before going to your husband's apartment?"

"An hour or so before, yes."

"And you had a couple of glasses after you got to his apartment, didn't you? A Clos du Bois?"

"I believe I had one glass."

"Are you sure it wasn't two?"

"One."

"So you were a little . . . under the influence at the time, weren't you?"

"No, I was not."

"Your doorman says you appeared intoxicated."

"I was not."

"Were you steadying your nerves for what you had to do?"

"That's ridiculous."

"Is it?"

"Yes."

"Do you *usually* have three glasses of wine around midnight?"

"No . . . This was . . . I mean, I—"

"How did you get the knife out of the bag?"

"—I . . . What?"

"The knife, Mrs. Fratt, the eight-inch knife: How did you get it out of the bag?"

"I don't understand."

"Well, you testified that when your husband grabbed you and tried to rape you, you stabbed him in the neck."

"Yes. That's true."

"Well, where did you get the knife from?"

"From . . . from the bag."

"You looked around for the bag, found it, went over and got it, opened it up, reached inside, found the knife, and pulled it out?"

"Yes."

"And you did all of this while a two-hundred-and-twenty-pound man had ahold of you and was trying to rape you?"

"Yes . . . Yes."

Dowd looked across the table at Julie Blackman. She sensed him, turned to meet his gaze. They knew they were both feeling the same thing: the embarrassment of having to watch a human being humiliated. And the realization that there were a lot of gaping holes in Louann's testimony.

Dowd was beginning to wonder if he had made a mistake in arranging for this practice run at cross-examination. There was a fine line between preparing your client for the rigors of cross and hitting her so hard that her confidence was completely shattered. Certainly, very few lawyers were so thorough in their preparation that they ran their client through a simulation like this. But then, very few lawyers worked as hard as Dowd at getting ready for trial. And he knew that there would be nothing in the coming trial even remotely as critical to the outcome as the cross-examination of Louann Fratt.

"How did you get into the apartment, Mrs. Fratt?"

"Get in?"

"Yes. Did your husband let you in or did you unlock the door?"

"Poe let me in. I don't have a key."

"Oh? You don't have a key?"

"No."

"You testified the door was locked when you returned with the police, is that right?"

"Yes."

"They had to break it down?"

"Yes."

"I assume, then, that *you* locked it when you left?"

"I . . . I really don't recall."

"Without a key."

"It . . . it can be locked without a key."

"Weren't you pretty upset after your husband tried to rape you?"

"Of course."

"And after you stabbed him three times?"

"Yes."

"Yet you calmly locked the door after leaving."

"I . . . I said I don't remember. I mean, I suppose I did."

Mogulescu stopped pacing, put his hands on the table, and leaned toward Louann Fratt. He suddenly spoke very slowly, spacing each word.

"Then . . . how . . . did . . . you . . . get . . . back . . . in . . . when . . . you . . . returned . . . the . . . second . . . time, . . . Mrs. . . . . Fratt?"

Louann Fratt closed her eyes for a moment, shook her head violently.

"You're confusing me!" she said.

"I repeat: If you had no key, how did you get back in when you went back to see if your husband was alive?"

"I . . . I . . . Maybe . . . I mean, I don't know if I locked it the first time. Maybe I locked it the second time." She shook her head again. "I don't know. I don't remember."

Mogulescu stood back up. He resumed his pacing, but always with his eyes on his prey.

"Why did you wash the murder weapon, Mrs. Fratt?"

"What?"

"The knife—you took it back to your apartment and washed it."

"Yes."

"Why? Isn't it a fact that you were trying to destroy evidence?"

"No. No, I . . . It was . . . so ugly . . . Poe's blood . . . I—"

"And you washed your clothes—washed your husband's blood away?"

"It was Poe's blood. . . ."

"Why did you wash it *before* calling the police?"

"I . . . don't know."

"Do you recall leashing the dog?"

"The dog?"

"Your little dog, Mrs. Fratt. You put a leash on him before leaving your husband's apartment, didn't you?"

"I think so, I'm not sure."

Mogulescu suddenly walked around the side of the table and quickly approached the woman. He stopped just two feet from her, then leaned forward, his face inches from hers.

"You had just stabbed your husband to death after he tried to rape you. You were hysterical, you say. And yet you calmly put a leash on your dog before leaving?"

"I . . . You don't understand. . . . It was—"

Mogulescu straightened up, looked down at Louann with contempt. He turned, began walking back toward the far end of the table.

"When you went to your husband's apartment the third time, with the police . . . the door was jammed closed, wasn't it?"

"I'm sorry?"

"With the police—they broke the door down because it was locked?"

"Yes. Yes, they did."

"But then they still couldn't get in, could they?"

"No. Poe's body . . . it was against the door."

"And it took two officers, two large officers, to force the door open wide enough to get in?"

"Yes."

Mogulescu reached the end of the table and suddenly turned around and almost yelled the next question at the woman.

"Then how did *you* get in when you went back the *second* time?!"

"The second . . ."

"Your husband was *dead* when you went back the second time, wasn't he?"

"Yes, yes, he was."

"So he didn't *move* after your second visit?"

"I don't . . . no, he . . . no."

Louann Fratt was now staring wide-eyed at her tormentor, transfixed like a small bird about to be swallowed by a snake. Yet, there was still no sign of any feeling on her face.

"And *you* didn't move him?"

"No."

"Then I repeat, Mrs. Fratt: How did you get in and out during that second visit?"

"I . . . I don't . . . know."

"You don't know," he repeated, sneering.

Dowd looked down, unwilling for the moment to continue watching. He couldn't decide what was worse: the total destruction Mogulescu was wreaking on his client, or her complete lack of any emotional response. Either would be deadly in front of a jury. He took a deep breath, then let it out. He reached in his pocket for a fresh cigarette, then looked across the table at Julie. She was looking at him, then quickly looked down at her notes.

"How much money did you make from murdering your husband, Mrs. Fratt?"

"What?"

"Was there life insurance?"

"Yes, of course, but—"

"How much?"

"I don't . . . maybe two hundred thousand, I'm not sure."

"You're not sure?"

"You see—"

"And the co-op, isn't it worth a couple of million?"

"I think . . . about that, maybe more."

"And the investments . . ."

"I don't know."

"A month or two more, and the divorce would have been final, wouldn't it?"

"A few months, I'm not sure."

"And your husband would have gotten half of everything."

"We hadn't . . . The lawyers hadn't yet agreed—"

"But with him dead, you get everything, don't you?"

"That's not why . . . You don't understand. Poe was trying to rape me."

Mogulescu suddenly stopped pacing, smiled broadly at Louann.

"Whose idea was the rape?"

"Whose idea?"

"You never mentioned rape during your call to the police, did you?"

"No, I guess not."

"You *guess* not?"

"No, I didn't."

"And you never mentioned it to the detectives when they showed up?"

"No."

"And you never mentioned it later at the police station, when you were questioned?"

"No, but . . ."

"In fact, the rape *story* never came out until after you had seen your *lawyer*, isn't that right?"

"It's not a story. Poe really did try to . . . to . . ."

"Was it *your* idea, Mrs. Fratt, or your *lawyer's*?"

Louann shook her head. "No, it was my idea . . . I mean, it happened."

The lawyer resumed his pacing.

"You were pretty surprised when your husband left you, weren't you?"

"When he left me? Yes. Yes, I was."

Mogulescu again walked along the side of the table toward Louann. This time, the woman looked away from him nervously. He stopped halfway.

"Thirty years of marriage." He shook his head sadly. "Then to be abandoned. You must have been quite upset. Hurt."

"Yes."

"And angry."

"Not really."

"Not angry? At being suddenly abandoned after all those years? For no reason?"

"I was . . . not angry."

"You went back to make sure he was dead," the lawyer said softly, "didn't you?"

"I . . . what?"

"When you went back to your husband's apartment the second time—it was to make sure he was dead, wasn't it?"

"No, no, that's not true."

"You were afraid he may still be alive, and you were going to finish him off."

"No, of course not."

He smiled again.

"Then please explain to the jury why you didn't call Emergency Services."

"Emergency . . ."

"Were you planning on giving him medical treatment yourself when you went back?"

"No, no, I was just . . ."

"Well, if you thought he might still be alive, why didn't you call an ambulance?"

"I . . . don't remember. I was confused."

Louann Fratt suddenly looked to Dowd for help.

Mogulescu pounded the table with his fist. "Your lawyer can't give you the answer, Mrs. Fratt!"

Dowd said nothing. She was on her own. She had to learn that there would be no help from anyone when Brownell had her on the stand.

"The fact is, you didn't call nine-one-one until *after* you had gone back and made sure he was dead, isn't that so?"

"That's not what . . . I mean, I was . . . so . . . confused. I don't remember. . . ."

Mogulescu leaned forward, his hands on the table.

"Tell me, Mrs. Fratt, did you *feel* anything when you stabbed him?"

"Did I feel . . ."

"Yes. Did you feel *anything*?"

"I felt . . . I felt . . ."

"Do you feel anything *now*?"

"I . . . Yes, of course, I . . ."

"*Do* you? Do you really?"

Louann Fratt sat silently, staring at the lawyer, her face stonily impassive. She would not speak, would not answer the question.

The room was uncomfortably silent for a long moment.

Dowd suddenly rose to his feet with a sigh. "All right," he said. "That's enough for now."

Julie Blackman stood and walked over to Louann. She put one arm around a shoulder gently, saying nothing. The seated woman did not seem to notice.

Dowd walked over to Mogulescu, extending his hand. "Thanks, Billy."

The tall, curly-haired lawyer smiled, shrugged. "Pulling wings off butterflies is what I do best," he said.

"I mean it. It was a real help." Dowd looked back at his client. Then, in a low voice, "I guess I have my work cut out for me."

"When's the trial?"

"Next week."

Mogulescu shook his head slowly. He slapped Dowd on the back. "Good luck, Mike."

"Thanks."

Mogulescu looked back at Louann Fratt for a moment, then turned and walked out of the room.

Dowd watched Louann as Julie stood silently next to the woman. His client was still staring straight ahead, her face empty of any expression.

Dowd knew that Brownell was no Mogulescu. But if Mogulescu could do this to his client after only a brief review of the case, what would the prosecutor do after months of careful preparation? And what would a jury think if Louann took the stand and showed absolutely no feelings about killing her husband?

Louann Fratt remained in her chair, staring vacantly at the coffeepot.

CHAPTER 15

"Congratulations."

Dowd smiled at his receptionist as the elevator doors closed behind him. "Thanks," he said tiredly, setting his battered leather satchel down on the polished hardwood floor. "Any messages?"

The young woman handed him a stack of paper slips. As usual, Dowd stuffed them unread into his coat pocket.

"Debbie around?" he asked.

The woman nodded toward the library.

Dowd picked up the satchel and walked into the library. Debbie Cohen was seated at the far end of the conference table, buried in a thick volume of New York appellate cases. Another dozen or so books were opened and spread across the table around her, along with a cup of coffee and a yellow legal pad with coffee stains on it.

Debbie looked up, startled. "Oh, Mike." She grinned. "Hey, congratulations. I heard over the news."

"Thanks, Debbie." Dowd wearily set the heavy satchel down on the floor and reached for one of the coffee mugs in the middle of the table. "Working on that psychiatric notice thing?" he asked, pouring himself a cup from the stainless-steel coffeemaker. It had been a long day and it was going to be a long night.

"Yeah."

Dowd had just finished another trial—days before the Fratt trial was to begin. It had been a tough one. Of course, murder cases usually were. But this one was special.

Dowd's client was a pretty woman, soft, gentle, with a happy, infectious laugh. At five feet one, tiny L'Tanya Gaskins looked more than anything like a small, fragile doll. She was also a prostitute. And she had been charged as an accomplice to her brother in the murder of one of her johns.

The police reports were clear: On the morning of March 15, 1988, L'Tanya and her brother Ornie were taking a walk near their parents' house in Brooklyn. Joseph Francis, a Jamaican and a former customer of L'Tanya's, approached the two with a knife. Ornie confronted Joseph and there was a struggle.

At this point the stories of four nearby witnesses clashed in one important detail. One claimed she heard L'Tanya yell out, "Kill the motherfucker!" The others never heard this—but all four saw Ornie somehow get the knife and stab Joseph in the heart. And all four then heard L'Tanya cry out, "If my brother's going to jail, then I'm going"; they saw her pick up the knife, and stab the unconscious man in the thigh.

Ten or fifteen minutes later, the police approached her on the street for questioning as a witness. "I'm not a witness," she told them. "*I'm* the one who killed him." When Ornie was picked up, he also claimed sole responsibility for the killing.

Ornie was charged with murder. Although the medical examiner determined that the thigh wound had not contributed to Francis's death, L'Tanya was charged as an accomplice to murder; under New York law, shouting encouragement constituted "acting in concert."

But L'Tanya told Dowd a much different story.

She had first met Joseph Francis in August 1986. She was a part-time prostitute who turned tricks when she needed the money; Joseph was a customer on two or three occasions. When he started to become obsessive about her, she refused to have any further dealings with him.

But Joseph would not leave her alone. The diminutive L'Tanya seemed to trigger a need in him to dominate, to control. He began to follow her wherever she went—to the store, to a show, to visit friends or family. If he missed her, he would wait outside of her apartment for her to return. Then he would confront her, demand to know where she had been.

Joseph became increasingly possessive of L'Tanya. He would tell her what kind of clothing to wear, where she could go and where she couldn't. He would tell her that she was "his woman" now. If she argued, he would slap her around. On one occasion, she had him arrested for pistol-whipping her; later, frightened by his threats, she dropped the charges.

For over a year and a half, Joseph continued to stalk the increasingly terrified woman. L'Tanya began to find it easier to simply do what she was told. But in November 1987, she again had him arrested—this time, for hitting her with a metal pipe. When he was released on bail, the judge issued an "order of protection." But Joseph ignored the order and jumped bail. A bench warrant was issued, but no attempts were ever made to find Joseph or serve it on him; the protective order was permitted to lapse. And he continued stalking L'Tanya.

By now L'Tanya felt helpless. The police wouldn't come, the courts were useless—no one could protect her. She was at Joseph's mercy. She was trapped.

It was then that Joseph confronted L'Tanya and her brother Ornie on the street.

When L'Tanya Gaskins came to Dowd with her story, he agreed to represent her without fee.

When trial finally began in Brooklyn Supreme Court, Dowd was faced with a very tough decision: Should L'Tanya take the stand? If she did not, then the jury would learn little of the strange "fatal attraction" that led to the killing. They would never learn of the conditions which created a kind of mental "enslavement," a state of mind very similar to that of the battered wife syndrome—a physically and emotionally beaten woman with a perceived lack of options and a sense of helplessness. Without such evidence, a finding of self-defense under the circumstances was unlikely.

But if she *did* take the stand, L'Tanya would have to testify to a damning fact unknown to the prosecutor and unseen by the witnesses: She had been carrying a knife—and had handed it to her brother during his struggle with Joseph. It was *this* knife—not Joseph's—that was the murder weapon. And supplying the weapon used in a murder was much stronger evidence of "acting in concert" than simply yelling out encouragement.

Tough decision.

When it came time for the defense case, Dowd kept his client off the stand. Fortunately, he was able to get enough of the "fatal attraction" evidence in through the testimony of eyewitnesses to be able to paint a fairly accurate picture for the jury.

The jury returned with verdicts that afternoon. Ornie Gaskins was found guilty of manslaughter in the first degree. L'Tanya was acquitted.

The Gaskins verdict was a victory for Dowd. But there was no time to bask in the glow: The Fratt trial started in a few days. And, as usual, there was more to do than time in which to do it.

"What do you have on the notice?" Dowd asked Debbie Cohen.

"Well, Brownell's right. There aren't any cases on it. But . . ."

"Yeah?"

"Well . . . the *purpose* of the statute is to give notice only when the defense is going to be psychiatric in nature."

"Uh-huh." Debbie was following the old law-school problem-solving technique, Dowd thought to himself: When the language of a statute is unclear, and there are no appellate decisions interpreting it, then look to the purpose of the statute—the legislative intent in passing the law. Fine in theory, but in real life, judges didn't want to know about ethereal purposes and intent; they wanted a solid case to point a finger at.

"What's your point?" Dowd asked.

"Well, you're not offering Dr. Rosen's testimony to establish a psychiatric defense."

Dowd waited. He reached into his coat pocket, pulled out a mangled pack of cigarettes, extracted one, and lighted it.

"I mean," she continued, "you're offering her testimony

to explain why Louann Fratt went to her husband's apartment *before* the killing—you know, 'her master's voice.' "

"Before the killing . . ."

"And why she showed no emotion *after* the killing."

"What you're saying is . . ."

"What I'm saying," the young lawyer said, warming to her theory, "is that you're not offering it to show her state of mind *at the time* of the killing."

"We're not offering Dr. Rosen on the issue of Louann's state of mind at the time of the killing," Dowd said slowly, almost to himself.

"Right."

"The defense is *self-defense*, not 'extreme emotional distress.' " In New York, "extreme emotional distress" had supplanted insanity as the legally recognized psychiatric defense to murder.

"Right."

"Dr. Rosen's testimony is offered to explain Louann's state of mind *before* and *after* the killing."

Debbie Cohen just nodded as Dowd continued trying it on for fit.

"Not to establish a psychiatric defense, not to show her state of mind *at the time* of the killing."

"What do you think?" she asked.

Dowd just looked at her for a moment. Then, "The statute just refers to . . ."

"You've got to give notice of evidence of a psychiatric nature relating to a defense."

"And there aren't any cases . . ."

"Nope."

"So what does the statute mean by 'relating to a defense'?"

"Louann's state of mind before or after the killing doesn't constitute a defense."

Dowd nodded slowly. "I agree."

"So Dr. Rosen's testimony doesn't 'relate to a defense,' " she said. "It's that simple."

Dowd just kept nodding. "If you're right . . ."

"I'm right."

Dowd grinned at the young lawyer's cockiness. If she *was* right, however, then he would not have to identify Dr. Rosen to Brownell. He would not have to tell him what she would be testifying to. He would not have to tip his hand to the prosecutor; Brownell would go on thinking Dowd was going to present a battered wife defense.

But if she was wrong about the notice statute, Dowd would not know until it came time to call Dr. Rosen. And by then it would be too late: Judge Goodman would not permit the testimony—or *any* testimony of a psychological nature. Dr. Rosen would be out. Julie Blackman would be out. And that stuff about rape trauma syndrome—that would be out.

Rape trauma syndrome, Dowd thought to himself. Damn it! He was supposed to have called that psychologist. What was her name? Veronen?

Dowd looked at Debbie Cohen. "Good work," he said. "Let me think about it."

The young lawyer shrugged, then went back to her books as Dowd picked up the heavy satchel and walked out of the library. He paused again at the receptionist's desk on the way to his office.

"Do you still have that phone number of the psychologist down in South Carolina? She's a professor at some college down there."

"Uh, yes, it's here somewhere," the young woman said. She began sorting through a small stack of notes.

"Try to get hold of her for me, will you? I think one of the numbers is her home. Try that."

"Sure."

Dowd continued on into his office, satchel in one hand, cup of coffee in the other, and a burning cigarette dangling from his lips. He set the satchel down on the floor next to the desk, shoved two stacks of papers apart to make way for the coffee, then collapsed in the green leather chair.

A long day.

Dowd continued to mull over Debbie Cohen's thoughts about the notice statute. And the more he thought about it, the more he realized she was right. The language of the statute was vague, but the purpose was clear: to give notice of evidence concerning a defendant's state of mind *when that state of mind constituted a defense.* Any evidence offered by Dowd to explain Louann's conduct before or after the homicide had nothing to do with a defense based upon state of mind—such as "extreme emotional distress." State of mind was a defense only when it existed at the time of the homicide.

But it was a hell of a gamble. And the stakes were high. If he did not give Brownell the information, and he was wrong . . . Well, there wouldn't be much of a defense left.

Dowd suddenly realized that if he decided not to give the assistant D.A. the information, he would have to immediately withdraw his previous notice, which Judge Goodman had ruled was too general in nature. The reason was simple: When the issue came up in trial, Dowd could not very well argue that the statute did not require notice of Dr. Rosen's evidence—if he had, in fact, complied with the statute by sending the general notice.

But if he withdrew notice . . . Brownell would then realize that the defense was not based upon battered wife syndrome. And he would quickly realize that the only other possibility was self-defense.

Knight to queen's bishop three.

Dowd sighed deeply. He closed his eyes and massaged them slowly.

When he opened them, the intercom light on the telephone was flashing.

He depressed the button. "Yes?" he said.

"Dr. Lois Veronen on line one," the receptionist said.

"Thanks."

Dowd paused for a moment, took a deep drag from the cigarette, then wearily pushed the first button. "Dr. Veronen?"

"Yes. Mr. Dowd?"

"Yes. I'm really sorry—"

"Dr. Blackman said you'd be calling."

"I—what?"

"Dr. Blackman. She said you'd be calling."

"Oh. Julie's already talked to you about the case, then? About Louann Fratt?"

"Yes, she did. Three or four weeks ago."

"Okay. Well, then, I guess you know why I'm calling."

"She said you were concerned about what a jury's reactions might be to some of your client's behavior."

"That's about it. I was hoping you could shed some light."

"I'll try. Let's see . . . please refresh my mind. Your client . . . Mrs. Fratt . . . was at her former husband's apartment. . . ."

"They were in the middle of a divorce, actually. But yes, she was at his apartment a few blocks away from her own."

"And he, as I understand it, he tried to rape her."

"Yes."

"Hadn't he raped her once before, a few months earlier?"

"Yes."

"And he tried it again."

"Yes."

"And she stabbed him with a knife."

"Uh-huh."

"And he's dead."

"Very."

"Yes. Now, what was it again you wanted to know?"

"Well, two or three things, really. An hour or so after the homicide, Mrs. Fratt called the police. The conversation was tape-recorded. And on it . . . well, she just sounds like—"

"Calm? Flat? Unemotional?"

"Yeah," Dowd replied, surprised.

"Blocking."

"What?"

"Blocking," the psychologist repeated. "A common reaction to rape. Repression. The rape incident is too painful to deal with, too painful emotionally. So the victim blocks the incident, represses the feelings. It's a method of emotional self-protection."

"Uh-huh."

"This is part of something we call rape trauma syndrome."

"Rape trauma syndrome. Yes, Julie mentioned that."

"It's just a term for a cluster of different symptoms, really."

"Uh-huh."

"You see, we've found that victims of rape experience similar psychological reactions."

"Uh-huh."

"Blocking, or repression, is a common one. Deal with the horror of the experience by blocking it out of your memory."

"Kind of like blowing a safety fuse."

"Yes, I suppose you could say that."

"Yeah . . . But . . . Mrs. Fratt told the police about the *stabbing*, even about being beaten up by her husband. She didn't block any of *that*."

"She didn't block it from her memory, no. But she blocked the *feelings*, the emotions."

"Well, why didn't she mention the rape? Why did she tell them about stabbing him, and about being hit by him, but nothing about the attempted rape?"

"Minimization."

Oh, God, Dowd thought to himself. "Minimization," he repeated dubiously.

"Another common reaction in the cluster."

"Uh-huh."

"The victim tends to recall what happened, to characterize it in a way that minimizes the trauma."

"Yeah."

"It's like denial. She denies the horror of the rape by characterizing it as an 'assault.' She wasn't *raped* by her husband—she was *beaten up*."

"Uh-huh."

"Emotionally, assault is much easier to deal with than rape, you see."

Actually, it was beginning to make a little sense to Dowd. His first reaction had been that it sounded like a lot of psychiatric garbage. He always distrusted anyone who used ten-dollar words, especially when a two-bit word would do the job. But what Dr. Veronen was saying was beginning to have the sound of truth. And it fit.

"Okay," he said. "Look, Mrs. Fratt doesn't seem to recall a lot of what happened. I mean, for example, she stabbed him three times. She remembers the two relatively minor wounds, but doesn't recall the lethal blow—a direct frontal blow deep into the heart. I wouldn't think she'd forget *that*."

"It could be repression, certainly. Traumatic amnesia. Stabbing your husband to death would be something you would want to repress, to forget. It could also simply be the effects of adrenaline."

"Adrenaline?"

"The so-called 'fight or flight' reaction. Confronted with rape, her body pumps out adrenaline. Blood rushes to the muscles, everything accelerates. All of this impairs the brain's ability to process events. The result: Perception and memory are defective."

"Adrenaline," Dowd repeated. "Fight or flight."

"Yes."

"And . . . there are a lot of other things she can't recall. Like, locking her husband's door . . . getting home to her apartment afterwards . . . where she put a nightgown . . . washing the knife . . ."

"I would imagine that there are many things that she can't—or won't—remember, Mr. Dowd."

Dowd was beginning to feel excited. Dr. Veronen was handing him the missing piece in the puzzle. Something called "rape trauma syndrome."

"Doctor?"

"Yes."

"Would you be willing to testify at Mrs. Fratt's trial?"

"Testify?"

"Yes."

"Oh, dear. I've never really—"

"It could mean a lot."

"I've never—"

"It could mean the difference."

"Well . . . I suppose I . . ."

"Great!"

"Well . . . When is the trial?"

"Next week."

"Next *week*?" the voice repeated in horror. "Oh, dear."

There was one more question Dowd had to ask. He had been holding back, afraid to ask it, afraid that the answer would destroy the last desperately needed piece of the puzzle.

"Doctor."

"Yes?"

"Uh . . . this rape trauma syndrome . . ."

"Yes?"

"Well, I don't know if I was clear."

"Clear?"

"The fact is, Mrs. Fratt wasn't actually raped."

"I don't understand, Mr. Dowd."

"I mean, it was an *attempted* rape. Her husband only *tried* to rape her. There was no . . . completion."

"Oh, I see."

"Uh, does this mean—"

"A victim experiences an attempted rape in much the same way as a completed one, Mr. Dowd," Dr. Veronen explained patiently. "The key is the *violence* involved."

"Uh-huh."

"There is a common misunderstanding that the trauma of rape stems from the sexual violation," she continued. "It is the violence, the perceived threat to life that is traumatic—not any actual sexual penetration."

"Then . . ."

"It would make no difference whether she was a victim of rape or of attempted rape."

"Uh-huh."

"The trauma is the same. And the emotional consequences the same."

"I think I understand."

Sitting there in the green leather chair, holding the phone in his hand, Dowd suddenly experienced a tremendous sense of elation. The puzzle was solved. He had found all the missing pieces and they fit. His client was no longer a mystery, an enigma: She was a sad, pathetic woman who had suffered long and silently and, pushed beyond the limit, finally broken.

Michael Dowd felt he finally understood what had happened that night when Louann Fratt had stabbed her husband to death.

Now he had to convince a jury.

PART TWO:
TRIAL

CHAPTER 16

T he tall man in the tan over-
coat walked slowly in the cold darkness of the winter morning,
his collar turned up and his shoulders hunched against the
icy chill. One gloved hand was stuffed deeply into a pocket of
the tightly wrapped overcoat, the arm pressed hard against
his body for warmth; the other carried a leather satchel, filled
with notes, documents, law books, and other weapons of trial.
Around him, horns shrieked and air brakes hissed as taxis
fought with trucks for control of the grim street. Other lone
figures bundled in coats and shawls hurried silently past the
man, warm vapor exploding in short bursts from their
mouths. But the man seemed oblivious to them, his eyes staring unseeing at the dirty pavement ahead as he walked. When
he finally approached the gray monolith that towered ominously over everything around it, he stopped and looked up.

Michael Dowd stood for a moment in the leaden gloom,
his eyes locked on the massive blocks of somber granite that
loomed over him. The Criminal Courts Building seemed to
him even more malevolent than usual on this cold, bleak winter day.

It was December 5, 1989. The second day of trial.

Dowd drew his overcoat more tightly around him, took a deep breath that chilled his lungs, then walked up the granite steps and through one of the revolving glass doors. Inside, he found himself in the huge, dimly lit foyer he knew so well. The floors were of cold marble, and marble columns rose high into an ornately decorated ceiling. At one time this had been an impressive setting, designed to instill in visitors a sense of grandeur and gravity. But times and attitudes change. Now, the majestic foyer was fast becoming just another gloomy relic, its dignity tarnished by peeling paint and obscene graffiti. In place of reverence and respect were barricades, metal detectors, and armed police.

Dowd was funneled by ropes and wooden barricades toward a long line of people waiting their turn to go through what looked like a door frame. Lounging around this device, a metal detector, were four uniformed court officers. As each visitor approached the detector, he emptied his pockets into a basket; these items were returned to him after he passed through the device without setting off alarms. Inevitably, the detectors were triggered by a forgotten pen or a pair of metal-tipped shoes. The shrill alarms, echoing deafeningly in the vaultlike marble foyer, destroyed any lingering sense of decorum.

With a wry smile, Dowd recalled the fine-sounding phrase chiseled over the entrance just outside. "Every place is safe to him who lives in justice," the words promised.

Dowd passed through the detector without incident, stuffed his belongings back into their respective pockets, and headed for the elevators. When a set of doors opened, he joined a waiting crowd and quickly jammed into the elevator. When no one else could squeeze in, they all stood, packed tightly together in the tiny cell, until at long last the doors decided to close. Then silence, the awkward silence of strangers suddenly forced into an unwanted intimacy.

When the elevator finally reached the sixteenth floor, Dowd got out, turned right, and began walking down a long, harshly lighted corridor. Lying along the freshly waxed floor was a jungle of thick black cables, twisting and winding their way toward the end of the corridor. There, just outside of

Judge Goodman's courtroom, was a confusion of television cameras, remote monitors, technicians, and reporters.

Dowd loosened his coat as he walked, carefully stepping over the cables, then shifted the heavy satchel to his other hand. As he approached the scene, he noticed that one of the television monitors was displaying a shot of the judge's bench inside the courtroom. A technician was speaking into a walkie-talkie as he watched the scene on the monitor.

"Yeah, yeah, a little more to the left," the technician said. "No, to the *left* . . . Yeah, yeah, that's it, that's it. . . ."

He looked up as Dowd approached him. Dowd nodded politely, but the technician ignored him and went back to the monitor.

Dowd opened one of the double doors leading into Part 62 and stepped inside. The scene that confronted him had changed drastically since the day before.

The case of *The People of the State of New York* vs. *Louann Fratt* had been called for trial early on the previous morning. In his usually efficient manner, Judge Goodman had seventy-five members of the jury panel brought in and seated in the audience, and Dowd and Brownell had spent the rest of the day choosing a jury. There had been no television cameras, only a couple of reporters and a few stray spectators. But that was yesterday. Since then, the courthouse grapevine had been busy. Word was out that jury selection in the Park Avenue murder case would be finished sometime today—and the lawyers would then give their opening statements: Brownell would tell the chosen twelve why the wealthy socialite had murdered her husband, and Dowd would blow the lid off with stories of weird sex and wife beating in high society.

Every pew in the gallery was now packed, and there was a sense of excitement in the low buzz of conversation. The left half of the gallery was filled with spectators, eagerly awaiting the beginning of hostilities; dozens of others had been turned away at the doors. The first two rows on the left had been reserved for newspaper reporters and photographers. At the far end of the first row was a large, high-mounted television camera pointing toward the judge's bench; each of the networks would take turns covering the trial and sharing the taped footage. The right half of the gallery was filled with men and women making up the panel of potential jurors. The front row had been reserved for those who had already been accepted by the prosecution and defense to sit as jurors; four men and four women sat stone-faced in the pew.

On the other side of the wooden railing, Daniel Brownell was sitting at the counsel table, going over some last-minute matters with an older, white-haired investigator seated next to him. He suddenly sensed rather than saw Dowd, turned to look behind him. Dowd nodded toward the prosecutor with a smile. Brownell returned the nod, slowly and solemnly, then turned back to his investigator.

Judge Goodman was nervously pacing back and forth in front of the bench, a white-shirted bailiff frantically following and listening as the judge issued rapid-fire instructions.

"Hey, isn't that her lawyer?" a reporter in the second row said loudly, pointing at Dowd as he walked down the aisle. "What's his name? Dowd?"

Dowd spotted Louann Fratt sitting in the third row on the left side, next to two of the children, Laura and Poe Jr. She was wearing a navy blue wool suit, with a white blouse and an ever-present Gucci scarf, and sat staring blankly into space. He unbuttoned his overcoat and walked toward her as two reporters confronted him.

"Mr. Dowd, can you tell us—"

Judge Goodman suddenly spotted Dowd. He stopped, almost causing a collision with the bailiff. "Mr. Dowd!" he called out above the low din of conversations.

Dowd looked up at the judge in his unbuttoned black robe. "Yes, Your Honor?"

"Let's get on with this!" Goodman nodded at the bailiff, then turned and stepped up behind the bench.

"All rise!" the bailiff yelled out.

Dowd leaned toward Louann Fratt and smiled as everyone in the courtroom stood up. He motioned for her to follow him.

"Part Sixty-two of the Supreme Court of New York is now in session," the bailiff continued, "Honorable Budd G. Goodman, presiding."

Goodman sat down. Immediately, he shifted in his seat, then leaned forward, then back. Judge Goodman strongly resented being confined to the chair. Seated behind the bench, his intense black eyes darting quickly from one face in the courtroom to another, he looked like nothing so much as a jittery, caged ferret desperately seeking an escape.

"Be seated," the bailiff called out. There was a low rumble as the audience settled into their seats.

"People versus Fratt," the judge said quickly, grabbing for a file. He looked down at Brownell. "Ready for the People?"

The young prosecutor rose. "Ready, Your Honor."

"Defense?" Goodman demanded, looking at Dowd.

Dowd guided his client to the defense table, pulled out the chair farthest from the jury for her. Goodman was wasting no time in applying the lash, he thought. "The defense is ready, Your Honor," he replied calmly as Louann Fratt sat down. Then he took off his overcoat, draped it over his own chair, and sat down.

Goodman looked at the clerk seated behind the large desk to his left. "Call the names," he said.

Dowd leaned over to Louann as the clerk began drawing names on strips of paper one by one from a small round drum. "You look great," Dowd whispered to his client. "You really look terrific."

Louann Fratt tried to smile, but managed only a quick, hard little grimace.

Like a caller at a bingo game, the clerk loudly began announcing the names as he drew them from the drum of the next twelve jurors to be questioned by the two attorneys. From their ranks, it was hoped, four would be chosen to join the eight already seated in the front pew as the jury that would try the case.

"Louisa Francini, West Forty-ninth Street."

A short, heavy-set older woman with a tight, wispy bun of graying black hair hesitantly stood up in the fifth row. The bailiff guided her into the far seat in the second row of the jury box. The ritualistic process of jury selection had resumed.

". . . Joan P. Clinton, West Eighty-fourth . . ."

Dowd looked back at the audience for a moment, searching for a face that he could not find. Then he turned back around. She would be there. She had never failed him before.

". . . Barry Feinstein, North Lexington . . ."

One by one, men and women rose from the right side of the audience as their names were called, walked through the swinging gate, and took seats in the jury box. Dowd was now writing down the names on a white sheet of paper as the clerk read them. The sheet of paper was actually a schematic diagram depicting two horizontal rows of six large boxes. Each box represented a juror's seat, arranged as the seats were in the jury box. As each potential juror was called, Dowd wrote the name at the top of the box corresponding to the seat in which that juror sat. As Dowd observed or learned things about each of the jurors during the next few hours of selection, he would write notes in the boxes. One potential juror's box might, for example, end up with scrawled notes reading "Upper West Side . . . CCNY . . . broker . . . divorced 2× (says amiable) . . . 2 kids (w/mother) . . . no eye contact . . . BMW . . . dad plumber/mom housewife . . . 2 trials/1 verdict . . . doesn't like psychs."

". . . Wendell George, East 104th . . ."

Dowd appeared casual, almost unconcerned, as the ritual continued. In fact, he was carefully studying the jurors for any sign, any facial expression, any body language that could be a clue to their attitudes toward him or his client. Some of them were already looking at Louann Fratt, trying to figure out who she was and what she had done. Others made concerted efforts to look everywhere but at the woman who was so obviously the defendant. Dowd knew that jury selection was one of the most critical stages of the trial; many lawyers believed that the outcome of a trial was 80 percent determined once the jurors were chosen. He also knew that jurors would rarely admit to biases or preconceptions, and that these often had to be detected through instinct, through observing a tight-lipped smile, an averted glance, an almost imperceptible frown.

". . . Grace Helen Papadakis, West Thirty-second . . ."

Dowd looked back at the audience again. A sea of faces. But not hers.

When the twelfth name had finally been called and the juror was seated, Judge Goodman asked this latest group of potential jurors to reply in turn to seventeen questions on a form they had each received when they had entered the courtroom. These questions addressed the basic personal information commonly asked by attorneys: Occupation? Are you married? Spouse's occupation? Divorced? Children? Do you have any friends in law enforcement? Have you or a close friend or relative ever been a victim of crime? Accused or convicted of a crime? Have you served as a juror before? Was it a criminal or civil case? Were you able to reach a verdict?

When the last juror had finished answering the written questions, Goodman looked with undisguised irritation at Brownell and nodded. The assistant D.A. stood and walked over to the railing separating him from the jurors. By Goodman's rules, each lawyer had one half hour in which to question each new group of jury panel members.

"Good morning, ladies and gentlemen," Brownell said pleasantly, leaning on the railing.

Close contact. Establish intimacy. But that was a two-edged sword: Some jurors resented the intrusion into their space.

"As you probably heard yesterday, my name is Daniel Brownell, and I'll be representing the People in this case."

I'm one of you, folks. It's us—"the People"—against them.

"And again, as I'm sure you heard, this is a murder case. Mrs. Fratt, seated there next to her attorney . . ."

Point to her. Force a confrontation. Make them take a long, hard look at her. See the expressionless, unfeeling face. This is what a murderer looks like.

". . . is charged with the murder of her husband, Charles Kennedy Poe Fratt. She is, of course, presumed at this point to be innocent, and you should not forget this . . ."

Fairness. Impartiality. Trust me.

"But I will present evidence to overcome this presumption, evidence which will convince you that this woman stabbed her husband to death in cold blood . . ."

Fair, but firm. Confident.

"It is now our job to ask questions of you, questions about your backgrounds, your experience, your attitudes—things that may affect your ability to sit as fair and impartial jurors . . ."

Both lawyers knew better, of course: Neither wanted a truly impartial juror. Brownell would like to have seen twelve

N.Y.P.D. narcs in the jury box, and Dowd would have been delighted with twelve members of the local Hell's Angels chapter. But that is not what you tell potential jurors.

"Some of these questions may seem very personal at times, they may concern very private matters. For that, I apologize. I don't want to embarrass you. But please understand that this is a very serious matter, and that these questions are necessary . . ."

Sensitive guy. Caring, concerned. But responsible. Trust me.

Brownell now wound up the brief introductory phase of the process known as *voir dire*. The main phase—the actual questioning of the twelve individual jurors—would now begin. The purpose of *voir dire* was to detect bias, prejudice, or other attitudes that would render an individual unfit to serve on the jury. In actual fact, however, experienced trial lawyers used the procedure for much more than that. While carefully couching their questions in ways that made them *seem* to address the personal attitudes of a potential juror, a skillful attorney could actually *change* those attitudes. This was done through "preinstruction"—a technique that was officially not tolerated but nevertheless widely employed. This involved the subtle implanting of information in the mind of the juror, information contained in the "question" itself that may concern facts in the case, or the law that applied. It may be designed to *create* a prejudice in the mind of the juror, rather than to detect one. Or the "question" may simply be intended to take the shock value out of the opponent's evidence.

A clever defense attorney in a drunk driving case, for example, might ask, "Mr. Ortega, there will be evidence that my client drank three cans of beer before driving. You realize, of course, that it is not against the law to drink and drive—only to drive under the influence?" Mr. Ortega will agree with the lawyer, since he will not want to show his ignorance by admitting he thought it *was* against the law to drink and drive. More important, the lawyer has accomplished a number of things with this "question." First, the shock value of the prosecutor's evidence when he presents it is gone: Every juror in the courtroom will already know that the defendant had three cans of beer. Second, the lawyer has countered the common misconception that it is unlawful to "drink and drive." Third, a "fact" has been implanted because it is assumed by the lawyer: Three cans of beer is not enough to render a person "under the influence." The one thing the lawyer has *not* done with the question is determine whether Mr. Ortega is biased or otherwise unfit to serve as a juror.

"Ms. DeLong?" Brownell said.

In the second row a young woman wearing a Syracuse sweatshirt lifted her head slightly. "Yes?"

"Ms. DeLong, I'm sure you understand that before you can convict Mrs. Fratt, you must be convinced of her guilt beyond a reasonable doubt."

"Yes. Yes, I understand that."

"It is the People's burden to convince you of her guilt beyond a reasonable doubt."

"Yes."

"Would you demand *more* of the People?"

The woman suddenly seemed confused. "I . . . I don't understand."

Dowd smiled slightly. The line of "questions" was designed to lighten the prosecution's burden of proof in the jurors' minds.

"Well," Browning continued, "you wouldn't insist that the People remove *all* doubt before you convicted, would you?"

"I . . . suppose not. No, of course not."

"You *do* realize, don't you, Ms. DeLong, that all things are subject to *some* doubt?"

"Yes, of course."

"Your duty is to convict unless there is a *reasonable* doubt?"

"Yes."

"So, Ms. DeLong, if after hearing all of the evidence, you still had a doubt about whether Mrs. Fratt was guilty of murder, could you still vote to convict—if the doubt was not big enough to amount to a *reasonable* doubt?"

"I . . . well, yes, if it was just . . . a small doubt."

"If you had a small, nagging doubt, you could still vote for conviction."

"Yes, I think so."

Clever. Dowd knew that every juror in the room was now rethinking his concepts of reasonable doubt. During the deliberations at the end of the trial, there would be jurors who would remind the others that doubt as to Louann Fratt's guilt was not enough to prevent a conviction. Dowd would have to ask questions during his own *voir dire* to counter this, questions designed to emphasize the "reasonableness"—whatever that was—of even small doubts.

"Now, Ms. DeLong, please take a look at the defendant, seated over there."

Hesitantly, the woman looked across the room at Louann Fratt. Dowd smiled again, but his client remained impassive, staring straight ahead at the judge's bench, apparently oblivious of the procedures. Brownell was once again creating a confrontation, forcing jurors to face the accused. More important, he was showing them a defendant who avoided eye contact. He was also showing them a wealthy, privileged woman who seemed aloof, who perhaps considered herself better than others.

"Ms. DeLong, looking at her now, do you feel you could vote to convict her of murder?"

"I'm sorry?"

"If, after hearing all of the evidence, you felt she was guilty of murdering her husband, could you vote for conviction?"

"I . . ." The woman looked back at Brownell.

"No, please," the prosecutor said, "look at her."

The woman looked back at the still-impassive Louann Fratt.

"Could you convict this woman of murder?" Brownell repeated.

Again, the "questions" *appeared* to address the issue of whether this juror was capable of sitting on the case. But the real purpose was get her used to the idea of convicting, to confront and overcome the emotional resistance to condemning another human being.

"I . . ." The woman turned her eyes away from Louann Fratt for a moment, then looked at her again. "Yes, I think so."

"You understand that you will take an oath to follow His Honor's instructions, and that he will instruct you not to be guided by emotion or sympathy?"

"Yes," the woman said, looking back at Brownell, "I understand that."

"Do you feel sympathy for Mrs. Fratt?"

"What?"

"Please look at her again, Ms. DeLong."

Once again, hesitantly, the woman looked across the room at Louann Fratt.

"Looking at her now," Brownell said, "do you feel any sympathy for her?"

"Well, I . . . I mean, maybe . . . Maybe some, yes."

"That's natural, Ms. DeLong. That's a normal human feeling. You may feel sorry for her. You may feel compassion."

"A little, maybe, yes."

"But let me ask you: Could you convict this woman of murder—even if you felt sorry for her?"

"Well—"

"Think about that for a moment, Ms. DeLong. Take a good, long look at Mrs. Fratt. Could you feel sorry for this woman—and still vote to convict her? Think about that for a moment."

The woman continued to stare uncomfortably at Louann Fratt. Dowd's client continued to stare blankly off into space.

"Now, Ms. DeLong, assuming the evidence is sufficient, *can you convict this woman?*"

"Yes," the woman replied finally, her eyes not moving from the seated defendant. "Yes, I can."

Brownell was good, Dowd thought to himself. He knew how to handle a jury. And while he lacked any noticeable sense of humor, he had an earnest, respectful, sincere manner that instilled a sense of trust in jurors. Unlike many lawyers, he did not seem to be trying to sell a used car: Brownell appeared to *believe* in his cause. And Dowd knew that this was a key to success in trial. Jurors were not always bright, but they were very good at sensing whether you really believed in what you were doing. And if you did not believe in it, neither would they.

Dowd looked back at the audience, again trying to find the familiar face he needed so much. Nothing. He returned to the sheet of paper that lay in front of him, then looked up at the twelve people in the jury box as Brownell continued his *voir dire*.

" . . . able to follow His Honor's instructions, Ms. DeLong?"

"Yes."

"Fine. I'm sure you can. Now, I'd like to talk with you about another . . ."

The young prosecutor's voice faded away as Dowd studied the twelve faces, trying to find some sign, some indication of what was in their hearts. He looked back down at the sheet of paper containing the schematic. Four more jurors to be chosen. And then probably two alternates—two who would sit with the jury in case one of the regular jurors became ill or otherwise be unable to continue with the trial. Four more jurors and two alternates. And he had used up sixteen challenges.

In a murder case in New York, each side was given twenty "peremptory challenges" and an unlimited number of "challenges for cause" to use in excluding jurors from sitting on the jury. Challenges for cause were used to dismiss a juror whenever he or she appeared to have a clear bias against one or the other side; the judge determined whether such a bias did, in fact, exist. A peremptory challenge, on the other hand, could be exercised for no apparent reason at all: Brownell and Dowd each had the absolute right to excuse up to twenty jurors without giving any reason. This was done in chambers, after the lawyers had finished their questions of each group of twelve.

The use of peremptory challenges usually developed into a chess match of its own. The tactics were clear: Force the opponent to use up his allotted challenges first. This placed him in the unpleasant situation of having to accept whatever new jurors were called from the panel, no matter how bad they were, leaving the attorney with remaining challenges firmly in the driver's seat.

The defense had four challenges left. The prosecution had six.

Brownell's voice drifted back." . . . your feelings about self-defense, Mr. Tanny?"

"My feelings?" The voice came from a burly, semibald man in the center of the front row wearing a red cardigan sweater, white shirt, and tie.

"Yes. If someone hits you with his fists, do you think you should be able to hit him back?"

"Well, sure, I guess so."

"And if someone hits you with his fists, do you think you should be able to stab him with a knife?"

"Well . . . a knife, no, I guess not."

"Not even if you were a woman?"

"A woman?"

"Yes. If you were a woman, Mr. Tanny, and a much larger man struck you with his fists, do you think you should have the right to stab him with a knife?"

"A woman . . . Well, I don't know about that, I don't know."

Brownell was preparing the jury for Dowd's evidence of self-defense. Dowd had withdrawn his notice of psychiatric testimony, so the young prosecutor was now taking the emotional impact out of any evidence that Poe Fratt had beaten his wife. At the same time, he was going to get the jury members to accept a legal fact that many people might find disquieting: A woman could not defend herself with a knife against the fists of a much larger man. Of course, Brownell did not know of the attempted rape; that was Dowd's ace-in-the-hole. But then, Dowd still did not know what Brownell's evidence of *motive* was—and the assistant D.A. had been careful so far not to disclose it during his *voir dire*.

"You will be instructed by the judge on the law of self-defense, Mr. Tanny."

"Yes, sir."

"He will instruct you that Mrs. Fratt could use deadly force, such as a knife, *only* if her husband had first used deadly force against her."

"Yes, sir."

"Can you follow this instruction?"

"I guess so, yes, sir."

"So if the evidence shows that the defendant's husband struck her two or three times with his fists, and she then stabbed him to death with a kitchen knife, would this be self-defense?"

The man thought about this for a brief moment, obviously not entirely pleased with the required answer. "I guess not."

"And if that was the evidence, would it be murder?"

Reluctantly, "I guess so."

"So if you heard evidence that the defendant . . ." Brownell paused, then pointed at Louann Fratt. "If this woman stabbed her husband to death, after he hit her with his fists, you would vote to convict her of murder?"

The man shrugged uncomfortably. "If that's what the law is, I guess so."

Dowd knew as well as Brownell that this man was history: The prosecutor would use one of his remaining peremptories to keep him from serving on the jury. He did not want a chauvinist there applying some unwritten "law of the Old West" to the case. But Brownell was continuing his questioning of the man so that he could educate the rest of the jurors on self-defense.

Dowd looked back at the audience again. Still no sign of her. He returned his attention to Brownell as the young prosecutor continued questioning the doomed juror.

"Mr. Tanny, do you think a woman has a right, in defending herself against two or three blows, to stab her husband *in the back?*"

A slight, muffled sound behind Dowd suddenly distracted him. He turned, but saw only Louann Fratt sitting next to him, her expressionless face still rigidly facing straight ahead. He was about to turn back to Brownell's questioning when something caught his eye. He looked more closely at his client. Then he saw it.

A tear was running down her cheek.

C. K. Poe Fratt in his college days before meeting Louann. A 1951 All-American nominee as a tackle at Cornell, Fratt was also a National Scholar and eventually earned a master's degree in business administration. In later years, Fratt rarely missed a chance to attend football games at his alma mater. It was at one of these games that the prosecution contended that Fratt and his youngest son got in a fight over an attractive blond girlfriend the father had brought to the game. Two days later, Louann stabbed Poe to death.
Courtesy of Cornell University Athletic Department

Louann Fratt's graduation picture from the 1951 yearbook of Weatherwax High School in the small lumber town of Aberdeen, Washington. The popular and attractive Louann was known for her habit of boldly approaching boys and asking them out. She was described by her friends as a "social climber" and a "designing woman" who was "very much in control of the situation." Her best friend recalled that "Louann wanted to marry the right kind of man. She wasn't going to live in Aberdeen. . . . I wasn't surprised at all when I heard that she was living on Park Avenue." Courtesy of Weatherwax High School

LOU ANN JOHNSON
Tri-Hi-Y I ·V. P. 4; Honor Society 2, 3, 4; Pep Club 2, 3 V. P. 4; Senate 4; Golden Finns 2, 3, 4.

Michael G. Dowd at a press conference shortly before trial. The former lawyer for I.R.A. terrorists had become widely known as a defender of abused women. At the time of the Fratt trial, Dowd had an unbroken string of victories in murder cases involving battered wives. But Louann Fratt turned out to be a mystery even for Dowd. Courtesy of the New York *Daily News*

Charles Kennedy Poe Fratt, wealthy senior partner of the largest accounting firm in the nation and an influential director of the National Democratic Committee. After thirty years of marriage and three children, Fratt
suddenly announced to his wife that he was leaving her.

ABOVE: At a dramatic moment during cross-examination, Louann Fratt describes how her estranged husband tried to rape her for the second time. In her hands is a police photograph of the death scene—Poe's apartment off Park Avenue.   Courtesy of the New York *Daily News*

FACING PAGE: In the predawn hours of November 22, 1988, Louann Fratt is arrested for the murder of her husband and taken away in handcuffs. After stabbing him through the heart, the Park Avenue socialite had returned to her two-million-dollar condo, calmly laundered her bloody clothes, washed and dried her hair, and then called the police.
Courtesy of the *New York Post*

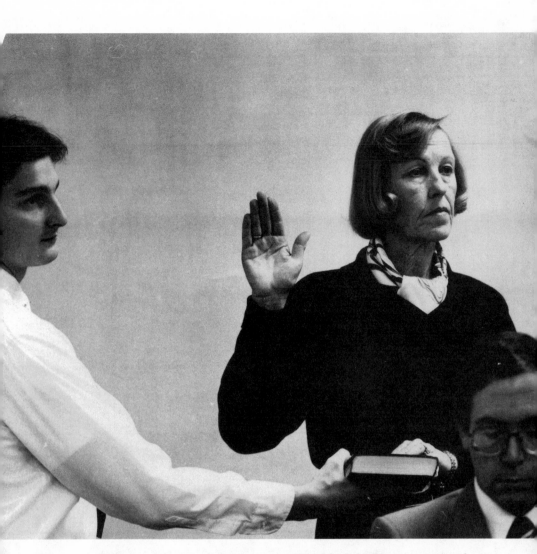

ABOVE: Louann Fratt being sworn in. Dowd had tried to prepare her for this critical moment by putting her through a searing cross-examination by an expert criminal lawyer. But the effort had failed: Louann's story was torn to pieces and her confidence badly shaken.

Courtesy of the New York *Daily News*

Enigma: Louann Fratt appears lost in thought as her attorney cross-examines a police officer.   Courtesy of the New York *Daily News*

Louann Fratt leaving lower Manhattan's Criminal Courts Building mid-way through the trial. To her left is her daughter, Laura, who had flown in from San Francisco for the trial; to her right is Poe Jr., a graduate student at Cornell University. It was Poe Jr. whom the prosecution contended was a key to the murder motive. Courtesy of the *New York Post*

CHAPTER 17

"What do you think of a person who sees a psychiatrist, Mrs. Francini?"

"A psychiatrist? I don't know, I guess it's okay."

"Do you think less of them?"

"I don't know, I never thought about it."

"Well," Dowd continued, pacing slowly back and forth in front of the jury box, "do you think it's any different than going to see another kind of doctor, say an orthopedic surgeon if you broke an arm?"

"It's different, sure."

"How?"

"Huh?"

"How? How is it different?"

"Well . . . In one, you break an arm, you got to get it fixed. In the other, well, there's nothing broken, you know? I mean there's nothing to fix."

"Can a person be broken *inside*?"

"Inside?"

"Can a person be injured in her heart, in her mind? Do you think a person can be damaged emotionally?"

"Well, sure, I guess so. They say so."

199

"What do *you* think, Mrs. Francini?"

"Myself, I don't know. I guess there's something to it."

Dowd stopped in front of the woman. He just stood there for a moment, smiling. Then, gently, he said, "Mrs. Francini, you have a son, and I know you love him very much."

The woman nodded silently.

At that moment Dowd sensed movement near the doorway. He looked out at the audience, then saw her walking silently up the aisle toward him. Dr. Julie Blackman.

Dowd's eyes met those of the psychologist. She smiled, shrugged apologetically, then stepped through the swinging gate and sat down in a chair next to Louann Fratt. She pulled out a legal pad, then leaned back slightly and began studying the jurors one by one.

Dowd continued as if nothing had happened. "What would you do if one day your son did not recognize you, Mrs. Francini, if one day he started seeing strange beings crawling on the walls, and if he believed he were someone else?"

The woman thought for a moment. "I'd pray," she said finally.

Dowd nodded, seemed to think about that for a moment. Then he turned to the woman seated next to her. "Mrs. Clinton?"

"Yes?"

"What do you think of Mrs. Francini's answer?"

"Oh, goodness, I . . . if it were my son?"

"Yes."

She shook her head. "Well, I think praying's fine, but . . . I just think I'd get help for him."

"What kind of help?"

"Psychiatric help, I suppose."

"Why?"

"Why? Because that's what he needs, I think. I mean, I'm not an expert, but—"

"But a psychiatrist is?"

"Yes, of course."

"Do you think a psychiatrist might be able to help her son—help repair the emotional or mental damage?"

"Maybe."

This line of questions was designed, of course, to bring

out attitudes of jurors toward psychiatrists and psychologists: Dowd's defense would depend heavily upon the testimony of Dr. Rosen and Dr. Veronen. But the questions were also intended to detect attitudes about mental illness and emotional problems generally. Dowd knew from hard experience that many people were reluctant to believe in the existence of such things as rape trauma syndrome.

Dowd took a few steps to the right and looked at a juror seated in the second row.

"What about that, Mr. Unsoeld?" he asked. "Do you think a psychiatrist could help Mrs. Francini's son?"

"Yeah," the small, wiry man with thick bifocals said. "I guess they can help some."

"What would you think if the psychiatrist told you this boy was a schizophrenic—that he had two completely different personalities?"

"I don't know."

"Would you think she knew what she was talking about?"

"She?"

"Yes, the psychiatrist."

"Oh, yeah. Well, I don't know. Probably. I don't know." He grinned. "Sometimes I don't think any of them really know what's going on, to tell you the truth."

"Would it make any difference if the psychiatrist were a woman?"

"Huh? Well, I don't know. I guess not."

Dowd's technique in conducting the *voir dire* of a jury was one that very few lawyers attempted, one that required a tremendous amount of skill, and it could backfire disastrously. Rather than question one juror at a time in isolated sequence, he would try to get the different jurors to talk about *each other*. Where other lawyers would ask a juror a series of questions and then move on to the next juror, Dowd would ask a question of one juror and then ask another to comment upon the answer—and then ask a third what he thought of the second juror's comments. In effect, Dowd was directing traffic—setting up the subject matter and then skillfully maneuvering the flow of conversation. The entire effect was not unlike a large group-counseling session.

The benefits of this approach were considerable. For one

thing, when the jurors began to focus upon others rather than upon themselves, they tended to become less guarded, more open and honest. Another benefit was that it avoided yes or no answers; rarely was such an answer very helpful in understanding the attitudes or character of the juror. Dowd realized that to understand who the juror really was, he had to get him talking—about some subject, about another juror's answers, eventually about himself.

Still another benefit to the "group dynamics" approach was that Dowd could remove himself from the judgmental and potentially confrontational role of advocate. By guiding the conversations, he could get the jurors themselves to condemn a particular attitude expressed by one juror. This meant that Dowd did not make an enemy, but instead enlisted other jurors as allies.

Mr. Unsoeld, for example, would have to go: He held a low opinion of psychiatry and he was prejudiced against women as professionals. But before spending one of his challenges to get rid of him, Dowd could use Mr. Unsoeld to bring out some of these attitudes—to air them and let other jurors condemn them.

Dowd had walked toward his counsel table as he continued talking with the juror. He looked down at the yellow pad of paper on Julie Blackman's lap, read the hastily scribbled question.

"Mr. Unsoeld," he said, looking up at the juror, "do you think girls are raised to listen to the men they marry?"

"Huh?"

"Do you think girls are raised to listen to the men they marry?"

The man shrugged. "I guess so. Sure."

The word "girls" had been circled by the psychologist. The question was designed to get the jurors talking about a critical issue in the trial: the role of women in a marriage. And it was designed very cleverly. The word "listen" could trigger very different reactions: It could be interpreted as "obey" or as something much less. But Dowd knew that the key to the question was the use of the word "girls," rather than "women" or "females." How an individual might use such terms could say a lot about his true attitudes.

"What do you think of that?"

"What do I think of it?"

"Yes."

He shrugged again. "I don't know. Somebody's got to wear the pants, don't they? I mean, the man is the head of the family, right? Girls . . . It's best they learn early, I guess."

Dowd nodded again, apparently considering this answer. Then he turned and walked slowly along the jury railing until he came to the end. He stopped in front of the last two chairs, smiled at the woman seated in the first row. She was young, maybe twenty-eight, with short reddish hair and wore a stylish gray herringbone wool pantsuit.

"Ms. Green?"

"Yes."

"Do you agree with Mr. Unsoeld?"

She grinned. "No, I don't."

"Oh? Why not?"

"Well . . . it's a typically chauvinistic attitude."

"What do you mean?"

"I mean that attitude went out years ago."

"You don't feel girls should be raised to listen to the men they marry?"

"Of course not."

"How should they be raised, Ms. Green?"

"*Women* should be raised to think for themselves. They have equal rights, they are equal human beings."

"How do you see marriage, then?"

"A partnership," the young woman replied confidently. "Two equal partners."

"Well, what do you think of a woman who *has* been raised to obey her husband, Ms. Green?"

"I feel sorry for her."

"You feel sorry for her."

"Yes," she said. "The woman was taught to be a servant. It's not her fault, of course. That was another time, another age. Things have changed."

"Yes," Dowd agreed. "Things have changed." And he made a mental note to kick this woman off the jury.

Most lawyers would have considered Ms. Green an ideal juror for the defense in this case. She clearly had enlightened views, and seemed to be a person who would prove very sympathetic to Louann Fratt's plight. But Dowd did not want her. She lacked what he felt to be the one essential quality in a juror.

Every lawyer had his own theories as to who the "perfect juror" was in any given case. In criminal cases, for example, defense attorneys generally sought out minorities and younger people—individuals who may have less respect for authority. Prosecutors, on the other hand, tended to like Asians and whites, preferably older, and middle or upper class. A defense lawyer might look for those in people-oriented professions such as teaching and social work, while an assistant D.A. would prefer the more disciplined thinking of engineers and retired army officers.

Dowd was different. He didn't believe in stereotypes. For him, the most important quality in a juror was to be *nonjudgmental*. He knew that the key to winning an acquittal for Louann Fratt was in the willingness of the jurors to put themselves in her shoes. The juror *had* to be able to empathize—to ask himself, "If I had been through what this woman had been through, what would *I* have done?" Without jurors like this, Louann Fratt was doomed. And Dowd was confident Ms. Green would not be able to do this. She was judgmental. She felt sorry for women who had been raised like Louann Fratt, but she also had contempt for them. She would be sympathetic to Dowd's client, but not *empathetic*. Ms. Green would never be able to put herself in Louann Fratt's place. She would never be able to understand what Louann Fratt felt the night she killed her husband.

"Thank you, Ms. Green," Dowd said with a smile.

The woman smiled back warmly.

Dowd looked up at the heavily bearded man seated directly behind her. "Mr. Karpov?" he said.

"Yes," the man replied. Like most people, the man found himself pleased that the lawyer somehow knew his name. Dowd had long ago learned the benefits of quickly memorizing the names of four or five jurors at a time.

"Mr. Karpov, what do you do when you feel sad, really sad, when you feel like crying?"

"Do?"

"Yes. Do you cry?"

"I . . . I don't know. It depends."

"If someone close to you suddenly died—your mother, your son—do you think you would cry?"

The man looked at Dowd for a moment without answering. He was remembering something from long ago. "Yes," he said finally.

"Do you think you would cry in front of other people?"

The man thought again. "No," he said. "I would wait."

"Uh-huh. And what do you think other people would think of you—that you didn't feel anything about the loss?"

"I don't know. Maybe."

"Do you think it's possible for someone to feel pain inside, tremendous pain, without showing it?"

"I think it's possible, sure."

Dowd suddenly looked at the woman seated next to Mr. Karpov. "What do *you* think, Mrs. Keough?"

The older black woman was startled. "What?"

Dowd smiled gently. "Do you think some people are raised to show no feelings? To keep things inside?"

The woman nodded. "Sure, there's lots of people like that."

"Uh-huh. Well, do you think—"

"Time!" Judge Goodman suddenly said loudly. The half hour of *voir dire* was up.

Dowd smiled at the woman. "Thank you, Mrs. Keough." She nodded, and the lawyer walked back to his seat.

Goodman looked at the jurors. "The court will now be in recess for fifteen minutes. Please be back here in your seats by then." Rising quickly to his feet, he looked down at the two lawyers. "I'll see you both in chambers." Then the judge stepped down from the bench and almost ran through the rear doorway.

"Sorry," Julie Blackman said to Dowd. "Got hung up in traffic."

"No problem," Dowd said. "I just used the same stuff you gave me yesterday."

Dowd had enlisted Julie Blackman's help in picking juries

in most of his recent murder cases involving battered women. He had quickly learned the value of her insight, both in framing revealing questions and in detecting hidden attitudes.

"Any feelings on these twelve?" he asked.

She shook her head. "Only the obvious."

"Gentlemen," the bailiff announced impatiently to Dowd and Brownell.

Dowd picked up his sheet of paper and followed the prosecutor out the rear door. They walked in silence down a short, empty corridor and into Judge Goodman's chambers. The room was lined along one side with hundreds of volumes of law books; two other walls were covered with framed diplomas and awards. A neatly arranged desk stood near the center of the room, with three chairs in front of it and a small couch to one side. Judge Goodman sat behind the desk. The court reporter was busily setting up his stenotype machine in front of one of the chairs.

"Well?" Goodman asked.

Dowd and Brownell each took one of the chairs and sat down. This was the time for the two lawyers to exercise their challenges. The prosecution was required to challenge any of the twelve new jurors for cause first, giving the reasons. After the judge ruled on these challenges, the defense offered its challenges for cause. It was then the prosecution's turn to exercise any peremptory challenges. When Brownell had excused all of the jurors he wished, Dowd would then use his peremptory challenges. The jurors who were left would then be sworn and added to the eight who had already been accepted.

The chess match resumed.

"No challenges for cause," Brownell said.

Goodman looked sternly at Dowd.

There were certainly jurors among the twelve who were biased or prejudiced. But Dowd knew that the bias or prejudice had to be made obvious by the juror and that the judge had to decide that it would clearly prevent him from following the court's instructions. Invariably, if a juror admitted a bias of some sort, the judge would ask him if he would nevertheless be able to decide the case fairly; the juror would, of course, rarely admit to being unable to be fair.

"No challenges for cause," Dowd said.

Goodman looked sharply back at Brownell.

The assistant D.A. glanced at the notes on his lap. "People's peremptory challenges on three, seven, and eight, Your Honor."

Dowd checked his sheet. There were three he wanted off the jury, too, but one of them was number seven. That was the tactical advantage to being second in exercising the peremptories: The prosecution very often wanted the same juror dismissed, though for very different reasons. Brownell had just saved him from using one challenge.

"Mr. Dowd?" the judge demanded.

"Peremptories on one and six," Dowd said.

"Let's see, that's five," Goodman muttered to himself, writing some notes on a pad. "Gives us seven left. And we need four, right?"

Both lawyers nodded silently.

"Then it's done," the judge said triumphantly. "We've got a jury. And I'm putting on three alternates, just to be safe. Any questions?"

The two men shook their heads.

"Good." The judge suddenly sprang to his feet. "I'll swear them in, then we'll recess until tomorrow morning." He looked at Brownell. "Your opening statement will begin at nine o'clock."

"Yes, Your Honor," the assistant D.A. said as he stood.

Goodman looked at Dowd as the defense lawyer slowly rose to his feet. "Will you be giving an opening?"

Brownell quickly looked toward his opponent.

Dowd just grinned and said nothing. The defense had the option of giving the opening statement immediately after the prosecution had finished giving its own, of saving the opportunity until the prosecution had rested its case and it was time for the defense to put on evidence, or of waving the statement altogether. But Dowd was not required to inform the court of his decision until after Brownell had finished his opening statement. There was a tactical advantage to not tipping your hand until the last minute: Brownell would not know when he would learn the details of the defense. And this could affect the preparation of his case. The advantage was a small one, but in trial you took every edge you could get.

"That's your privilege, Mr. Dowd," Goodman said testily. He walked past the two men and out into the corridor. "I'll see you two gentlemen bright and early tomorrow morning," he called back.

Dowd and Brownell looked at each other for a brief moment, then filed out of the room. They walked quietly down the empty corridor and out into the courtroom. The judge was already on the bench and the bailiff was calling the court back to order. As the judge began swearing in the new jurors, the two lawyers sat each lost in thoughts of opening statements and critical strategic decisions. They knew that with the giving of the statements the next day, the die would be cast.

Unlike the summation at the end of the trial, where the lawyers tried to persuade the jury to convict or acquit, an opening statement was intended as a more objective presentation of what the case was all about. It served as a road map, a preview of what the evidence would be and how it all fit into a bigger picture.

As with most things in trial, there were many tactical considerations involved in the giving of opening statements. For his part, Brownell would have the benefit of being the first to tell the eagerly awaiting jury just what this case *was* all about. His representation of the facts would tend to be accepted by the jurors; it was a psychological truism that they would be more resistant to later versions of the facts. And so Brownell would want important details to be etched into their memories at this impressionable time—details such as *motive*. But was it worth tipping off Dowd as to what the motive was? The longer he could keep the defense in the dark, the less time it would have to counter.

Dowd, too, had decisions to make. Should he give the opening statement immediately, save it for later, or not make it at all? Some lawyers thought the most effective approach was to waive the statement; testimony would then have more dramatic impact on the jury than if they had been told ahead of time what it would be. Others felt that the statement was more effective if it was reserved until the prosecution had rested its case, thus preserving the element of surprise and at the same time allowing for changes in the defense case caused by unforeseen prosecution evidence.

Dowd believed it was important to paint a defense version of the "big picture" for the jury. And he felt it was important to give a second view of what had happened that night in Poe Fratt's apartment as soon as possible. If the jury did not hear a second version of the facts until later, the prosecution version would tend to become set in their minds like concrete—and would become just as hard to change. However, a key weapon in the defense arsenal was surprise: The prosecution had no idea that the defense was based upon an attempted rape. Like Brownell, Dowd was torn between playing his ace now or holding it back a little while longer.

As he sat half listening to the swearing-in of the jurors, Dowd made his decision.

CHAPTER 18

Judge Goodman paced nervously back and forth between the bench and counsel tables, his dark, intense eyes darting around the crowded courtroom. Spectators were talking excitedly about the trial, and reporters were conducting interviews of witnesses and family members. As usual, Goodman's black robe was wide open and flowing behind him as he walked, exposing a white shirt, a thin red paisley tie, and light gray slacks. Every few seconds he stopped, glanced up at the clock on the wall as it grew nearer 9:00, then down at his wristwatch before resuming his frantic pacing. Periodically, he would stop and just stare at an individual as if he or she were some strange animal, then continue pacing. Goodman showed a special interest in the reporters and photographers, and particularly in the television camera, though it was difficult to tell whether this interest reflected fascination or his usual annoyance.

The jurors sat in their respective chairs in the jury box, five men and seven women chatting amiably among themselves. Two alternates were also seated at the far end; an additional chair had been found for the third alternate.

Brownell and Dowd were seated at their counsel tables,

each lost in last-minute reading of notes they had prepared for their opening statements. Debbie Cohen sat at the far end of the defense table; an empty chair stood between her and Dowd, waiting for their client.

Louann Fratt was standing in the aisle between the pews, surrounded by Peggy Keating and four other friends. She was wearing a dark gray Chesterfield coat over a light gray wool suit, with black pumps, black leather gloves, and the ever-present matching silk scarf. The other women were similarly dressed in the conservatively fashionable style of their age and class, each wearing a nearly identical dark gray wool overcoat. Laura and Poe Fratt, Jr., were standing nearby, lost in conversation with an older, balding, and red-faced man. Laura Fratt, with her long patrician face, narrow eyes, and fine ash-blond hair, looked like a clone of her mother; the effect was heightened by her Chesterfield, black wool suit, black pumps and gloves, and silk scarf. Poe Jr. and the elderly man were both dressed in the uniform of Park Avenue: black or dark gray wool overcoats, dark gray wool suits, neatly pressed white shirts, the mandatory dark red tie, black leather gloves, and cordovan or black wing-tip Oxfords.

The friends and relatives of Louann Fratt seemed happily lost in renewing acquaintance and making pleasant conversation, an occasional restrained laugh rising above the chatter. The scene was of a Christmas cocktail party, not a murder trial.

The gaiety was a front, of course, a shield thrown up by this modern-day aristocracy against the ogling spectators and prying reporters who pressed in from all sides. One of their class might be getting dragged publicly through the mud, but the world would not get the satisfaction of seeing any sweat or tears. Appearances had to be maintained. Marie Antoinette would ride to the guillotine with her head held high.

Judge Goodman suddenly stopped pacing and almost ran up to the bench. "All right, all right," he yelled out. "Sit down and let's get started."

For his own reasons, Goodman usually preferred to dispense with most of the formalities of court, such as having the bailiff call everyone to order and announce the session.

"I said let's get started," Goodman growled, his eyes glaring at the audience.

There was a low din of rustling and murmurs as the audience slowly took their seats. Poe Fratt, Jr., opened the swinging gate for his mother as she stepped through and took her seat at the defense table.

Goodman looked at Brownell. "You may begin."

Brownell stood up slowly, then walked over to the wooden railing encircling the jury.

"Ladies and gentlemen," he began, "at about one-thirty on the morning of November twenty-second of last year, the defendant in this case . . ."

Brownell stopped and looked at Louann Fratt. She was sitting in a rigid position of attention facing the judge's bench, her eyes locked on some distant object.

". . . the defendant, Louann Fratt, carefully placed an eight-inch kitchen knife in a small bag. Then, carrying the bag, she left her elegant home on Seventy-ninth Street, near Park Avenue, and walked a few short blocks to a small apartment on Seventy-eighth. In that apartment a man was asleep. The man was Poe Fratt, her estranged husband. She and Mr. Fratt were in the middle of a particularly bitter divorce."

Brownell walked along the railing, looking at each of the jurors as he passed them.

"The defendant silently entered the apartment. Then, as her husband slept . . ." He looked back at Louann Fratt again. ". . . she took the knife from the bag . . . and stabbed him to death."

Dowd leaned back, studying the assistant district attorney as he presented his opening statement. Brownell was good, Dowd thought to himself. The eyes of each of the jurors were locked on the young prosecutor as he passed by. His sincere and straightforward manner was effective. But Dowd was more concerned with what Brownell was *saying*. He was listening very carefully for the prosecutor to show his cards, to spell out just what his client's *motive* was for killing her husband.

There were many different theories as to what an opening statement should be. Some lawyers felt that the entire case should be spelled out in detail—who every witness would be and exactly what they would testify to; this gave the jurors a detailed road map to follow as evidence was presented. Others felt that you should just recount for the jurors everything that happened, as if you were telling them a story, without mentioning witnesses or testimony; this approach had the benefit of burning one version of the facts in their minds without weighing them down with too much detail. Still others believed that the jury should be told as little as possible—enough to give them the "big picture," but not enough to tip off the other side or to take away from the dramatic impact of the testimony when it was presented.

"The defense," Brownell continued, "will try to convince you that she killed Poe Fratt in self-defense. They will try to convince you that her husband called her up in the middle of the night and told her to bring his mail over. They will try to convince you that, in the middle of this bitter divorce, Louann Fratt readily complied, that she walked alone, in the middle of the night, to deliver mail to him. They will try to convince you that Poe Fratt then tried to beat her up, that they got into a fight and he tried to beat her up."

The assistant D.A. stopped and looked once again at Louann Fratt sitting impassively in her chair.

"But ladies and gentlemen, you will hear evidence that will convince you beyond a reasonable doubt that she did *not* kill him in self-defense. You will hear evidence that the defendant did not reach for a knife that was lying there in the apartment, but rather that she *took* the knife *with* her—that she had *planned* the murder long before sinking that knife deep into her husband's heart."

He looked back at the jury. "You will hear evidence that there were no signs of a struggle in that apartment that night, no indications of any fight. And you will hear evidence that there were *three* stab wounds to Poe Fratt's body—each of them carefully directed to a lethal point."

Brownell once again walked along the jury railing, then to his chair. He put his hands on the back of the chair and looked back at the jury.

"At the end of this case, ladies and gentlemen, you will be

convinced, beyond a reasonable doubt, that *this* woman . . ." He looked directly at Louann Fratt, seated a few feet away from him. ". . . is a cold-blooded murderess."

The courtroom was deadly silent as the prosecutor pulled back his chair and sat down.

Dowd got slowly to his feet. Brownell had played it close to the vest, he thought to himself as he walked to the jury box. The assistant D.A. had offered nothing more than a brief glimpse into the People's case, giving no hint to Dowd of what the motive was or what evidence he would produce. He put his hands on the railing and stood there in silence, looking at each of the twelve faces, one at a time. When he had finished, he turned and looked at his seated client. Louann had not moved since taking her seat, nor had there been any hint of an expression.

Each of the jurors looked from Dowd to the impassive woman, then back to the lawyer.

"Louann Fratt killed her husband," Dowd said finally. "She stabbed him to death with a kitchen knife."

The jurors quickly looked back at the seated figure. Still no change of expression on her face.

"The defense does not dispute that," Dowd continued. "But the question in this case is not whether Louann Fratt killed her husband. The question is: Was she *forced* to kill him to save herself?"

Dowd walked along the railing, seemingly lost in thought. Then he stopped. "Because, ladies and gentlemen, late on that night of November twenty-second . . ." He slowly scanned the twelve faces again. ". . . Poe Fratt tried to *rape* his wife."

Out of the corner of his eye, Dowd could just see Brownell's head snap up from his notes and quickly turn toward the defense lawyer. The young prosecutor stared in near disbelief at Dowd as the defense attorney continued his slow pace in front of the jury box. Just as quickly, Brownell recovered and adopted a look of casual disinterest.

"The issue in this case, obviously," Dowd went on, "is what happened in apartment 9B sometime after midnight on November twenty-second, 1988. But ladies and gentlemen, there is also a long and winding road that leads to that apartment."

Dowd turned slowly, looking once again at each of the jurors. "And it begins someplace on the West Coast," he continued, "in the state of Washington, where Louann Fratt grew up in a different time, in a different place . . ."

Sergeant William Nevins leaned back in the witness chair, a cocky smile on his face, and unbuttoned his badly strained brown sport coat. He was of only average height, but a huge belly, a fat face, and a full brown beard and moustache gave one the impression of a much bigger man.

"After getting the radio call," he said, "we responded to the location, One Fifty-one East Seventy-ninth."

"We?"

"Yeah, me and my partner, Officer Lapinski."

"I see," said Brownell, leaning against the jury railing. "And what happened after you arrived, Sergeant?"

"We went up to the fifth floor. I knocked. The defendant . . ." He nodded toward Louann Fratt. ". . . opened the door. She let us in. She said she just stabbed her husband. She said she thinks he's dead."

"Now, when she said this, Sergeant, how did she appear to you?"

"Appear?"

"Was she upset? Hysterical? Crying?"

Nevins shook his head, his fat jowls shaking like jelly. "Calm," he said. "She was real calm."

"Calm," Brownell repeated, looking again toward the jury. Then he looked back at the officer. "What else did she say?"

"I asked her why, and she says they were divorcing and they had a fight."

"Was this a *physical* fight, or a verbal one?"

"She didn't say. Just a fight."

"Did she ever say, at any time that evening, that he had *hit* her?"

Nevins thought for a moment. "She may have said something like that."

"Well, did you notice any bruises on her face or body, Sergeant?"

"No, I didn't."

"Did you notice anything else unusual about her?"

"Unusual?"

"Did you notice anything about her *breath*?"

"Oh, yeah. I smelled alcohol on her breath."

"I see." Brownell walked over to the swinging gate. "And what happened next, Sergeant Nevins?"

"Well, I ask her, what did you stab him with? And she says a knife, and she points to this bag on the table. And so my partner goes over there and looks inside, and he pulls out this knife. A long kitchen knife."

Brownell walked over to his table and picked up a brown and gold Louis Vuitton bag lying on the floor. He carried the bag to the witness stand, holding it up so both the jury and the witness could clearly see it.

"Showing you what has been marked People's number four, is this the bag she pointed to?"

The fat man with the full beard looked at it for a moment. "Yeah."

Brownell reached inside the bag and pulled out a long-bladed kitchen knife. He handed it to the officer, handle first. "Showing you People's number three, is this the knife you found?"

Nevins pretended to study the knife. "Yeah," he said finally, "this is the knife."

Dowd realized that it was doubtful whether the officer had the slightest idea if it was the same knife; after the passage of a year, he would probably have identified anything the prosecutor handed him. But the identity of the knife was not an important issue in the case.

Brownell again reached inside the bag and pulled out a pair of white Reebok sneakers. "Sergeant Nevins, do you recognize what has been marked People's six?"

"Yeah. Those are the shoes Lapinski—Officer Lapinski—found in the bag with the knife. With blood on them."

The assistant D.A. once again reached into the brown bag. This time, he extracted a shiny white garment and held it up. "Do you recognize what has been marked People's five?"

The witness nodded. "That's the nightgown he found inside the bag, along with the knife and the shoes." He paused. "It had blood on it, too."

Dowd still had no answer for why the shoes and the nightgown were in the bag that his client had taken to her husband's apartment. Louann Fratt had told him that she had *not* put them in the bag: She had taken off her shoes in the bathroom before washing her hair, and the nightgown had been hanging next to a towel. The lawyer was left with two theories. One, his client had irrationally gathered the objects and put them in the bag, and later did not remember having done so; the nightgown would have gotten blood on it from the shoes and the blood left in the bag from the knife. Two, Lapinski found the bloody shoes and nightgown in the bathroom, not in the bag, and put them in the bag himself to transport to the station; Louann could have gotten blood on the nightgown while changing and cleaning herself in the bathroom, leading Lapinski to think that it was evidence worth taking. Later, when crime reports were made out, either Nevins or Lapinski could have mistakenly recalled the items being found in the bag.

The fact that Louann had acted irrationally in washing the knife and replacing it in the bag before calling the police tended to support the first theory. But Dowd had also learned to be suspicious of police procedures and officers' memories.

The problem with having two theories, Dowd realized, was that a jury would accept neither. The key to winning an acquittal was in presenting a single, coherent picture to the jury: *This* is what happened, ladies and gentlemen, and this is *why* it happened. Giving them different possibilities simply did not work.

Most lawyers defended criminal clients by trying to punch holes in the prosecution's case and nothing more; the prosecution built a structure of facts and the defense tried to tear it down. But Dowd had learned that the path to acquittal lay in building a *second structure*—one that made more sense than the first. It was not enough just to tear holes in the prosecution's version of what happened. To win, the defense had not only to show the defects in that version, but to give the jury a believable version of its own. Put another way, it was not enough to run down the competitor's product; you had to convince the consumer that your product was better.

Dowd had to choose: Louann had irrationally placed the shoes and nightgown in the bag, or Nevins's recollection was inaccurate. If the jury did not accept the defense version, then they would adopt the probable prosecution version: Louann Fratt had taken the nightgown to her estranged husband's apartment that night—possibly to seduce him and then murder him in his sleep.

Brownell put the knife, shoes, and nightgown back in the bag. He walked back to the counsel table, his expression intent and darkly brooding as always, and set the bag down. Then he turned back to the huge-bellied man in the sport coat.

"What happened next, Sergeant?"

"We drove over to her husband's apartment." Nevins looked at a report lying in his lap. "Fifty-two Seventy-eighth, apartment 9B." He looked back up.

"And what happened then?"

"The door was locked."

Brownell looked meaningfully at the jury. "The door was *locked*?"

Had Louann Fratt locked the door when she left? Dowd wondered to himself. If it locked from the outside, then she would have to have had a key. Maybe the door locked automatically. He should have checked it when he was at the apartment. She might have set it to lock after the door closed. But if she had done this after leaving the second time, why hadn't she done it after leaving the first time? And if she had locked the door after the first visit, how had she gotten back in the second time?

Theory: Louann Fratt had been too hysterical when she left after the first visit to remember to lock the door.

"Yeah," Nevins said. "There was some uniformed officers who met us there, and I ordered two of them to break the door down."

"And they did break it down?"

"They kicked it in. Broke the lock. But I still couldn't get in."

"Why was this?"

"The door was jammed against something. I could see a pair of legs through the opening. Looked like a body on the floor. And a lot of blood."

"What did you do next?"

"I had a couple of the guys force the door open some more. Then I went in."

"Where was the defendant at this time?"

"She was out in the hallway. She stayed out there, with my partner and the other officers. I was the only one went in."

Brownell walked toward the witness, his hand sliding along the jury railing. He stopped, turned to look at the jurors.

"Tell us, Sergeant," he said, "what did you find once you were inside?"

"A dead body. The victim, Charles Kennedy Poe Fratt. Lying face down. He was lying against the door."

"Against the door."

"Yeah."

"Preventing anyone from getting in—or out."

"Looked like it."

Dowd considered this. How *had* his client gotten back in the second time? For that matter, how had she gotten *out* after the first visit? Theory number one: Poe Fratt was not dead when she left the first time, and had crawled to the door. But then how had she gotten in the second time? Maybe he was *still* alive, and crawled to the door after she left. But she said he was dead. Theory number two: Poe died immediately, but Louann was able to squeeze through the door both times; Nevins had to weigh at least twice as much as the slightly built woman.

"Sergeant," Brownell continued, "would you please describe what the inside of the apartment looked like?"

"It's a small apartment, a studio, I guess you call it. Small kitchen, bathroom. The living room has a couch, a bureau . . ." He looked down at the report in his lap for a moment, then looked back up. ". . . a small desk, a small table, a lot of books, a bed . . ."

"What kind of bed was this?"

"One of those things that folds out."

"I see. Now tell us, what condition was the room in?"

"Well, there was a lot of blood."

"Where was the blood?"

"There was some on the bed, and then a trail of blood from the bed to where the body was. A few footprints, bloody footprints. Some blood on the phone. And a pool of blood around the body, a lot of blood around the body."

A sudden chill went through Dowd. Blood on the phone?

he thought to himself. Had someone used the phone—someone with blood on their hands? Had Louann Fratt calmly made a phone call after stabbing her husband? Or had Poe lived long enough to call someone? Was *that* the evidence Brownell was holding back? A witness who had heard Poe Fratt's dying accusation over the telephone?

Brownell once again leaned against the jury railing. "Sergeant, would you please describe the condition of the furniture and personal effects in the living room."

"Everything seemed pretty neat, pretty much in order."

"Pretty much in order," the prosecutor repeated.

"Yeah."

"The phone wasn't knocked off the table."

"No."

"The books weren't scattered across the floor?"

"No."

"Well, Sergeant Nevins," Brownell said, walking back toward the counsel table, "was there *anything* about the condition of the room that looked like there had been a violent fight there earlier that morning?"

The officer again shook his huge head. "No."

"I see." Brownell rested his hands on the back of his chair, leaned forward. "What happened next, Sergeant?"

"Well, the emergency medical guys come after a while, and I let them in. Then, about an hour or so later, the nightwatch detectives. Then I took the defendant to the station and booked her."

"Thank you, Sergeant." Brownell started to sit down, suddenly stopped. "Oh, by the way," he said, as if he had just thought of something, "did the defendant ever mention to you anything about her husband trying to *rape* her that night?"

Nevins shook his head, a big grin spreading across his bearded face. "No. No, she never said anything like that."

"She mentioned *nothing* about any rape attempt?"

"Nothing."

"I see." He looked up at Judge Goodman. "No further questions, Your Honor."

Goodman glared down at Dowd.

"Sergeant," Dowd said, rising to his feet, "you said Mrs. Fratt did not have any bruises on her face?"

"That's right."

"Or anything else that indicated she may have been hit by her husband?"

"That's right."

"Well, after taking her down to the station, isn't it true that she was then taken to the hospital?"

"Yeah. There was some friends that come down to the station, or relatives, and they wanted her to get medical treatment."

"If there was nothing unusual about her appearance, why did they think she needed medical treatment."

"Her finger was cut. Knife cut."

"Sergeant," Dowd said, standing in front of the jury, "isn't it true that the hospital reports indicate that she had swelling and bruising around the right eye and in the area of—"

"Objection!" Brownell said quickly. "Calls for hearsay."

Judge Goodman thought for a moment. "Sustained."

"Well, Sergeant Nevins," Dowd continued, "photographs *were* taken at the station of Mrs. Fratt's face, weren't they?"

"I think so, yeah."

"And you still say you didn't see any swelling or bruises on her face?"

"I didn't notice any at the time."

Dowd decided not to confront the officer with the photographs. Dowd's own photographs, taken by the attorney John Kelly, would not be helpful, since they had been taken a few days after the arrest. The photos taken by the police at the station were in Brownell's possession. Although Dowd could ask the prosecutor to produce them, he decided to force Brownell to offer them himself; if he withheld them, Dowd could obtain the photos and point out to the jury that the prosecution had been hiding evidence.

"Sergeant," Dowd said, trailing his hand along the jury railing as he walked toward the witness stand, "you testified that you couldn't get into apartment 9B after kicking the door in."

"Yeah."

"Poe Fratt's body was blocking anyone from getting in."

"Yeah."

"Anyone?"

Nevins looked at the lawyer without comprehension.

"Sergeant," Dowd said, "take a look at Mrs. Fratt over there."

The officer shifted his bloated body in the chair, then looked across the room at Louann Fratt, seated with her eyes turned away.

"How much would you say she weighs?" Dowd asked.

Nevins shrugged. "A hundred, hundred ten."

"Is it fair to say that *you* weigh considerably more than that?"

"Me?" The sergeant chuckled. "Yeah, that's fair."

"You wouldn't describe yourself as slim, would you?"

"No."

And leave it right there, Dowd thought to himself. He knew that a big secret to cross-examination lay in not asking one too many questions. If he went on to the next subject, the jury would be able to see the point: Louann Fratt might have been able to slip through the door opening even though the huge-bellied sergeant could not. A point was always more effective if the individual juror could discover it himself, rather than have it spelled out for him. But if Dowd continued the questioning by asking, "Well, Sergeant, what makes you think a much thinner person couldn't have fit through that opening?" he knew he would be violating the two cardinal rules of cross-exam: Know the answer, and don't ever ask a question that calls for anything but a yes or no reply. Violate those rules and Nevins's answer would probably be something like, *"Nobody* could fit through that opening—it was only a couple of inches wide."

"You mentioned that the room appeared neat and in order, didn't you, Sergeant?"

"Yeah."

"Well," Dowd said, walking toward his table, "isn't it a fact that there were books strewn about the floor?"

"They weren't strewn."

"Oh?" Dowd said, picking up a report in his hand and

reading it. "Are you saying they were all neatly stacked in bookcases?"

"No, some of them were stacked on the couch and on the furniture."

"On the couch."

"Yeah."

"And weren't some of them on the floor?"

"Some, I think."

"And isn't it a fact that the chair in the living room was nearly knocked over, with one of its legs resting on an athletic bag?"

"I think so, yeah."

"And you consider that to be neat and orderly?"

"Yeah."

Dowd had a few other subjects he wanted to question Nevins about, but none of them would produce anything significant. He decided to save them for his partner, Lapinski, and follow another cardinal rule of cross-examination: Leave the jury with a final question and answer that makes an important point or tends to discredit the witness.

"Nothing further," Dowd said, returning to his seat.

Nevins lumbered off the witness stand and walked out through the swinging gate as Brownell called out a name.

"Dennis Marousek."

The bailiff repeated the name into the hallway as Nevins walked out. Within seconds, a man in his thirties of medium height and build, with a moustache and wearing a dark blue suit, entered and walked confidently down the aisle and up to the witness stand. He took the oath, spelled out his name, and sat down.

"It's *Detective* Marousek, isn't it?" Brownell asked.

"Yes."

"Detective, calling your attention to November twenty-second of 1988, did you have occasion to be called to an apartment 9B located at Fifty-two East Seventy-eighth Street?"

"Yes, I did."

"What time was this?"

"I arrived at approximately five thirty-five A.M."

"At this time, you were a member of the crime scene unit?"

"Yes, I was."

Brownell walked toward the witness. "What was the purpose of your visit to the apartment?"

"The purpose was to secure the scene, then to collect evidence—take photographs, draw diagrams, take fingerprints, footprints, have blood samples analyzed . . . that sort of thing."

"I see." Brownell stepped behind the witness stand and pulled out a large cardboard diagram mounted on an easel. The diagram was a floor plan of apartment 9B. Overlaying the diagram was a clear plastic sheet with markings; one of the markings appeared to be an outline of a body.

"Do you recognize this diagram, Detective?" Brownell asked as he walked back to his table.

"Yes. That is a reproduction of the floor plan of the apartment."

Brownell picked up a stack of 8 × 10 photographs and walked back to the witness. "Showing you what has been marked as People's number thirteen, Detective Marousek," he said, handing him the top photo, "do you recognize it?"

"Yes. This is a photograph of the body, taken from next to the bed."

Brownell moved the diagram so that the jury could see it.

"Would you point out on the diagram where the body in the photograph is," he said, "indicating from where in the room you took the picture."

The officer stepped down from the stand and pointed to a marking on the diagram. "Here . . . and this is where I was standing."

Brownell took back the photograph, then looked up at Judge Goodman. "May I show these to the jury, Your Honor?"

Goodman nodded.

Brownell handed the top photograph to the juror closest to the witness stand. The middle-aged woman looked at it for a moment, an expression of revulsion quickly appearing on her face. She passed it on to the woman seated to her right.

"Now, Detective," Brownell continued, "showing you another photograph, marked People's twelve . . ."

Dowd's mind began to drift as he watched Daniel Brownell continue to paint a graphic picture for the jury of the crime scene. This was a mechanical part of the prosecution's case; it would do very little damage to the defense and would require very little in the way of cross-examination. And so Dowd found himself thinking about something else as he watched the prosecutor. He found himself wondering once again what evidence of *motive* Brownell was holding back. And why was Brownell so confident that Louann Fratt's claim of self-defense would fail?

Dowd kept seeing an image of a bloody telephone.

CHAPTER 19

"And approximately how many autopsies have you performed as a forensic pathologist with the medical examiner?"

"Approximately nine hundred."

"Nine hundred," Brownell repeated, standing next to the jury box. "Now, Doctor Charlot, when was the first time you saw the body of Charles Kennedy Poe Fratt?"

"It was . . ." The young woman glanced down at a written report lying in her lap. "I believe it was during the early morning hours of November twenty-second."

"And where was this?"

"It was at the deceased's apartment."

"This was shortly after the death of the . . . victim?"

"That is correct."

"Now, sometime after this you conducted an autopsy on Mr. Fratt?"

"I did."

"When was this?"

The woman again glanced down. "November twenty-third," she said, looking back up.

Brownell walked over to the counsel table and picked up

an 8 × 10 black-and-white photograph. After showing it briefly to Dowd, he approached the witness.

"Doctor Charlot, I'm going to show you what has previously been marked People's exhibit number twenty-eight, and ask you to look at it." He handed her the photograph.

Dr. Waglae Charlot took the picture and pretended to study it, though she had seen it only moments before taking the stand. The tall, slender, strikingly attractive young black woman, elegantly dressed in a form-hugging peach dress and matching pumps, looked more like a high-fashion model than a forensic pathologist. The contrast was heightened by a pleasantly lilting accent, reminiscent of the Caribbean; in fact, she had immigrated from Haiti after graduating from medical school there three years earlier. It was somehow difficult to imagine this woman cutting open Poe Fratt's body.

"Yes?" she said, waiting for her cue.

"What does that photograph depict?"

"This shows the wound to the neck."

"Please describe the wound."

"An apparent knife wound, three and one half inches in depth. Entry from front to back, right to left, and downward."

"*Downward?*" Brownell repeated, acting mildly surprised. "As if the assailant were standing *above* the victim?"

"Yes, that is possible."

"I see," Brownell said, walking back to his table. "And was this wound fatal?"

"No. It was not fatal. It missed both the carotid artery and the jugular vein."

Brownell picked up a second 8 × 10 glossy from a stack of photos on his table and again approached the witness. "Showing you People's exhibit number twenty five, would you please look at it and tell the jury what it depicts?"

"I object!" Dowd said loudly, getting to his feet.

"Grounds?" Goodman demanded.

"The prejudicial effect outweighs any probative value, Your Honor," Dowd said. "The D.A. has a whole pile of these pictures, and they're gruesome, they're disgusting. The only purpose here is to inflame the passions of the jury with gory autopsy photos of Mrs. Fratt's husband."

"Your Honor," Brownell replied calmly, "these are photographs taken by the office of the medical examiner. They are relevant in helping the jury understand the *path* of the knife wounds."

"The path?" Goodman repeated. He leaned toward the witness and grabbed the photograph, began studying it.

"Yes, Your Honor, the direction the knife took after entering the body. This can indicate the relative positions of the assailant and the deceased at the time of the stabbing."

"That's not the purpose," Dowd said angrily. "This witness can *testify* to what the paths were. Look, I'll *stipulate* what the paths of the knife wounds were! Then there'll be no need for these repulsive photos."

Dowd fully realized that he and Brownell were arguing about the admissibility of the evidence in open hearing of the jurors. This often rendered the point moot, since the jury learned all about the offensive evidence whether it was admitted or not. The safer approach would have been to have a "bench conference"—to discuss the objection at the judge's bench, out of hearing of the jurors. The problem with this was that it was a time-consuming procedure, requiring the court reporter to move and set up his stenotype machine at the bench each time; if this were done with every objection, the trial would proceed at a snail's pace. The judge had the difficult job with each objection of trying to weigh expediency against the possibility of jurors hearing damaging statements.

The plain fact was that Dowd wanted the jury to hear the reasons for his objection.

"The defense is willing to stipulate to the path of the knife wounds?" Goodman asked, looking up from the photos at Dowd.

"We are, Your Honor."

"Mr. Brownell?"

"Your Honor," the prosecutor said, "the People do not have to accept offered stipulations."

"Well, damn it, he's willing to admit what you're trying to prove."

"He can't tell us *how* to prove it," Brownell said. "We feel that the photographs will be more effective in proving the point than a stipulation will."

Goodman looked back at the photo, then shrugged. "A

photograph of a body in a state of decay is not repulsive," he decided finally. "Objection overruled."

Dowd sat down. He had lost, as he had known he would. But he had accomplished his real purpose in objecting: He had let the jury know what the assistant D.A. was really trying to accomplish with the photographs. As happened so often in trial, the objection had been directed not at the judge, but at the jury.

Brownell turned back to the witness, again handed her the photograph. Dr. Charlot took the photo and looked at it. "This is the second wound."

"Please describe it."

"A stab wound to the back. Approximately one and three quarters inches in depth. Downward thrust."

"Downward," Brownell repeated, walking back to the counsel table.

"Yes."

"Indicating, once again, that the assailant was standing above the victim?"

"It could indicate that."

"Was *this* wound lethal, Doctor?"

"No."

Brownell picked up a third photograph and once again approached the woman with it. "Showing you People's twenty-four, Doctor Charlot, please tell us what it represents."

The pathologist studied the picture briefly, then looked toward the jury. "This shows the deceased's chest area, and the third wound," she said, following the unwritten script.

"Please describe the wound."

"Apparent knife wound, approximately five and one half to six inches in depth. The blade entered the fifth intercostal space, left of midline—"

"Could you interpret that, Doctor?"

"I'm sorry. The fifth space between the ribs, just below the mammary line. On the left side of the chest."

"Thank you."

"After entry, the blade pierced the right ventricle—the right side of the heart—then went on through the heart, through the diaphragm, and finally into the liver."

Dowd glanced back at the audience. A sea of anonymous

faces. A photographer taking pictures with a still camera. Reporters writing on tiny pads of paper. A television camera—pointed directly at Louann Fratt. Dowd looked back at his client, seated next to him. She seemed completely impassive, her face expressionless as the witness continued testifying to the damage her knife had done.

Debbie Cohen, sitting on the other side of Louann Fratt, looked at Dowd until she caught his eye, then at the jury. Dowd followed her gaze out of the corner of his eye. Two jurors were busily studying his client, looking for some reaction.

"I see," Brownell continued. "Now, Doctor, was *this* wound lethal?"

"It was."

"And how soon after sustaining the wound would the victim have died?"

"Immediately. I would say . . . within seconds."

Brownell turned back to his table. "And," he said without turning back, "was this also a downward thrust?"

"It was."

"Indicating, once again, that the defendant was standing *above* her husband when she stabbed him?"

"It could indicate that."

"Thank you, Doctor." The assistant D.A. picked up another photograph, approached the witness with it. "I now ask you to look at what has been marked People's twenty-six and tell us what it depicts."

Dr. Charlot glanced at the picture. "The deceased's left arm, showing a superficial incised wound to the distal portion of the forearm."

"In other words, a cut to his forearm."

"Yes."

"As if he were fending off a knife attack," Brownell said, again returning to a pile of photographs on his table.

"It would be consistent with that."

Brownell carried the next picture to Dr. Charlot. "Showing you People's twenty-nine, do you recognize it?"

"This is the deceased's other arm, the right arm. Incision wounds to the right hand."

"Consistent with grabbing for the blade of a knife?"

"Consistent with that."

"Thank you, Doctor," Brownell said. "Nothing further."

Brownell began walking back to his table as Dowd slowly rose to his feet. The prosecutor stopped, then turned back to the witness.

"Oh, incidentally," Brownell said, "there was a serology test done on the victim, wasn't there? A blood test?"

"Yes, there was."

"And the report from that showed a blood alcohol concentration of point eleven percent, is that right?"

"That's correct."

"Thank you," Brownell said, sitting down. "Nothing further."

Dowd smiled in amusement. The young assistant D.A. had just pulled one of Dowd's favorite tricks: "taking the wind out of the enemy's sails." Brownell knew Dowd would have read the autopsy report carefully, would have noticed the presence of alcohol in Poe Fratt's body. And he knew the defense lawyer would have skillfully built Dr. Charlot up in his cross-examination to a point where the revelation would be disclosed to the jury in some startling fashion. By asking the question himself during direct examination, however, the dramatic impact was lost. Further, by treating the subject in such an offhand manner, the seeming importance of the evidence was minimized.

Dowd walked slowly over to the jury box and leaned against the wooden railing.

"Good morning, Dr. Charlot," he said in a pleasant tone. "My name is Michael Dowd and I'd just like to ask you a few questions, okay?"

The pathologist nodded. She had testified in murder trials before, and was not fooled by friendly defense lawyers.

"If there's any question you don't understand," Dowd continued, "please just let me know, and I'll try to make it clearer."

She nodded again. Sure, buster.

"Now, let's see . . . This first wound you mentioned, the one to the neck?"

"Yes."

"This would not have impaired the deceased, Poe Fratt, from moving and functioning, would it?"

Dr. Charlot thought about this for a moment, looking for some trick. Then she shook her head. "No."

"So he would still have been capable of beating Mrs. Fratt with his fists?"

"He would have been capable."

"By the way, what did Poe Fratt weigh at the autopsy, Dr. Charlot?"

The attractive young woman glanced down at the notes in her lap, then looked back up. "Two hundred twenty-one pounds."

"Uh-huh. Now, this *second* wound, the one to the back?"

"Yes."

"This was rather superficial, wasn't it?"

"It was."

"So this wound would also not have kept Poe Fratt from continuing to beat his wife?"

"Objection," Brownell said from his chair. "Assumes facts not in evidence." Brownell was right: Dowd's question required the witness to assume that Louann Fratt *had* been beaten by her husband, even though there had not yet been any testimony to that effect.

"Sustained," Judge Goodman said.

"Let me rephrase that, Doctor," Dowd said. "*Hypothetically*, would this second wound have kept a two-hundred-and-twenty-one-pound man from assaulting with his fists a woman who weighed only half that much?"

Dowd had sidestepped the objection by using the technique of asking a hypothetical question. While a witness could not be asked her opinion about actual facts that had not been proven, she *could* be asked to give an opinion about *theoretical* facts; in other words, she could be asked, "What if . . . ?" Technically, the answer would be no less hypothetical than the question, but juries were good at ignoring legal niceties.

"No," Dr. Charlot replied, "it would not."

"And, hypothetically, would the combination of these two wounds keep such a man from beating such a woman?"

"They would not."

"Thank you." Dowd walked along the jury railing, making eye contact with as many of the jurors as possible. "Incidentally, Doctor, the third wound, the lethal one?"

"Yes?"

"This entered *between* the ribs, then went through soft tissue and organs, is that correct?"

"That is correct."

"So, although it went quite deep, it would not have taken very much force, am I right?"

"It would not have taken much force, that is correct."

Dowd now walked over to his chair, glanced at some notes on the table. Louann Fratt was still seated rigidly in her chair, staring straight ahead as if she were bored with the proceedings. Debbie Cohen was busily writing down notes about any apparent reactions of jurors to the testimony. At the end of the day, she would review her observations with the defense lawyer.

Dowd looked back up at Dr. Charlot. "You testified that the three wounds were caused by downward thrusts."

"Yes."

"Doctor, if the knife were brought down in an overhand motion, like this . . ." Dowd acted out a person with a knife held high and stabbing down. ". . . wouldn't the path of the knife inside the body be downward?"

The attractive young physician shifted in her seat. "Yes, it would."

"But the person with the knife would *not* have been standing above the person being stabbed?" Dowd began walking toward her.

"That is correct."

"And if the deceased, Poe Fratt, had been bending forward, reaching for Mrs. Fratt, like this . . ." Dowd demonstrated again, reaching toward Dr. Charlot. ". . . wouldn't the path of the knife inside the body indicate a downward thrust?"

"It would, yes."

"But the *actual* thrust of the knife, by Mrs. Fratt, would *not* have been downward, correct?"

"Correct."

"Well, as I understand it then," Dowd continued, acting somewhat perplexed, "you can't really tell much of *anything* from the path of the knife wound, is that right?"

Dr. Charlot uncrossed her legs, then recrossed them. "One can tell from the path of the knife what possible relative—"

Dowd stopped, looked her directly in the eyes. "Doctor,"

he said in a suddenly low voice, "can you tell these ladies and gentlemen of the jury whether Mrs. Fratt was, in fact, standing above her husband when she stabbed him?"

The woman paused, then said, "No."

"So when Mr. Brownell here asked you if the wounds were consistent with Mrs. Fratt standing above her husband, they could *also* be consistent with her standing level with him, couldn't they?"

"They could be consistent with that, yes."

"And they could be consistent with him reaching for her, attacking her?"

"They could."

"Thank you." Dowd turned away from her, looked again at a number of the jurors. Most were watching him, while a few were looking at the witness; one was still studying Louann Fratt. Dowd took a few steps, then turned back to Dr. Charlot.

"Doctor, you testified that Poe Fratt had a blood alcohol level of point eleven percent at the time of the autopsy."

"That is correct."

"What does that mean exactly?"

"It means that point eleven percent of his blood, by weight, consisted of ethanol."

"Ethanol?"

"Ethyl alcohol."

"Drinking alcohol."

"Yes."

"So, what you're saying is, Poe Fratt was *drunk* at the time of the—"

"Objection!" Brownell yelled out, jumping to his feet.

Judge Goodman glared at the two lawyers for a moment. "Approach the bench," he said finally.

Dowd and Brownell crossed the courtroom to the far end of the bench, then waited for the court reporter. When the reporter had moved his stenotype machine from its stand in front of his chair to the top of the judge's bench and indicated he was ready, Goodman looked at Brownell.

"Your Honor," the prosecutor said in a hushed voice, "there is no evidence the victim was drunk. And this witness is not qualified to testify that he was."

Goodman looked at Dowd.

"She testified he had a level of point eleven percent," Dowd said quietly. "Under our drunk driving statute, a person is under the influence of alcohol at point ten percent."

"Yes," Brownell said, "but this isn't a drunk driving case. And 'under the influence' isn't the same as 'drunk'—they're two different legal concepts."

Dowd looked around him as Brownell argued his point, looked at the jury, then out at the audience and the cameras. He found himself faintly surprised to find that they were all looking back at him. It suddenly struck him as absurd that three grown men should be whispering to each other in a huddle while a roomful of people and a television audience watched.

"Mr. Dowd?" Goodman hissed. "Are you with us?"

"Your Honor," Dowd replied smoothly, "the blood alcohol level, by itself, means nothing to the jury. I am simply trying to give them some frame of reference. The simple fact is that a person with that level is considered a drunk driver under our laws."

"Your Honor," Brownell said, "this witness can't testify to what the law is. She is a physician. All she can do is testify to the blood alcohol level."

Goodman nodded to himself for a moment. "Very well," he said finally. He leaned back, indicating the conference was over.

Dowd and Brownell returned to their seats while the reporter moved his machine back to its stand and sat down in his chair near the witness stand.

"Ladies and gentlemen," Goodman said, "you are hereby instructed that under the laws of New York, a driver of a motor vehicle is presumed to be under the influence of alcohol if he has a blood alcohol level of point ten percent or more at the time of driving. You are also instructed that the terms 'under the influence' and 'drunk' are legally distinct." He looked at Dowd. "Proceed, Counsel."

"Thank you, Your Honor," Dowd said. He walked toward Dr. Charlot. "Now, Doctor, as a physician, you are familiar with the effects of alcohol on a human being?"

The woman paused. Then, cautiously, she answered, "Yes."

"And isn't it a fact that alcohol can make an individual aggressive?"

"That is possible. It can also make him more passive."

Dowd turned away and again made eye contact with some of the jurors. Without looking away, he said, "I notice your report indicates that there were some marks on the deceased's chin."

"Abrasions, yes."

"Abrasions. Would you please describe them?"

"Yes." She again glanced at the report in her lap, then looked up. "Curved, semilunar, approximately one-quarter inch in length."

"Curved?" he repeated, still looking at the jurors. "Semilunar?"

"That is correct."

Dowd turned from the jury to the witness. "That sounds like fingernail scratches, Doctor."

"The abrasions are highly suggestive of being inflicted with fingernails."

"And how many of these marks were there?"

"Three on the left of the chin, two on the right."

"Consistent with a hand—four fingers and a thumb?"

"Consistent with that."

"And consistent with Mrs. Fratt defending herself against her husband by scratching at his face?"

"Objection!" Brownell cried out. "Calls for speculation."

"Sustained," Goodman growled.

"Thank you, Doctor," Dowd said, smiling at the woman. "Nothing further."

CHAPTER 20

T he fourth day of trial began
ominously.

Dowd was seated at the counsel table reviewing a police
report, waiting for the trial to resume, when Judge Goodman
walked up to him.

"Mr. Dowd."

The lawyer looked up.

"Mr. Dowd," Goodman continued irritably, "I understand
you intend to call expert witnesses to testify concerning your
client's state of mind?"

"Yes, Your Honor," Dowd said. "But it doesn't relate to
her state of mind at the time of the homicide."

"You chose not to give notice."

"We withdrew notice, but—"

Goodman nodded. "I'll expect a written brief from you on
the admissibility of that testimony."

"A written brief . . ."

"In two days." Then Goodman quickly turned away and
looked at the bailiff. "All right," he said to the bailiff. "Bring
them in."

The uniformed bailiff walked out the rear door. Within

seconds, the jurors were filing in and taking their seats in the jury box, nervously shepherded by the bailiff.

Dowd was still recovering from Goodman's little bomb-shell. The lawyer was confident that he had been right in withdrawing the notice to Brownell of psychiatric testimony: The notice statute applied only to cases where the defense itself involved state of mind, such as insanity. Louann Fratt's defense was the traditional one of self-defense. But if Good-man ruled against him, neither Dr. Rosen nor Dr. Veronen would be able to testify concerning Louann Fratt's strange conduct before and after the killing—and the defense would be left in shreds.

"Call your next witness," the judge said impatiently to Brownell.

The prosecutor stood up. "David Schlessinger," he said loudly.

Within seconds, a young man in a blue patrolman's uni-form stepped into the courtroom and walked up to the witness stand. After being sworn in by the clerk, he sat down.

"Please state your name, spelling the last," the clerk said.

"David Schlessinger. S-C-H-L-E-S-S-I-N-G-E-R."

Brownell walked toward the jury box, leaned against the railing. "What is your occupation and employment?"

"Police officer, Nineteenth Precinct."

"Now, Officer Schlessinger, calling your attention to No-vember twenty-second of last year, at approximately three forty-eight A.M. . . . Did anything unusual occur?"

Dowd smiled to himself. He knew that the question "Did anything unusual occur?" was a well-known code, cueing the officer to begin his recitation. The rules of evidence prohibited a lawyer from simply cutting a witness loose with an open-ended question like, "What happened that day?" To guard against objections that the witness was simply giving a re-hearsed speech, the prosecutor would periodically interrupt his testimony with, "And then what happened?" Dowd knew this was a transparent mechanism designed to circumvent the rules of evidence, permitting the witness to do exactly what was objectionable: ramble on with a prepared story. But, Dowd thought, that was one of the benefits of having experi-enced witnesses. They knew how the game was played.

"At approximately three forty-eight A.M., we were on patrol when we got a radio run to respond to . . ." Schlessinger glanced at a small notebook on his lap. ". . . One Fifty-one East Seventy-ninth, fifth floor."

"Who is 'we'?" Brownell asked. His job now was to sit back as Schlessinger told his story, cleaning up details that a jury might find confusing.

"I was in a patrol unit with my partner, Officer Louis Teodoro."

"And what is a 'radio run'?"

"A radio call from the dispatcher."

"What happened next, Officer Schlessinger?"

"We arrived at the location, and met Sergeant Nevins and his partner, Officer Lapinski. We then went with them into the building and up to the fifth floor. Sergeant Nevins knocked on the door, and the defendant answered."

"And then what happened?"

"There was a conversation between Sergeant Nevins and the defendant. The defendant said, 'I stabbed my husband, I think he's dead.' She also said something about they were going through a divorce. She pointed to a small bag and said the knife she used was in the bag."

"What happened next, Officer?"

"We left and drove to her husband's apartment, at . . ." Again he glanced down at his notes. ". . . Fifty-two East Seventy-eighth, apartment 9B."

"You were all in the same car?"

"No. The defendant was with me and my partner. Sergeant Nevins was in another car, with Officer Lapinski."

"Was Mrs. Fratt under arrest at this time?"

"No, she was not."

"And then what happened after you left her apartment?"

"We drove to her husband's apartment. We met Sergeant Nevins there, and Lapinski. Also, Officer Totten and Officer Crespo responded to the location. The door was locked, so Sergeant Nevins told me to go get the keys from the super. I went to look for the super, but I couldn't find him. When I got back to the apartment, the door was open. All I could see from the hallway were the legs, a pair of legs lying on the floor inside. Behind the door."

"Did you go inside?"

"No. I stayed out in the hallway for about forty-five minutes, with the defendant, while Sergeant Nevins was inside."

"Who went inside the apartment?"

"Only Sergeant Nevins. And two guys from Emergency Medical Services who showed up later."

"What happened next, Officer Schlessinger?"

"When Sergeant Nevins authorized it, I arrested the defendant, and placed handcuffs on her. Then I read her her rights under *Miranda*."

"Did she say anything?"

"No."

"Did she ever mention anything about being raped?"

"No, she did not."

"What happened next, Officer?"

"I left the scene with the defendant at . . ." He glanced down. ". . . four fifty A.M. I drove her to the station, where she was booked. My partner stayed to guard the crime scene."

"Fine," Brownell said. "Now, did you notice any marks or bruises on the defendant's face that morning?"

Dowd smiled. The young prosecutor was again taking the wind out of the sails of Dowd's cross-examination. He knew that Dowd had read Schlessinger's crime report and that it contained an observation that there were bruises on Louann Fratt's face.

"Yes," Schlessinger said. "I noticed a slight swelling on her right cheek, and a cut on one finger. Later, at the station, I noticed a bruise also."

"Thank you," Brownell said, sitting down. "Nothing further."

Dowd rose. There was no point in attacking the officer or cross-examining him at length: There was little that he had said that had hurt the defense. Many lawyers would attack the witness for no other reason than that it was expected, or because he was "the enemy"—a police officer and a prosecution witness. But Dowd realized that if he attacked every witness, the jury would come to expect it—and the impact of a later attack on a *critical* witness would be lost. It was far better to treat most witnesses with respect and consideration, saving the ammunition for targets worth shooting at.

"Good morning, Officer," Dowd said with a smile.

Schlessinger nodded silently.

"My name is Michael Dowd, and I just have a couple of questions, okay?"

Schlessinger nodded again.

"Now, you testified that you observed bruises and swelling on Mrs. Fratt's face. Is that correct?"

"Yes."

"Are you aware that Sergeant Nevins has testified that *he* observed *no* bruises or swelling on her face?"

Schlessinger just stared at the defense lawyer for a moment. "No," he said finally. "I was not aware of that."

"Uh-huh." Dowd walked over to the jury box, looked some of them in the eye. "Officer," he continued, without looking away from the jurors, "you didn't smell any alcohol on Mrs. Fratt's breath that evening, did you?"

Rule number one of cross-examination: Don't ask a question if you don't already know the answer. And the plain fact was that Dowd did *not* know the answer to this question. He was gambling. But the odds were good. Something like alcohol on the breath would be important enough to put in a crime report, and there was no mention of it in Schlessinger's report. If the officer suddenly testified there *was* an odor of alcohol on Louann Fratt's breath, Dowd could shove the report down his throat. Still, it was a gamble.

"No," Schlessinger said.

Dowd turned to look at the officer. "Are you aware that Sergeant Nevins has testified that *he* smelled alcohol on her breath?"

Schlessinger cleared his throat. "No."

"Officer, you and your partner were the ones who drove Mrs. Fratt from her apartment to her husband's apartment, weren't you?"

"Yes."

"And you were with Mrs. Fratt in the hallway for forty-five minutes while Sergeant Nevins was inside apartment 9B?"

"Yes."

"And I believe you testified that you were the one who arrested her and drove her to the station?"

"Yes."

"So . . . you had plenty of time to observe Mrs. Fratt's face?"

"I guess so, yes."

"And you had more than enough time to smell her breath?"

"Yes."

"While Sergeant Nevins was with her for only a couple of minutes or so?"

"Something like that, yes."

So much for the imperious Sergeant Nevins, Dowd thought. He realized, of course, that Nevins had probably been partially right. Louann Fratt had admitted to Dowd that she had consumed not only the glass of wine at Poe's apartment, but two additional glasses earlier at her own apartment; there may well have been alcohol on her breath. But Dowd felt justified in impeaching Nevins's credibility. The sergeant's testimony that Louann had no swelling or bruises could have been damaging if the jury believed him. In any event, Dowd did not feel he could afford the luxury of weighing ultimate "truth": Nevins had hurt the defense, and it was Dowd's job to discredit him.

"Now, you testified that after you gave Mrs. Fratt her *Miranda* warning, she didn't say anything, right?"

"Yes."

"Didn't she tell you that she wanted to talk with her son?"

Schlessinger thought for a moment. "Yes, she did. Later, back at the station, she said she wanted to talk to her son."

"Thank you, Officer," Dowd said. "No further questions."

Brownell stood up as Schlessinger quickly rose from the witness chair and headed for the door.

"Louis Teodoro," the prosecutor called out.

A stern-faced, dark-haired man in a blue police uniform stepped through the door and, with a military bearing, marched quickly to the witness stand. Oddly, in the stifling heat of the courtroom, the officer was wearing a bulky blue bulletproof vest under his uniform jacket.

Officer Teodoro came to rigid attention as he took the oath, then quickly sat down, back ramrod straight.

"Louis Teodoro," he said brusquely. "T-E-O-D-O-R-O. Badge number seven nine three nine, Nineteenth Precinct."

Brownell walked over to his favorite spot next to the jury box. "Officer Teodoro?"

"Yes, sir," the witness said, his dark eyes locked intently on the assistant D.A.

A former sergeant in the marines, Dowd thought to himself. Maybe a Vietnam vet. There were a lot of ex-marines in the department.

"Calling your attention to November twenty-second of last year," Brownell continued, "at approximately three forty-eight A.M. did anything unusual occur?"

"Yes, sir. My partner and I, Officer David Schlessinger, received a radio call to respond to One Fifty-one East Seventy-ninth Street, fifth floor, possible homicide. We did respond and, upon arrival at the building, met Sergeant Nevins and Officer Lapinski. The four of us then rode in an elevator to the fifth floor, where Sergeant Nevins knocked on the door. The defendant—"

"What happened next?"

"Yes, sir," Teodoro said. "The defendant, Mrs. Fratt, opened the door. She advised Sergeant Nevins that she had just stabbed her husband, and she thought he was dead. She said they were involved in a divorce. Sergeant Nevins asked her where the knife was, and she pointed to a brown bag and said it was in there."

"And then what happened?"

"Officer Schlessinger and I drove the defendant to her husband's apartment, sir. Fifty-two East Seventy-eighth Street, apartment 9B. When we arrived, we met Sergeant Nevins and Officer Lapinski and proceeded to the ninth floor."

Teodoro was an impressive witness, Dowd thought to himself. Respectful, concise, confident, professional. And he was testifying without having to refer to any notes. That meant he was conscientious enough to have carefully studied his report before testifying. He would be tough to cross-examine.

"Then what happened, Officer?"

"At Sergeant Nevins's request, sir, Officer Schlessinger and I went to find the superintendent to get the keys. When we returned, the door was open and Sergeant Nevins was inside. Shortly after that, Officers Totten and Crespo arrived. After approximately forty-five minutes, Sergeant Nevins came into the hallway. At this point, my partner, Officer Schlessinger, arrested the defendant and read her rights in accordance with the *Miranda* decision. He then transported her to the station, while I stayed to keep the crime scene secure."

"Thank you," Brownell said. "Now, Officer Teodoro, did you notice anything unusual about the defendant's appearance?"

The officer sat there at rigid attention, thinking for a moment. "Yes, sir."

"Yes?"

"She seemed shook up."

Dowd looked up quickly at the witness. Shook up? This was the first evidence he had heard that his client had felt *anything*.

"Shook up?" Brownell repeated. The horror of every trial lawyer: the wrong answer.

"Yes, sir."

"Well, she wasn't crying, was she?"

"No, sir."

"All right."

Dowd smiled to himself. He knew that a lawyer could not attack his own witness. This fact of trial life led to cardinal rule number 36: If your own witness hurts you, get onto another subject—quickly.

"Well," Brownell said, getting back on track, "did you notice anything unusual about her *physical* appearance?"

"Yes, sir. I noticed a bruise on her right cheek."

"Just a bruise."

"Yes, sir."

"Thank you, Officer." The prosecutor looked at Judge Goodman. "Nothing further, Your Honor."

Goodman scowled at Dowd.

The big defense lawyer thought for a moment. "I have no questions, Your Honor," he said finally.

Cardinal rule number 21: If it ain't broke, don't fix it.

Goodman looked at Brownell. "Call your next witness."

Teodoro almost sprang to his feet, then marched stiffly out of the courtroom.

"Your Honor," Brownell said, pulling out an audio tape

from his briefcase, "at this time, the People would like to play the following tape recording for the jury."

Dowd jumped up. "What is this? What . . ."

"This is the conditional examination of Susan Wise, Your Honor, the manager of the apartment—"

"Wait a minute!" Dowd interrupted angrily. "May we approach the bench?"

Goodman stared at the two men, then nodded slightly. Dowd and Brownell walked up to the bench. When the court reporter was ready, Goodman looked at Brownell expectantly.

"This is a one-half-hour tape, Your Honor," Brownell said. "Susan Wise. She is—was—the manager of the apartment building where the victim was living at the time he was killed. I conducted a conditional examination three months ago, since she was going to be out of the state during the trial and unavailable for testimony."

"So what's she got to say?" Goodman asked.

"On the tape, Mrs. Wise testifies that she had inventoried all of the furniture and appliances of apartment 9B before renting it to Mr. Fratt."

"So?"

"You see, Your Honor, the apartment was *completely* furnished—including kitchen utensils, like dishes, pots, forks . . . and knives. And the knife that the defendant stabbed Mr. Fratt with was *not* in the inventory."

"So?" the judge repeated.

"Well, Your Honor, it proves that the defendant did not pick the knife up from the kitchen to defend herself with. It proves that she *brought* the knife *with* her."

"Of course she brought it with her," Dowd said. "We've said that all along."

"Yes, Mr. Brownell," Goodman said irritably. "What's the point?"

"Your Honor," the prosecutor continued, "this tape was made three months ago. And, of course, defendant's counsel knew about Mrs. Wise."

"Get on with it, Mr. Brownell."

"Yes, Your Honor. Well, the point is, Mr. Dowd's client *now* admits she brought the knife over with her."

"*What?*" Dowd said.

"She admits it *now*," the prosecutor repeated. "But would she have admitted it if we hadn't questioned Mrs. Wise three months ago? Would she be admitting it in this trial if we didn't have this tape?"

"Let me see if I understand this. . . ." Goodman said.

"I want the jury to know *why* the defendant admits taking the knife with her," Brownell said. "I want them to know that if I hadn't come up with this tape, she would probably have denied taking the knife over with her. She would have said she just grabbed the knife from his kitchen when he attacked her."

"That's ridiculous," Dowd said. "That's just pure speculation." Louann Fratt had, in fact, told him about taking the knife to Poe's apartment long before the questioning of Susan Wise. But the jury might well believe Brownell's theory—that Louann had only admitted taking the knife because she knew of this witness. The truth was that the tape could hurt the defense.

Goodman thought about this for a moment. "Mr. Dowd?"

"Your Honor," Dowd said, "the tape is irrelevant."

"Irrelevant?"

"Sure. It's offered to prove something that's just not an issue. I mean, we've said all along that she took the knife with her. We'll even *stipulate* that she took the knife to the apartment. So there's no issue: Both sides agree she took the knife."

"The People don't have to accept the stipulation," Brownell said. "We can independently prove she took the knife if we want."

Goodman pondered this, his face a dark frown. "No," he said finally, "I'm not going to let you take a half hour to prove something that's already been admitted."

"But Your Honor," Brownell said, "the point of the tape—"

"I have ruled," Goodman growled. "Now call your next witness."

Dowd felt a sense of relief as the two men walked back to their tables. He realized that Brownell had been legally correct: The tape should have been played—not to prove that

Louann Fratt had taken the knife with her, but to explain to the jury why the defendant was now *admitting* it. Dowd had just won a battle he should have lost. And he had a nagging feeling that events down the road would more than make up for this small victory.

"Walter Lapinski," Brownell announced loudly.

CHAPTER 21

"Then he asked her how many times she stabbed him."

"And what did she reply?"

"She said she couldn't remember."

"All right," said Brownell. "And then what happened, Officer Lapinski?"

"Sergeant Nevins asked her where the knife was."

"And?"

"And she pointed to a brown bag in the living room. I retrieved the bag and found the knife inside."

Brownell picked up the brown and gold Louis Vuitton bag lying on the counsel table and carried it to the officer.

"Showing you what has been marked People's number four, is this the bag she pointed to?"

The tall, husky young man with the huge moustache looked at it for a moment. "Yes, sir."

Brownell pulled out the knife and handed it to the officer. "Showing you People's number three, is this the knife you found?"

"Yes," he said, "this is the knife."

Brownell again reached inside the bag and pulled out the pair of white shoes. "Officer Lapinski, do you recognize what has been marked People's six?"

"Yes, sir. Those were in the bag with the knife."

Finally, the assistant D.A. held up the nightgown. "Do you recognize what has been marked People's five?"

Lapinski nodded. "It was in the bag, too." He paused. "It had blood on it."

"Now, Officer Lapinski," Brownell said, walking back toward the large television camera that was zeroed in on his face, "please tell us, did the defendant ever mention that her husband had tried to rape her?"

"No, sir, she did not."

"She did not." Brownell turned and looked at the jury for a moment, then went on. "Now, can you recall how Mrs. Fratt appeared to you?"

"Appeared?"

"Yes. Did she seem upset? Hysterical?"

"Oh." Lapinski shook his head. "No. No, she wasn't upset. Not at all." He shrugged slightly. "She seemed to me to be sort of . . . reserved."

"Reserved," Brownell repeated. He leaned on the wooden railing, his eyes seeking out those of the jurors.

"Yes, sir," Lapinski said. "Not happy, not depressed. Just . . . answering questions."

Brownell nodded in silence. Then he turned and faced the witness again. "And how did she appear to you *physically*?"

Lapinski shrugged again. "Okay, I guess."

"Any marks on her face or body?"

"There was a slight discoloration on her right cheek."

"Just a slight discoloration? Nothing more?"

"No, that's all."

"I see. And did you notice anything unusual about . . . her breath?"

"Oh, yes. I noticed an odor of alcohol on her breath."

Brownell looked at the jury, then at Judge Goodman. "Nothing further, Your Honor."

Dowd rose to his feet as the prosecutor sat down. "Good afternoon, Officer Lapinski."

"Afternoon," the witness replied warily.

"My name is Michael Dowd, and I'm just going to ask you a few questions, okay?"

"Sure."

Dowd knew that Lapinski had probably talked with his partner before taking the stand. Nevins had probably told Lapinski what he had testified to. The officers would get their stories together: Lapinski would back up his partner's testimony. It was not that the two men were dishonest. It was more a question of habit, professional pride, and gamesmanship. Just as most lawyers unthinkingly attacked police officers on cross-examination, so those officers automatically closed ranks against any and all defense lawyers. But there were always cracks. And Dowd was good at finding them.

"Now . . . you said that Mrs. Fratt had alcohol on her breath?"

"Yes, sir."

"And I believe your partner testified to that, too."

Lapinski shrugged. "I couldn't say."

"Uh-huh." Dowd guessed that Lapinski had also heard that Schlessinger had testified there was *no* smell of alcohol. "Well, this evidence was pretty significant, wasn't it, Officer?"

"Significant?"

"Yes. I mean, this was a homicide investigation, wasn't it?"

"Yes . . ."

"And if the suspect had alcohol on her breath, this could indicate that she was a little drunk at the time of the stabbing, couldn't it?"

"Maybe."

"Isn't that a pretty important bit of evidence in a homicide investigation?"

"I guess so, sure."

"Important enough to write down in your crime report?"

Lapinski paused. The hook had been set and he knew it. He knew Dowd would have a copy of his report. He could not remember, but it was a pretty safe guess that the report must not have mentioned anything about alcohol on Louann Fratt's breath. But he was stuck: He could not very well claim that the fact was *not* important enough to be included in the report. Score one for the lawyers.

"Yes, it would be important enough."

Dowd picked up a copy of Lapinski's report and approached him with it. "Would you like to take a look at your report, Officer?"

The tall young man adjusted his tie, then accepted the report as if it were going to bite him. He glanced through it quickly, then looked up.

Dowd stepped back a few paces. "Do you find any mention of Mrs. Fratt having alcohol on her breath?"

"No, Counselor, I do not."

Dowd could always tell when he had finally gotten to a cop: They started referring to him as "Counselor"—a term of apparent respect in court, but of thinly veiled contempt among police officers.

"Well, I assume you asked Mrs. Fratt to submit to a blood or breath test, to find out what her blood alcohol level was?"

"No, we did not."

"You did *not?*" Dowd asked in mock surprise. "This . . . murder suspect had alcohol on her breath, and you didn't even try to find out if she was intoxicated or not?"

"As I said, Counselor, we did not."

Dowd nodded slowly as he turned away and walked back to the counsel table. He stood next to his chair in silence, as if trying to understand this strange contradiction.

"You testified that Mrs. Fratt never mentioned anything about a rape," Dowd said, quickly changing the subject.

"Yes, sir."

"She *did* mention that there had been a fight, didn't she?"

There had been no mention of this, either, in Lapinski's report, but Nevins had testified that Louann Fratt had said she and her husband had been in a fight. Dowd was forcing the officer into another untenable position: If he denied hearing her say it, he contradicted his partner's testimony; if he confirmed it, the lack of any mention of the fact in his report added to the appearance of sloppy police work.

Lapinski shook his head. "No, she never said anything like that."

"Are you aware that your partner, Sergeant Nevins, testified that she *did* tell him there was a fight?"

Lapinski paused for a moment, trying to decide if the

lawyer was setting him up with a lie. "No, sir, I'm not aware of that."

Dowd walked toward the jury box. "You were standing right next to him when he was questioning Mrs. Fratt, weren't you?"

"Yes."

"But *he* says Mrs. Fratt told him that she and her husband got into a fight—and *you* say she never said that, is that correct?"

Lapinski shrugged. "I don't remember her saying anything like that. She may have."

"She did appear to have been hit by *someone*, didn't she, Officer Lapinski?"

"Like I said, she had a slight discoloration over her right eye."

Dowd suddenly stopped. Something clicked in the back of his mind. Like a computer that had found an error, his brain was sending an irritating little signal. And, like a computer, Dowd's mind played back the witness's testimony almost as if it were reading a transcript. The lawyer had long ago discovered that he possessed a strangely selective memory—one that became almost photographic during the intensity of trial, but one that would, at the close of day, fail him when he was trying to find where he had parked his car.

He looked at Lapinski. "The right eye?"

The young officer paused for a moment before answering. "Yes, sir."

"Your testimony is that the discoloration was *over* the *right eye*?"

"Yes, Counselor, the right eye."

"Didn't you just testify, on direct, that the discoloration was on Mrs. Fratt's right *cheek*?"

Lapinski was silent for a moment. What *had* he said during direct examination? Was this defense lawyer bluffing him?

"The right eye," the officer repeated.

Wrong answer. Now Dowd had a choice. He knew the bloodthirsty approach would be to have the reporter read back the transcript and then shove it down the witness's throat, perhaps adding to his misery with a question like, "Well, now, Officer Lapinski, which version is the *truth*?" The second option was to drop the matter, then point out the inconsistency to the jury during the closing arguments at the end of the case. Although this was not as soul-satisfying as skewering a live witness, it had the great advantage of not giving the witness a chance to explain the discrepancy.

Dowd decided to save it.

"Officer Lapinski, do you recall Mrs. Fratt saying that her husband had called her and asked her to come over to his apartment?"

"No, she never said that."

"She never mentioned her husband asking her to come over?"

"No."

"You're *sure* of that?"

"Yes, Counselor, I'm sure."

As part of his discovery motion, Dowd had obtained a copy of Lapinski's crime report. But he had gone further: He had also asked for and received a copy of the officer's handwritten notes taken while at the scene. And this was where thorough pretrial preparation paid off. He had noticed that the report contained no mention of Louann Fratt saying anything about being asked to come to Poe's apartment. But the handwritten notes *had* referred to such a statement. As so often happened, the crime report had probably been prepared in a hurry and failed to include all of the facts in the notes. But Dowd knew that it was the crime report that Lapinski would probably review before testifying, since it was only the crime report that most defense lawyers read before cross-examining.

Dowd picked up the photocopies of the notes, walked over to the witness stand, and handed the notes to the officer.

"Do you recognize these, Officer Lapinski?"

The tall man tugged on his huge moustache as he glanced at the papers. "Yes, sir."

"And what are they?"

"These are my notes."

"You took those notes in the field—that is, at the scene?"

"Yes."

"So the events were fresh in your mind when you wrote them down?"

"Yes."

"Would you please read those notes now, Officer, and tell us if there is anything in there about Mrs. Fratt mentioning being asked to come to her husband's apartment?"

Lapinski began reading through the photocopies of his notes. He turned a page, then appeared to freeze. He looked up.

"Yes?" Dowd asked.

"I guess I forgot."

"You forgot."

"Yes, sir."

"Uh-huh. Well, has your memory been refreshed now?"

"Yes, sir."

"Then let me ask you again: Did Mrs. Fratt tell Sergeant Nevins that her husband had called and asked her to come over to his apartment that night?"

"Yes, sir, that's what she told him."

"Thank you, Officer," Dowd said, walking back to the table. "I have no further questions."

Cardinal rule number 11: If the horse is dead, stop beating it.

Judge Goodman looked at Brownell. "Call your next witness."

Lapinski shrugged again, then stood up and stepped down from the witness chair. The big man stared straight ahead, tugging at his moustache, as he walked past the jury and out through the swinging gate.

"Pedro Sanchez," the assistant D.A. called toward the bailiff standing at the door.

A short, slightly heavyset man in his forties, possibly Puerto Rican, stepped into the courtroom. He was wearing a cheaply made blue serge suit and a slightly frayed and heavily starched white shirt and tie. He seemed to flinch as all eyes turned to look at this newest actor in the play. He walked down the center aisle slowly, uncertainly, following the bailiff through the gate. The bailiff led him to the witness chair, and the man began to sit down.

"Raise your right hand," the clerk across the room said.

Confused, Sanchez looked toward the bailiff for help. The bailiff demonstrated by raising his own right hand. Sanchez looked back at the clerk, raising his hand also.

The clerk rattled off the litany. "Do-you-swear-to-tell-the-truth-the-whole-truth-and-nothing-but-the-truth-so-help-you-God?"

Sanchez looked again at the bailiff, then back to the clerk. "Yes, sir."

"Be seated," the clerk said. "State your name, spelling the last."

Sanchez sat down tentatively, began looking around the courtroom like a trapped animal.

"Your name," Judge Goodman growled.

The judge's voice startled him. "Sanchez, sir," he said, looking up at the black-robed figure. "Pedro Sanchez."

"Spell the last name."

"S-A-N-C-H-E-Z."

The man kept looking up at the judge, then sensed someone approaching. He turned in his chair, saw the assistant D.A. walking toward him.

"Mr. Sanchez," Brownell said, "where are you presently employed?"

"Employed? Ah, at One Fifty-one East Seventy-ninth Street, sir."

"That is where Mrs. Louann Fratt lives?"

"Mrs. Fratt, yes, sir."

"You are the doorman there, is that correct?"

"Yes, sir."

"And were you employed at that address as a doorman during the early morning hours of November twenty-second, 1988?"

"November twenty-second . . ."

"The morning the police officers came to arrest Mrs. Fratt."

"Ah, yes, yes. I am the doorman then, too."

"And what were your hours that night or morning?"

"Ah, from midnight to eight o'clock."

"I see," Brownell said, leaning against the jury railing. "Now, you are familiar with the defendant in this case, Louann Fratt?"

"Mrs. Fratt? Yes, yes, I am familiar."

"Would you point her out for us, please?"

Sanchez looked around the room in momentary confusion, then saw the woman seated at the table. He smiled broadly, nodding at her. "That is Mrs. Fratt," he said, pointing.

"Thank you. Now, during the night and morning hours of November twenty-second, did you have occasion to see Mrs. Fratt?"

"Yes, sir."

"And when was this?"

The man shrugged. "Two-fifteen, I think, maybe two-thirty. I open the door for her."

"And what was she doing?"

"She takes her dog out for a walk, like she always does. The little Chinese dog."

"She did this often?"

"Yes, sir. It's like I told you when we talk before, she takes the dog out for a walk about twice a week, around midnight."

"What was she wearing on this occasion?"

Sanchez shrugged again. "A dark coat, I think."

"Was she carrying anything?"

"No, sir, I don't think so."

Brownell walked back to the counsel table, held up the brown and gold Vuitton bag. "Do you recall if she was carrying something like this?"

"No, sir, I don't think so."

Dowd wondered for a moment if perhaps Louann Fratt had not taken the bag containing the mail and the knife with her that night. But he quickly concluded that the doorman simply did not remember. Like most witnesses, he was honest but his perception and memory were very far from accurate.

"All right. Now, when did you *next* see Mrs. Fratt?"

"The next time, it is . . . twenty minutes later. I open the door again, and she comes in, Mrs. Fratt and the dog."

"Now, Mr. Sanchez, tell us . . . Did you notice anything unusual about her face at this time?"

The man seemed to think about this for a moment, then shook his head slowly. "No, sir, it's like I tell you last week. I don't see nothing different."

"You saw no bruises?"

The man shook his head.

"You have to answer out loud," Brownell said, "so the reporter can take it down."

"No, sir, no bruises."

Brownell stepped away from the railing, seemingly lost in thought. He turned and looked at the witness. "Tell us, Mr. Sanchez, when Mrs. Fratt came back . . ."

"Yes, sir?"

"Did she seem . . . hysterical? Upset?"

"Upset?" Sanchez thought about this, then shook his head. "No, sir. She seem sad."

"Sad?"

"Yes, sir."

Dowd hurriedly scratched down some notes for cross-examination. The doorman was hurting the defense with his testimony that Louann Fratt appeared neither injured not particularly upset after returning from her husband's apartment. A woman who had just been forced to kill her husband to fight off a rape would appear hysterical or traumatically withdrawn. A woman who had just executed the father of her children might look no more than sad.

"All right," the prosecutor said, walking back to the jury box. "Now, Mrs. Fratt went out *again* that night, didn't she?"

"Yes, sir."

"When was this?"

"Ah, I think twenty minutes later."

"And was the dog with her this time?"

"No, sir."

"She was alone?"

"Yes, sir."

"Was she wearing the same dark coat?"

"Yes, sir."

"Was she carrying anything?"

"No, sir."

"And when did she return this time?"

"Twenty minutes, like before."

"Each time, she was gone for about twenty minutes?"

"Yes, sir."

Brownell walked over to his chair, placed his hands carefully on its back. He looked to his right at Louann Fratt, seated stoically in her chair. "And Mr. Sanchez, how did Mrs. Fratt appear *this* time? Was she upset?"

Sanchez shook his head again. "No, sir, she is sad."

"Just sad."

"Yes, sir."

Brownell looked down at his chair, nodding his head in silence. Then he looked back up at the witness.

"When was the next time that night you saw Mrs. Fratt?"

"Some policemen, they come and they go up. And maybe seven or eight minutes later, they come back down, with Mrs. Fratt. And they take her away."

"Thank you, Mr. Sanchez," Brownell said, sitting down. "Nothing further."

Sanchez nodded, then stood up to leave.

"Just a couple of questions, Mr. Sanchez," Dowd said, walking toward the man with a smile.

Sanchez appeared confused. He looked at the judge, then back at Dowd. Slowly, he sat down.

"Mr. Sanchez," the lawyer continued, "my name is Michael Dowd and I'd just like to ask you a few questions, okay?"

"Okay," the man said hesitantly.

"Do you recall talking with my investigator a few months ago? A young woman?"

The man thought about this for a moment. "A young woman, yes," he said finally. "I remember this, yes."

"Do you remember telling her that Mrs. Fratt was gone for a *half hour* each time?"

"A half hour . . ."

"Yes. Do you remember telling her that?"

"Maybe. Maybe I tell her that, I don't remember."

"Well, Mr. Sanchez, which is it? Was she gone for twenty minutes or for thirty minutes?"

The man shrugged. "Twenty minutes, maybe thirty minutes."

"So you're not really sure."

"Twenty minutes, maybe thirty, I think."

"Uh-huh." Dowd walked back to the gate, swung it back and forth. "Now you testified that you've seen Mrs. Fratt walking her dog twice a week for . . . how long has it been?"

"I think six years now."

"You've worked there, and seen Mrs. Fratt walking her dog late at night, for six years?"

"Yes, sir."

"Tell me, Mr. Sanchez, what does Mrs. Fratt *usually* wear when she walks the dog late at night?"

Sanchez again shrugged. "The dark coat."

"And what does she *usually* carry—other than the dog leash?"

"No, she don't carry nothing."

Dowd kept swinging the gate back and forth.

"There wasn't anything unusual about *this* particular evening, was there?"

"No, sir. The police, maybe."

"But before the police arrived, Mrs. Fratt did the same thing she always did, twice a week for six years?"

"Yes, sir."

Dowd walked toward the witness chair, stopped in front of the jury. "Well, if there was nothing unusual about that evening, how is it that you're able to remember what she was wearing, and what she was carrying?"

Sanchez shrugged again.

"Mr. Sanchez," Dowd continued. "Think back, think way back. Can you really remember what Mrs. Fratt was wearing on *that* night? Or are you remembering what she *usually* wore?"

The doorman appeared to be concentrating very hard.

"Isn't it possible she was wearing something else that night?" Dowd asked.

Sanchez nodded slowly. "Maybe."

"And isn't it possible that she was carrying something in her hand, possibly a bag?"

Sanchez nodded. "Maybe. I'm not sure."

"And isn't it possible that her face was bruised or swollen, and you didn't notice it?"

The doorman shrugged again.

Dowd walked over to his table, looked down at Louann Fratt. Then he looked back at the witness.

"You said Mrs. Fratt looked sad to you that night?"

"Yes, sad."

"Mr. Sanchez, how would you say Mrs. Fratt looks right now?"

The man looked at the woman sitting next to the lawyer. Louann Fratt dropped her eyes down to the folded hands in her lap.

"Sad," Sanchez said finally, sorrow in his own voice. "She look sad."

Dowd walked toward the jury. "The same as she looked that night the police came?"

"Yes, sir."

"And the week before then, when she took her dog out for a walk, how did she look?"

"She look sad."

"And the week before *then*?"

Sanchez again shrugged his shoulders. "Mrs. Fratt . . . she always look very sad."

Dowd looked at the jury, then back at the witness. "Thank you, Mr. Sanchez." He walked back to his chair. "No further questions."

Sanchez began to get up, then looked hesitantly at the judge.

"You're excused," Goodman said.

Sanchez nodded, then quickly walked past the jurors, up the aisle, and out the door.

Goodman looked at Brownell. "Call your next witness."

The young prosecutor rose to his feet. "The People rest," he said simply.

Dowd was stunned. He looked in disbelief at Brownell. How could the prosecution be resting its case? There was too much missing. Where was the evidence showing what had actually *happened* in Poe Fratt's apartment? Where was the evidence of premeditation? Where was the refutation of self-defense? Most important, where was the *motive*?

"This court will be in recess until tomorrow morning," Judge Goodman announced, rising to his feet. He looked down at Dowd. "The defense will call its first witness at nine sharp."

Dowd lay in the darkness, his eyes fixed on the barely visible ceiling of the bedroom. The room was silent, save for an occasional rustle of the sheets as his wife, Irene, stirred in her sleep.

Where was the motive?

Dowd sighed deeply, then looked over at the glowing numerals on the clock radio: 3:31. Two more hours, he thought. Two more hours, then he would get up and begin to get ready for the day. Two more hours.

He looked back up into the darkness.

Brownell had rested his case without putting on all of his evidence. That much was clear. He had presented nothing more than a skeleton case: a body with three stab wounds, an ex-wife who admitted the stabbing . . . and little more.

Why?

The answer was simple—and disturbing.

Assistant District Attorney Daniel Brownell was sandbagging Dowd: He was holding back critical evidence until after the defense had taken its best shot. It was an old strategy, and one that was technically improper. The prosecution was supposed to present all relevant evidence during its case-in-chief. When the prosecution rested, the defense then presented its own case. When the defense rested, the prosecution was permitted to offer *rebuttal*—evidence that refuted any *new* issues brought up during the defense case.

This rebuttal case was supposed to be limited to just that: evidence that directly contradicted new issues raised by the defense. However, many clever prosecutors had come to realize that there were tactical advantages to holding back their big guns until after the defense was finished. First, it kept the opponent in the dark; the defense never knew exactly what evidence to present during its case. Second, the impact on the jurors of last-minute evidence was more dramatic—and much fresher in their minds when they began deliberations.

Dowd knew that there were risks in the sandbagging strategy, of course. First, the prosecution had to present *enough* evidence in its case-in-chief to make out a prima facie case against the defendant; if too much was held back, the judge could dismiss the case for lack of evidence. But Dowd was confident that Brownell had already offered enough evidence to support a second-degree murder conviction.

Second, there was always the risk that the judge would rule that the evidence was not proper for rebuttal, that it should have been presented during the case-in-chief, as required by the rules. This rarely happened, however, because most evidence was at least arguably offered to refute the defense, and few judges had the courage to keep out critical prosecution evidence.

The main risk with holding back evidence was the distinct possibility that the defense would counter with its own chess move: resting immediately after the prosecution rested, offering no evidence. That would force an abrupt end to the trial, with nothing left for the prosecutor but to argue his case to the jury, based only on the weak evidence he had already offered.

But Dowd realized that Brownell knew the defense could not rest without offering evidence. The simple fact was that Louann Fratt would probably be convicted on the basis of the evidence presented so far. She had admitted stabbing her husband to death. An acquittal depended upon producing evidence of self-defense. And there was only one living witness to what happened in Poe Fratt's apartment that night. Louann Fratt would have to testify, and Brownell knew it.

Yes, the assistant D.A. was holding back some big cards. What were they? And when would he play them?

Dowd looked at the glowing numbers again.

3:54.

CHAPTER 22

The morning of Thursday, December 7, had dawned another cold, bleak winter day in lower Manhattan. As spectators filed into Judge Goodman's stuffy and overheated courtroom, they shed their heavy overcoats and woolen scarves and quickly claimed places in the wooden pews by laying the bulky garments across the seats. Conversations were animated as an almost electric anticipation filled the air. On this morning, the defense in the case of *The People* vs. *Louann Fratt* would begin to present its evidence.

The audience section of the courtroom had rapidly become segregated into identifiable cliques as the trial wore on. The reporters and photographers took the first two or three rows on the left side of the courtroom, while spectators, always hungry for a sensational murder trial, settled into the rows behind them. The right half of the audience, directly behind the defense table, had broken down into three groups. The first two or three pews were taken by the "pro-Louann" faction—the friends and relatives who had come to lend support to the defendant. Among this clique were Louann Fratt's children, Laura and Poe Jr. (her third child, William, would fly out from his home in San Francisco just before his mother

263

was to testify). Behind the pro-Louann coterie were four more rows of spectators. Seated in the last two pews, insulated from the pro-Louann camp by the buffer region of spectators, were the members of the "pro-Poe" clique—a circle of friends and relatives of the deceased, come to see that justice was done.

In a strange and recurring ritual, the members of the two groups would warmly greet one another each morning, chatting amiably in the manner of a family reunion; most, in fact, knew each other quite well. Everyone put on a very civilized, convivial, even cheerful air, as if this were just another grand social affair—a gathering of the elite, the powerful, the wealthy, the men wearing their dark gray wool uniforms, the women their tailored suits and scarves, all busily ignoring the distasteful circumstances and plebeian atmosphere surrounding them. When the trial resumed, these finely dressed gentlemen and ladies of breeding would conclude their niceties and then silently reform into the two isolated camps.

The recognized leader of the pro-Poe group was Meade Emory, a cousin and the lifelong closest friend of Poe Fratt. The bald, distinguished-looking older man with his trademark bow tie was a tax lawyer and senior partner in one of the most respected law firms in Seattle. Like the Fratts in New York, Emory was influential in Seattle society, serving as a trustee of the Seattle Symphony Orchestra, a director of the Cornish Institute of Art, and a member of the prestigious Rainier and University clubs.

Meade Emory and Poe Fratt had shared an aristocratic heritage. Their mutual grandmother, Josephine deWolf, had come out to Seattle as a pioneer late in the nineteenth century, shortly before the great Seattle fire of 1889. There she had met and married George Meade Emory, a distinguished lawyer, Cornell graduate (Poe was to become the fourth generation alumnus of Cornell), and soon-to-be Superior Court judge. In rapid succession, the beautiful Josephine gave birth to six children—among them, Poe's mother, Laura Emory, and Meade's father, DeWolf Emory. In 1906, however, Judge Emory was murdered by a young man, in apparent retaliation for the judge denying the man the right to court his lovely niece.

Josephine Emory raised the six children alone for a number of years. Then, shortly before World War I, the beautiful widow met a prominent and handsome lawyer who had come out west from New England. Charles Kennedy Poe was a descendant of Edgar Allan Poe and a former law clerk of Chief Justice Oliver Wendell Holmes. The two married, and "C. K." proved to be both a prolific father—Josephine soon gave birth to three more daughters—and popular stepfather.

Laura Emory grew up and married an executive (later to become president) of the Seattle Gas Company, Norbert "Nubbs" Fratt. The couple had one child: Charles Kennedy Poe Fratt. Laura had named her only son after the stepfather she had grown to love and admire. When Poe Fratt later met and married Louann and had three children of his own, he would name two of them after his step-grandfather, Charles Kennedy Poe, and his mother, Laura Emory.

Meanwhile, DeWolf Emory had also grown up, married, and produced a son: Meade, named after the grandfather.

Meade Emory and Poe Fratt were born in the same year, cousins bonded within a tightly knit gentry. They were to become the closest of friends for their entire life, each an avid admirer of the other. Emory would often refer to Poe as "the finest gentleman I've ever known."

On the verge of retirement at the time of his cousin's death, Emory was about to accept a position as law professor at Duke University when he heard the shocking news. Within hours of Louann Fratt's arrest, Emory had flown to New York to make arrangements for the funeral. He spoke at the funeral, held in Seattle, where he commented upon the irony of Poe's still-living mother, Laura Emory, losing both her father and her only son to murderers. Two weeks after her son's death, Laura Emory died. Meade Emory spoke at that funeral as well, bitterly observing the fact that her death had been caused by her son's murder.

The elder statesman of the Emory-Fratt clan had again flown out from Seattle, this time for the trial of his dead friend's wife. Emory had actually flown to New York a few weeks before the trial and had lived at Daniel Brownell's home, familiarizing the prosecutor with the background of the case. The remaining time he had spent talking with family friends and relatives, seeking out witnesses to testify against his cousin's killer. And throughout the trial, the venerable lawyer would take notes during testimony and then confer with Brownell during recesses.

At 9:00 sharp, a glowering Judge Goodman stopped his pacing, loudly ordered everyone to their seats, and quickly mounted the bench.

"You may proceed," he told the seated Michael Dowd.

Dowd rose to his feet. "Peggy Keating," he said quietly to the bailiff.

Members of the Emory-Fratt camps were still offering their parting salutations and finding their claimed territories as Louann Fratt's friend entered the courtroom. Smiling and nodding to acquaintances in both groups, she walked down the aisle and through the swinging gate to the witness stand. The attractive older woman stood with her hand raised for the oath, her reddish-brown hair and plain black-framed eyeglasses seemingly coordinated with a simple but elegant red and black wool suit. When she had finished swearing to tell the truth, Peggy Keating graciously sat down and waited.

"Good morning, Mrs. Keating," Dowd said, walking toward the jury box.

The woman smiled. "Good morning, Mr. Dowd," she said pleasantly.

"Mrs. Keating, where do you presently reside?"

"Nine Thirty-five Park Avenue."

"And before living there, where did you live?"

"One Fifty-one East Seventy-ninth Street."

"That is the address where Louann Fratt lives?"

"Yes, it is."

"You know Mrs. Fratt?"

"Yes, I do." Peggy Keating looked across the room at Dowd's client, seated next to Debbie Cohen at the counsel table, and smiled. "She is a very dear friend."

"And for how long have you known her?"

"I have known Louann Fratt for nine years now."

"All right," Dowd said, his hand on the jury railing, "I'd like to take you back a few months, Mrs. Keating, to November twenty-first of last year."

"Yes."

"The day before Poe Fratt's death."

"Yes."

"Did you have occasion to see Mrs. Fratt on that day?"

"I did."

"When and where was this?"

"I met Louann at two-thirty in the afternoon, at my apartment."

"What was the purpose of this visit?"

"We were going to the Museum of Natural History, for the lighting ceremonies with the *origami* tree."

"The *origami* tree?"

"Yes. The Japanese art of making paper sculptures. The museum had an entire tree decorated with these sculptures. It was really quite beautiful."

"Uh-huh. And did you and Mrs. Fratt go to the Museum of Natural History that afternoon for the lighting ceremony?"

"Yes, we did."

"Where did the two of you go after that?"

"We returned to my apartment."

"What did you do there?"

"We made *origami* sculptures."

"And for how long did you do this, Mrs. Keating?"

"Oh, I'd say about an hour and a half."

"Now, please tell us, Mrs. Keating," Dowd said, walking toward that point where the jury railing met the audience railing, "how did Mrs. Fratt *seem* to you during this time? What was her mood?"

"Why, she was laughing, joking. Happy, I would say. We were both in a very good mood."

"She did not seem . . . depressed, or preoccupied?"

The woman shook her head. "No."

Dowd was now standing at the juncture of the railings, at the opposite end of the jury box from the witness stand. This was a technique the lawyer often used when a witness was either so soft-spoken that the jury had difficulty hearing her, as was the case with Peggy Keating, or when he wanted the jury to pay particular attention to critical testimony, as was also the case. By standing at almost the opposite end of the jury from the witness, Dowd forced the person to speak more loudly in order to be heard by him. More important, it forced the witness to face the jurors while testifying. Dowd knew that the psychological impact on a juror of a witness seemingly talking directly to him rather than conversing with a lawyer could be dramatic: The testimony would be much more likely to be heard—and *remembered*.

"She did not seem as if there were something very . . . upsetting on her mind?"

"No, not at all. Quite the contrary."

"I see." Dowd moved slightly away from the juncture of railings. The psychological effect of positioning was heightened if it was used sparingly. "Now, what did the two of you do next?"

"We went to Louann's apartment. She had a glass bowl I wanted to borrow for Thanksgiving. I stayed there for about ten or fifteen minutes."

"Then you left?"

"Yes."

"What time was this?"

"I believe it was about six o'clock."

"Six o'clock."

"Yes."

"And you did not see her again that evening?"

"No. No, I did not."

Dowd smiled. "Thank you very much, Mrs. Keating." He walked back to his seat.

The woman watched the lawyer sit down, then looked at her old friend seated next to him. An expression of sadness, of pain, seemed to come over Peggy Keating for a moment.

"Mrs. Keating," Brownell said, rising.

"Yes?" Peggy Keating's attention was quickly brought back to the proceedings.

"How often did you see the defendant?"

"The defendant? Oh, you mean Louann?"

"Yes."

"I'd say . . . oh, perhaps every two or three days or so."

"When was the last time you saw the defendant before November twenty-first?"

"Before November twenty-first? Let me see . . ."

"Didn't you see her four days earlier, on November seventeenth? At a patrons' dinner at the Metropolitan Opera?"

"Yes, yes, that's quite right."

"And isn't it a fact, Mrs. Keating," Brownell said, walking toward the witness chair, "you told your husband shortly after this dinner that Louann Fratt was drinking too much?"

"Objection!" Dowd said, jumping to his feet. "Not relevant."

Dowd rarely objected to questions asked by opposing counsel. Most lawyers objected at every opportunity, of course. Some did it to keep out as much potentially harmful evidence as possible. Others proceeded on the theory that the more objections the lawyer could make, the more he disrupted his opponent's case. Still others seemed to follow a game theory, believing somehow that having an objection sustained scored a point. Dowd felt strongly that objections should be used sparingly. He knew that jurors resented objections, viewing them as a shifty lawyer's way of keeping the jury from learning the truth; juries tended to be suspicious of a lawyer who was constantly objecting. Dowd also was aware that the vast majority of objections concerned testimony that had very little if any harmful effect. And the fewer objections he made, the more likely it was that the judge would sustain those he saved for more important evidence.

The trick in being this selective in objecting, of course, was the timing involved. When a question was asked that was technically objectionable, the lawyer usually had a second or less in which to object before the witness began his damaging answer. It was during this one second that Dowd had to make three lightning-quick decisions: Was the question, in fact, objectionable? Did the benefits of keeping out the answer outweigh the negative consequences of appearing to the jury to be an obstructionist? If the answers to the first two questions were yes, what were the technical grounds under the evidence code for objecting?

If Dowd were a second or two late in objecting, the damage could be irreversible. If the witness answered yes before Dowd could object, for example, the only remedy would be to move to have the answer stricken. The judge would instruct the jury that they were to disregard the answer. This was very much like telling the jurors not to think of a purple horse: It was guaranteed to get the jury thinking about nothing *but* a purple horse.

In that second after Brownell asked his question, Dowd

decided it was one of those times to object. He was fairly convinced that Louann Fratt did, in fact, have a drinking problem. But he could not afford to have his client's drinking habits become a focal point of the trial.

"Overruled," Judge Goodman said.

Dowd sat back down.

"Do you want the question read back, Mrs. Keating?" Brownell asked.

"I don't recall saying that," Peggy Keating said stiffly.

"You don't recall saying that you had often seen Mrs. Fratt intoxicated?"

The woman straightened her posture slightly. "I don't recall saying that." She paused. "I may have seen her a little tiddly, perhaps, but never intoxicated."

"A little . . . tiddly?"

"Yes."

"Nothing further," Brownell said, walking away with a slight smile.

"Nothing further," Dowd said, rising to his feet again.

Judge Goodman turned to the woman. "You may be excused."

"Thank you," Peggy Keating said, stepping down from the witness stand. She glanced quickly at Louann Fratt, then walked out through the gate and out of the courtroom.

"Laura Fratt," Dowd announced.

Louann Fratt's daughter and look-alike rose gracefully from the second row of the audience and edged her way past her younger brother and out into the aisle. The slender twenty-nine-year-old walked to the witness stand, took the oath, and sat down. She avoided looking toward her mother, keeping her eyes fixed on the big, heavyset lawyer approaching her.

"My name is Laura Fratt," she said softly. "F-R-A-T-T."

"Ms. Fratt," Dowd said, "you are the daughter of the defendant in this case, Louann Fratt?"

"I am."

"Now, on November twenty-first of last year, where were you living?"

"In Sunnyvale, California."

"And at about eight o'clock that evening—Pacific Coast time . . . that would have been about eleven o'clock out here in New York—did you have a telephone conversation with your mother?"

"Yes, I did."

"What did the two of you talk about, if you can recall?"

"I was flying to Seattle the next day, to spend Thanksgiving with my grandparents. My mother and I were discussing travel arrangements . . . who would be picking me up, with whom I would be staying, that kind of thing."

Dowd walked over to where the jury box railing met the audience railing.

"I see. And did either of you mention anything about your father?"

"No."

"Now, Ms. Fratt, would you please tell us, did you notice anything unusual in your mother's mood—anything in the conversation or in her voice that indicated there was something heavy on her mind?"

Laura Fratt shook her head slowly. "No. Nothing."

"Thank you." He walked back to his chair. "Nothing further."

Rule number 7: Keep it short, keep it simple.

Like Peggy Keating, Louann Fratt's daughter had testified that her mother had not seemed to be preoccupied or in an unusual mood on the evening of the killing; Dowd could argue that there was nothing to indicate that his client was planning to murder her husband later that night. Of course, the jury would discount the testimony of a best friend and a daughter. But there was a second, equally important, purpose to Laura Fratt's testimony. Dowd wanted the jury to see his client's daughter, to listen to her, to be able to recognize her seated in the second row, and to know that she would be sitting there when they came back with their verdict. He wanted the jury to absorb the reality that Louann Fratt was not just an abstract defendant, but a human being with daughters and sons who loved her and cared for her. He wanted the jury to know that the three children continued to love and support their mother even after she had killed their father—and to think about the possible implications of that.

Brownell stood up slowly, seemingly lost in thought. "I have no questions," he said finally, and sat back down.

Laura Fratt left the witness stand and, as she walked past the jury, Dowd announced his next witness.

"Charles Kennedy Poe Fratt, Junior."

Louann Fratt's youngest son stood up in the audience and edged his way out into the aisle. He held the gate open for his sister as she passed, their eyes meeting for only an instant. Then the ruggedly good-looking young man in the dark gray suit, white shirt, and red tie entered the inner sanctum, took the oath, and seated himself in the witness chair.

"Mr. Fratt," Dowd said, standing behind the counsel table, "you are the youngest son of the defendant, Louann Fratt, is that correct?"

"Yes, sir."

"Would you please tell us, on November twenty-second of last year, where were you living?"

"Ithaca, New York."

"And why were you living there?"

"I was attending graduate school at Cornell University."

The young man's soft-spoken, polite, and mannered voice seemed to Dowd as oddly out-of-place coming from the scarred and broad-boned face now as it had in his office.

"All right," Dowd said. He walked over to the gate, leaned against the railing. "Now, at about three-thirty on the morning of the twenty-second, were you awakened by a telephone call?"

"Yes, sir, I was."

"And who was it calling you?"

"It was my mother."

"Mr. Fratt, would you please tell us why your mother was calling you at this hour?"

"My mother . . ." Poe Fratt, Jr., stopped, looked down in his lap for a moment. A muscle in his massive jaw flexed once, twice. Then he looked up, his chin high, and turned to the jury. "My mother said she thought she had killed my father. She said she wasn't sure, and she was going to call E.M.S. Then she said she'd call back once she found out if he was alive or not." He looked back at Dowd.

"And did your mother call back?"

"No, sir," he said, "she did not."

"Nothing further," Dowd said, returning to his seat.

The assistant D.A. rose slowly, then walked over to the jury box.

"Mr. Fratt . . ." he began.

"Yes, sir."

"When was the last time you had seen your father, before that night?"

"My father? I . . ."

"Didn't you see him just two or three days earlier, in Ithaca?"

"I . . . yes, that's right."

"This was at the Cornell-Penn football game, wasn't it?"

"Yes, sir."

"And for how long did you see your father during his visit?"

"I believe it was for about . . . five minutes."

"Five minutes."

"Yes, sir, I believe so."

"This was during the halftime of the game, wasn't it?"

"Yes, sir, I believe so."

Dowd shifted uncomfortably in his seat. He did not know why, but he was beginning to have a bad feeling somewhere deep inside.

"Do you recall who was with your father at the game?"

"Uh . . . some friends, two or three friends."

"Who were these . . . friends?"

"I don't recall."

"Do you know a Jerry Grady?"

"Jerry Grady?"

"Yes."

"Yes, sir. He's a friend of the family. He was a classmate of my father's, at Cornell."

Brownell took a step toward Poe Fratt, Jr. "And, in fact, wasn't Jerry Grady one of those friends who was with your father at the football game?"

"Objection, Your Honor!" Dowd found himself rising to his feet without quite knowing why. An instinct, something, told him to try to stop this. "What is the relevancy?"

Brownell calmly turned to the judge. "The relevancy will very quickly become apparent, Your Honor."

"Very well," Goodman said. "Overruled."

Dowd slowly sat down.

Brownell turned back to the witness. "Do you want the question repeated?"

"No, sir." Poe Fratt, Jr., looked down at his lap for a second, then back up at the prosecutor. "I believe one of the friends was Jerry Grady."

"There was another . . . friend with him, isn't that right?"

"I don't recall, sir."

Brownell took another step toward the witness. "Mr. Fratt, do you know a woman named Joan Clark?"

Joan Clark, Dowd thought to himself. Joan Clark, Joan Clark . . .

"Yes, sir."

"And how do you know her?"

"I met her after my father's funeral."

"*After* his funeral?"

"Yes, sir."

"Mr. Fratt . . ." Brownell took yet another step toward the young man. "Isn't it a fact that Joan Clark was with your father at the football game?"

"Objection!" Dowd jumped to his feet this time. "Your Honor, this . . . May we approach the bench?"

Goodman thought for a moment, then waved the two lawyers toward him. When they were standing at the side of the bench farthest from the jury, and the court reporter was ready, Goodman looked at Dowd expectantly.

"Your Honor," Dowd said, "what is the possible relevance of all this?"

Goodman looked at Brownell.

"Your Honor," the prosecutor said calmly, "we have evidence that Joan Clark and Poe Fratt were . . . romantically involved."

Dowd felt it like a dagger deep into his heart. The cold, icy feeling of a long-awaited lethal blow. There it was, at last. The oldest motive in the world . . . The other woman.

"That's ridiculous," Dowd said angrily. But the conviction in his voice did not match what he felt inside. "Poe Fratt and my client had been separated for many months. What relevance is it to bring up evidence of boyfriends or girlfriends at this stage?"

"Your Honor," Brownell continued, "we will show—"

"No, no," Goodman said. "It's relevant, it's relevant."

Dowd protested. "But—"

The judge looked at Dowd. "Your client claims that her husband tried to rape her, right?"

"Yes, but—"

"Well, it seems to me that it's less likely he's going to rape anyone if he's already got a girlfriend."

"What?" Dowd was stunned by Goodman's archaic reasoning. Rape had long since been widely recognized as a crime of violence, not of passion or lust. Every study, every statistic pointed to the simple fact that the availability of sex to the rapist was not a significant factor in rape.

"There's less motive to do that," Goodman repeated, "to rape someone, than if he didn't have a girlfriend."

"Your Honor—"

Goodman leaned back. "I've ruled."

Brownell stepped back from the bench as the court reporter picked up his stenotype and walked back to his seat. Dowd just stood there for a moment, speechless. Then he slowly turned away and walked back to his seat.

Brownell walked over to the jury box, put a hand on the railing. "I repeat," he said to Poe Fratt, Jr., "was Joan Clark with your father at the football game?"

"I didn't see her at the game."

Brownell pulled a small snapshot from his coat pocket, walked toward the witness stand with it. "Showing you what has been marked People's number thirty-nine . . ." He handed the snapshot to the young man. "Do you recognize who the two people in the photograph are?"

Poe Fratt, Jr., smoothed his hair back with one hand as he stared at the photo. He looked up.

"Who are those two people, Mr. Fratt?" Brownell persisted.

"One is myself."

"Yes?"

"The other is Jerry Grady."

"And this photo was taken at the Cornell-Penn game, wasn't it? At halftime?"

"I don't recall if it was taken at the game."

"You don't recall."

"No, sir."

Brownell now pulled out another photograph, handed it to the witness. "Showing you People's forty, do you recognize this?"

"Objection, Your Honor," Dowd said, rising. "I haven't had a chance to see these photographs."

"Show counsel," Goodman said impatiently.

Brownell took the second photo from the witness as Dowd approached them, then handed it to the defense lawyer. Dowd looked at the snapshot. There were two people standing next to one another. One was a man he did not recognize. The other was a very attractive blond woman, possibly in her late forties.

"Thank you," Dowd said, returning to his chair.

Brownell again presented the photograph to Poe Fratt, Jr. "Who is the man in the picture, Mr. Fratt?"

Louann's son again smoothed back his hair as he studied the picture. "Jerry Grady."

"And the second person, the woman . . . who is she?"

Poe Fratt, Jr., looked up. "She looks familiar, but I can't say."

"You don't recognize Joan Clark, Mr. Fratt?"

"She looks familiar."

"You *did* say you met her at your father's funeral?"

"Yes, sir."

Brownell stepped back, looked at the jury. "Looking at those two photographs, Mr. Fratt, isn't it a fact that Jerry Grady has on the same clothing in each?"

Poe Fratt, Jr., looked at one picture, then the other. "Yes, sir."

"Then is it fair to say that both photos were taken at the football game, probably near the same time?"

"I can't say."

"And, therefore, that you and the woman were together, in Jerry Grady's company, for at least a short while?"

"I can't say."

Dowd kept studying Brownell, trying to understand where he was going with this. All right, maybe this Joan Clark had been having an affair with Poe Fratt. Maybe it had started before the separation. Maybe it was the *reason* for the separation. But what did Poe Fratt's son have to do with it?

"Mr. Fratt," the assistant D.A. said ominously, looking now at the jurors. "Is it not a fact that you went over to see your father at halftime because you were *angry* that he had brought this woman with him to the football game?"

"What?"

"Is it not a fact," Brownell repeated, looking now at the young man, "that you and your father had a heated argument because he had brought Joan Clark to the game—rather than your mother?"

"I . . ." Poe Fratt, Jr., once again smoothed his hair. "I said I saw him briefly, meaning about five minutes, during the halftime."

Louann's son had been evasive. Dowd realized that he was trying to protect his mother without committing perjury. He also knew that Brownell could press him, force him to answer. But he might deny having had the fight. Brownell would be better off to quit while he was ahead, leaving the obvious evasion hanging in the air.

"Nothing further," Brownell said. He walked to his chair, sat down.

Poe Fratt, Jr., began to step down.

"Just a minute," Judge Goodman said.

The young man seemed startled, then sat down hesitantly.

"You didn't answer the prosecutor's question."

"Sir?"

"The question was," Goodman continued, "during that five-minute period did you have an argument with your father or not?"

There was a long silence. Dowd realized that his client's son was trapped: He had to decide.

"No, sir," Poe Fratt, Jr., said finally. "I did not."

Dowd realized that everyone in the courtroom knew he was lying. He also realized that Brownell was beginning to build a very strong motive. The oldest motive in the world: the other woman. But with a twist.

If the motive was that Louann Fratt had killed her estranged husband because he had a lover, the assistant D.A.
would have difficult questions to answer. If Joan Clark was
a recent girlfriend, why would Louann Fratt have become
insanely jealous—months after the separation, and when she
and her husband were on the verge of a divorce? But if Joan
Clark had been Poe Fratt's lover before the separation, why
would his client wait all that time and then suddenly stab him
to death in a rage of jealousy or anger?

The answer suddenly became clear to Dowd. His client
might be able to accept her husband of thirty years seeing
another woman. But she might *not* be able to accept him
flaunting this woman in front of their friends and—what may
have been the final blow—flaunting her in front of their son.
At that point, the rage of a mother was added to that of a
scorned and publicly humiliated wife. Louann Fratt may have
finally reached her breaking point.

The simple, unavoidable fact was that Louann Fratt
stabbed her husband to death two days after he had taken Joan
Clark to the football game. Was the timing just coincidence?

Dowd realized with a sinking feeling that Brownell almost
had his motive. All the prosecutor needed was one more thing.
He needed to prove that Louann Fratt found out about the
football incident, and that she found out shortly before killing
her husband.

Brownell needed a witness. He needed the person who
told Louann Fratt what had happened at that game.

If there was such a witness, Dowd knew, his client would
be convicted of murder.

CHAPTER 23

"The court is now prepared to rule on the admissibility of psychiatric testimony offered by the defense."

Judge Goodman leaned forward slightly in his chair behind the bench and glared darkly out at the audience, waiting for the last of the spectators to take their seats. When the murmur had died down and the courtroom was finally silent, he cleared his throat.

"The court," he said again, "is now prepared to rule on the admissibility of psychiatric testimony offered by the defense."

Dowd sat rigidly in his chair, nervously tapping a pencil against the table. He looked across the table at Debbie Cohen. His young assistant's eyes were locked on Dowd, studying him. When she realized that he was staring back at her, she quickly looked away.

Debbie Cohen had spent most of the weekend trying to find out who Joan Clark was. All she had been able to discover was that Poe's girlfriend was a prominent member of Manhattan society, rumored to have recently been divorced from the heir to the Avon fortune. She had also recently been to the district attorney's office, accompanied by her lawyer.

Dowd had a much more pressing problem for the moment. His gaze returned to the quick, darting black eyes of the judge, trying to find in them some indication, some tell-tale sign of what the crucial ruling would be.

Seated at the next table, Daniel Brownell appeared calm as always. He was leaning back casually, his eyes wandering without apparent interest over the two rows of empty chairs in the jury box. Behind the tranquil facade, however, was a mass of nerves, finely tuned to every word that came down from the bench.

It was Monday, December 11. Judge Goodman had read the legal briefs submitted by both sides. Now he was about to announce his decision whether Dr. Rosen and Dr. Veronen would be permitted to testify. Both Dowd and Brownell understood that this ruling was critical to the defense. With expert testimony to explain Louann Fratt's strange conduct, Louann Fratt had a chance at an acquittal. Without it . . .

"I note that defense counsel previously served the required notice of intent to proffer psychiatric evidence in this case," Goodman said, looking out at the audience. "He then withdrew that notice. At that time, I cautioned him in this regard . . ."

Dowd suddenly felt as if the earth were falling out from under him.

"Defense counsel now indicates that the expert psychological testimony he seeks to introduce here is not intended to explain the defendant's state of mind at the time of the crime." Goodman paused, looked down at Dowd. He seemed to be talking directly to the defense lawyer. "He states that the purpose of this testimony is to explain the defendant's diminished reaction to having stabbed and killed her husband."

I've lost, Dowd thought to himself. He had lost the motion. He had lost the trial. He had lost Louann Fratt's life.

"Notwithstanding defense counsel's characterization of the proposed expert testimony," Goodman continued, again looking out at the spectators and reporters, "this court concludes that such testimony is indeed being offered to explain the defendant's state of mind at the time of the offense charged. . . ."

He doesn't understand, Dowd thought angrily. The sonofabitch doesn't understand. . . .

". . . and that notice of intent to proffer psychiatric evidence pursuant to C.P.L. 250.10 *is* required if defendant intends to call at trial an expert witness to explain that at the time of the offense charged, the defendant was suffering from so-called battered woman's syndrome. . . ."

Dowd slowly brought his right hand up to his face, began gently massaging his eyes. The sonofabitch doesn't understand, he kept thinking. This was *not* a battered woman's syndrome case. The two experts were *not* going to testify to state of mind at the time of the stabbing.

"Specifically . . ." Goodman looked down at the papers in front of him, reading something. ". . . defense counsel indicated that he intends to call the defendant's therapist, Dr. Rosen, to explain the nature of the defendant's relationship with the victim. And to explain that the flat affect or unemotional tone of defendant's conversations with the nine-one-one operator does not necessarily mean that she acted coldly, but could be a result of her emotional responses to the trauma of the incident, and of her family background where the expression of emotion was repressed."

Dowd looked at his client seated next to him. Louann Fratt was staring straight ahead, apparently uninterested in what the judge was saying.

"Defense counsel also proposed to call Dr. Rosen to explain what he felt would be the defendant's unemotional tone at trial, particularly with regard to her proposed testimony." Goodman looked down at the impassive woman seated before him. "All of us have observed defendant manifesting emotion, shedding tears at the beginning of trial. It was taped for television. . . ."

Dowd remembered the tears running down her cheek, remembered the surprise he had felt.

". . . Thus, it would be inappropriate now to allow comment on the defendant's nonexistent lack of emotion."

Dowd sat at the counsel table, absently leafing through his trial notes. The words on the sheets of paper swam up at him, but they did not come together into sentences. They were just words, and they made no sense.

"The prosecutor," Goodman continued, "has indicated that he does not intend to submit in evidence the tape recording of the nine-one-one call. . . ."

Dowd looked quickly over at Brownell. A slight smile formed on the prosecutor's face.

"... Accordingly, I will not permit Dr. Rosen or any other expert to testify about the alleged unemotional tone of the defendant's conversation with the nine-one-one operator, as she can't comment on something not in evidence."

The 911 tape, Dowd thought to himself. The 911 tape ... Brownell was not going to offer it into evidence. He was sacrificing the tape to keep Dowd's experts off the stand. But why was Goodman even mentioning this as a grounds for prohibiting expert testimony? He had already ruled that the failure to give notice resulted in an exclusion of the testimony. Dowd suddenly came to the realization that Judge Goodman was "building a record": Possibly unsure of the legality of his ruling on lack of notice, he was shoring up his decision with additional grounds for keeping the testimony out.

If he could knock out these additional grounds, Dowd thought to himself . . .

"Your Honor," Dowd said, rising quickly to his feet. "The defense will offer the nine-one-one tape."

Both Goodman and Brownell suddenly jerked forward in their seats.

"*You* want to offer the tape?" Goodman asked incredulously.

"Yes."

Goodman looked at the prosecutor. "Mr. Brownell? Do you want to respond?"

Brownell rose slowly from his chair. "It's pretty clear, Your Honor, why the defense now wants to offer the tape. With the tape in, they think they can put Dr. Rosen on, have her testify why the defendant sounds so unemotional on it." Brownell looked at Dowd. "The defense is setting up a straw man, so they can get their expert to testify, to knock it down. This is just a way of getting in through the back door what they couldn't get in through the front door."

Goodman nodded, thinking it over. "This is premature," he said finally. "I want to see what Mr. Brownell does on cross-exam, then I will consider it further."

"But, Your Honor—" Dowd protested.

"As to Dr. Veronen . . ." Goodman continued, ignoring

Dowd. "In the exercise of my discretion, I will permit Dr. Veronen to testify."

What was he saying? Dowd thought to himself. Veronen *could* testify? Did he say she *could* testify?

"However," Goodman continued, "this witness will not be permitted to comment upon *this* particular defendant's mental or emotional status. Furthermore . . ." Goodman once again began reading from the papers in front of him. "Defense counsel has proposed that this expert be permitted to testify in nine areas. As to those areas, I rule as follows:

"One, I will permit the expert to state that there has been research into the response of victims of sexual assault, and that this research demonstrates that many victims display certain common psychological responses. I will *not* permit the expert to discuss or otherwise summarize the research in this area."

Dowd tried to understand what the judge was saying. Dr. Veronen *could* testify. She could testify that research had been done, that there were common responses to rape. But she could *not* testify what the findings of that research were?

"Two, I will not permit the expert to testify as to the definition of rape.

"Three, I will permit the expert to *state* that some victims fail to report the sexual assault, and I will permit her to list briefly—and I stress *briefly*—the reasons why.

"Four, I will *not* allow the expert to testify about commonly held myths about rape. That is irrelevant."

Irrelevant? Dowd thought. How could mistaken beliefs about rape that were possibly held by the jurors be irrelevant?

"Five, I will permit the expert to *state* that persons of both sexes and of all socioeconomic classes are victims of attempted or actual sexual assault.

"Six," Goodman continued reading, "I will *not* permit the expert to discuss the short-term and long-term reactions to sexual assault. However, I will permit her to *state* that some victims of violent crime respond with emotional numbing and may describe the incident in a matter-of-fact manner and tone."

Dowd found himself wondering why Goodman was permitting Dr. Veronen to testify to anything. Was he fearful of being reversed on appeal, hedging his bets by permitting the defense to call one expert witness—but then restricting her testimony so severely that it was almost meaningless?

"Seven, I will *not* permit the expert to discuss scientific research that the nature of the relationship between the victim and the victimizer has a bearing on the intensity of the violence.

"Eight, I will permit the expert to *state* that many victims of attempted or actual sexual assault repress and block out the event, which leads to failure to report the event immediately.

"Nine, I will permit the expert to *state* that some victims of sexual assault by persons with whom they have had an intimate relationship may subsequently place themselves in a situation where that person may once again victimize them."

Judge Goodman looked up from the papers, first at Dowd, then at Brownell, then out at the audience and the television camera. He resumed reading aloud.

"I will instruct the jury that the testimony of this expert is solely for the purpose of providing them with information about psychosocial responses of some victims of attempted or actual sexual assault in general, and *is not evidence that this defendant is necessarily such a victim.*" Goodman looked up again. "The testimony is about the response of *some* victims, in general, and is *not* an opinion of the expert about *this* defendant."

Good God, Dowd thought. But it was better than having no expert testimony at all.

"That is the decision of the court with respect to psychiatric testimony," Goodman said, leaning back in his chair.

"Judge," Dowd said, standing, "can I be heard?"

"No, I made my ruling."

"I'd like to make at least a partial record about one thing."

Goodman glared at the big lawyer for a moment. "Go ahead," he said finally.

"You said Dr. Veronen could not testify about some commonly held myths concerning rape."

"Yes."

"The fact is, there are a lot of mistaken beliefs about rape, beliefs that could affect this trial. For example, the belief that having a sexual outlet means an individual is less likely to commit rape."

"Go on."

"What I'm saying is," Dowd continued, "that is a *myth*. There is a lot of research, a lot of documentation, that proves it's a myth. And there are other myths—for example, that the victim must be sexually attractive. The research consistently shows that rape has nothing to do with sex. It is a crime of violence and power."

"Mr. Dowd," Goodman said coldly, "I think we have reached that stage in life where I think everybody knows what rape is all about. Nobody assumes today that someone rapes someone else because they are attractive. It is clearly a crime of violence, and I think the jury is capable of understanding that without the help of an expert."

"But Your Honor, you may recall a conversation we had at the bench last week, a conversation about the relevance of evidence that the deceased had a girlfriend."

Goodman said nothing.

"You may recall that you said evidence that Poe Fratt had a girlfriend *could* be offered—to show that he had a sexual outlet, that there was no need for him to rape the defendant."

"I don't remember that conversation."

"But—"

"If the People offered evidence of a girlfriend, I assume that it would be to show motive."

Dowd knew he was at a dead end. "Well," he said finally, "if I can't offer evidence of the untruthfulness of commonly held myths about rape, the prosecution should not be able to argue those myths as if they were true."

Goodman thought about this. "I agree," he said, looking at Brownell.

The assistant D.A. shrugged.

"All right," the judge announced loudly, "bring in the jury." He looked down at Dowd. "Call your next witness."

As the bailiff went out of the courtroom, Dowd sat down and began to shuffle through his trial notes. But this was a show, a stall. He knew who his next witness was, who it *had* to be. Yet, he could not call her. For the simple fact was she would give the prosecution the missing piece to its case.

Dowd glanced at the woman seated next to him. With Rosen knocked out, and Veronen handcuffed, Louann Fratt's testimony was all that was left of the defense. But if he put her on . . .

After Poe Fratt, Jr.'s testimony at the end of the previous week, and the revelation about the existence of his father's girlfriend, Dowd had asked Louann Fratt about Joan Clark. She vaguely recalled having met the woman, but claimed to know little about her.

Then Dowd asked the critical question: Had she heard about Poe taking Joan Clark to the football game, and about the fight between him and their son? And if she *had* heard of it, *when*? Louann admitted knowing about the incident: Jerry Grady's wife, Susan, had called to report the affair to her old friend. Worse, the call had taken place on Sunday, the day after the game—and the day before Louann had stabbed her husband to death.

Brownell needed only one more thing to wrap the case up into one neat little package of premeditated murder: a witness who could confirm the motive for the stabbing—who could verify that Louann Fratt had heard about the football incident just before she killed her husband.

If Louann Fratt took the stand, he would have that witness.

The bailiff returned with the fifteen jurors in tow. As they were taking their seats, Judge Goodman glared at Dowd.

Dowd continued shuffling through his notes. There was no avoiding the fact that he was firmly impaled on the horns of a dilemma. If Louann Fratt testified, she would give Brownell his motive; it would be unethical for Dowd to permit his client to lie during her testimony. If she did not testify, however, there would be no way of informing the jury about the attempted rape. Without a finding of self-defense based on the attempted rape, a murder conviction would be automatic.

"Call your next witness," Judge Goodman repeated impatiently.

Dowd stood for a moment in silence. "Louann Fratt," he said finally.

There was a murmur in the audience, but another dark

scowl from Goodman brought a hush back into the court-room.

Dowd pulled the chair out for his client as she gracefully rose to her feet. Louann Fratt was wearing a simple black tailored dress, a white and gold silk scarf, a black leather belt, black stockings, and black pumps. But for the scarf, she appeared to be a widow still in mourning.

A small, forced smile briefly crossed the fatigue and sadness in her face as she nodded her thanks to the lawyer, then turned and walked toward the witness stand.

As his client raised her hand and took the oath, Dowd found himself wondering which Louann Fratt had shown up to testify—the unfeeling, cold-blooded murderer or the emotionally shattered woman who had finally found a few tears. After Judge Goodman's ruling, there would be no Dr. Rosen to explain his client's emotional mechanisms. He knew that if the wrong Louann showed up, the jury would very likely hang her.

Everything rested on Louann Fratt's testimony.

Dowd's client sat down in the witness chair, her posture rigidly erect and her head held high.

"My name is Louann Fratt," she said stiffly. "F-R-A-T-T."

CHAPTER 24

"It was about this time that Poe was transferred from Paris to New York."

"And you bought the co-op on Seventy-ninth Street?"

"Yes."

"Like the other property, this was in your husband's name?"

"Yes."

Dowd leaned back against the audience railing. He held a pencil in one hand, absently tapping it against the palm of the other.

"Mrs. Fratt . . . How would you characterize your marriage up until this point?"

"Characterize?"

"Yes. Was it a successful marriage? Were you both happy?"

Louann Fratt looked down at the hands carefully crossed on her lap. She was silent for a moment as she thought over this seemingly strange question.

"Yes," she said quietly, looking up at her lawyer. "Yes, I think it was a . . . successful marriage."

"And you were happy?"

288

Louann Fratt just stared at Dowd, as if not comprehending the question.

"And you were happy?" the lawyer repeated.

"I . . . Yes, I believe I was . . . happy."

Dowd turned and walked toward the jury.

"Now . . . At some point in time, this . . . happy marriage fell apart, isn't that true?"

"I suppose . . . Yes, that's true."

"And when was this?"

"In May of 1987. Poe told me . . . He told me he wanted a divorce."

"Were you expecting this?"

"No," Louann Fratt said, looking back down into her lap. As if suddenly remembering where she was, her head snapped back up, chin held high. "No," she repeated. "I was quite surprised."

"There had been no signs?"

"None. We had been married for thirty years." She looked away from her lawyer, an edge of bitterness creeping into her voice. "I could not understand why he suddenly wanted a divorce."

Dowd nodded, began walking back toward his chair. "And did your husband move out of the apartment?"

"Not at first. We lived together until November. We both retained attorneys in June, I believe, but Poe did not move out until November."

"November of 1987."

"Yes."

"And where did he move to?"

"The apartment on Seventy-ninth."

"All right." Dowd put his hands on the back of his chair, staring down at his trial notes on the table. "Now, did you have any occasion to meet with your husband after he moved out?"

"Yes."

"For what purpose?"

"There were always matters coming up, financial matters, investment decisions. . . ."

"And where were these meetings?"

"Sometimes at his apartment, sometimes at mine."

"When you went to *his* apartment, was this during the day or at night?"

"It was usually at night. He worked during the day."

"How did you get to his apartment?"

"I walked."

"Mrs. Fratt," Dowd said, looking at his client, "weren't you just a little afraid to be walking alone at night?"

"Yes, I was."

"Did you carry anything for protection?"

"Yes. I always took a large kitchen knife with me, in a bag."

"I see."

Dowd looked away for a moment, then turned and walked toward the jury. Out of the corner of his eye he saw a tall, handsome young man in an immaculate dark gray pin-striped suit, white shirt, and red tie walking down the aisle. In his mid-twenties, the neatly groomed man was wearing tortoise-shell-rimmed glasses and freshly polished wing-tip Oxfords; a cheap black plastic watch seemed oddly out of place on his left wrist. The young man had the slender face, fine hair, and telltale narrow eyes of his mother.

William Fratt spotted his brother and sister in the second row and quietly sat down beside them.

"Mrs. Fratt," Dowd continued, "I'd like to direct your attention to an evening in July of last year, an evening during which your husband paid a visit to you at your home."

Louann Fratt seemed to tense almost imperceptibly. "Yes."

"Do you recall this?"

"A Friday evening," she said tersely. "The Fourth of July weekend."

"And what was the purpose of this meeting?"

"Poe . . . I needed the car. Poe brought it over. It was about nine o'clock."

Dowd had reached the strategic point where the jury railing met the audience railing. He leaned back against the corner.

"Tell us what happened," he said.

"He . . . Poe came into the library. I was sitting on the loveseat. He sat down next to me."

"Yes?"

"He . . . We were talking. I don't recall. . . . Then he . . ."

Louann Fratt looked away from her lawyer, away from the jury, out toward the audience.

What was she looking for? Dowd wondered. He glanced back at the audience himself. Was she looking for her children?

"And what happened next?" he said, looking back at his client.

Louann Fratt was silent, her jaw locked tightly, her chin held a fraction higher.

"Mrs. Fratt?"

When she spoke, the words were barely audible. "He grabbed me."

"What?"

Silence.

"Mrs. Fratt," Dowd said, "I can't hear you."

She looked down, away from the audience, her eyes coming to rest once again on the folded hands in her lap. "He grabbed me," she repeated in a near whisper.

Dowd remained standing at the juncture of the railings. In a firm voice, he repeated, "I can't hear you."

Louann Fratt slowly lifted her head, looked at the big lawyer across the room. "He grabbed me," she said a little more loudly.

"And then what happened, Mrs. Fratt?"

"He . . ." Her eyes were locked on Dowd now, as if he were a life preserver in an angry sea. "He . . . tore my shorts off."

"And?"

"And . . ." She shook her head back and forth.

"And then what did your husband do, Mrs. Fratt?"

"He . . . Poe . . ."

"What did he do?"

"He . . . raped . . . me." Louann Fratt's head seemed to fall forward. Then she quickly lifted her head back up, up until she was looking at the pale salmon ceiling. Her jaw was clenched tightly, and she seemed to be fighting for control. She brought her head down and again looked out at the audience.

Dowd saw Laura, William, and Poe, Jr., sitting in the second row, listening to their mother describe how their father had violently raped her. Sitting without expression. Impassive. Nothing to give away their feelings.

Dowd looked back at his client. And then he saw it. A tear. And another. Her eyes glistened wetly. His client was crying. Louann Fratt was crying; she was showing pain. The woman on the stand was no longer a cold, empty, unfeeling aristocrat.

The woman on the stand was nothing more than a badly frightened, deeply scarred, very lonely human being.

A handkerchief suddenly appeared in Louann Fratt's hand. She dabbed at her cheek, sniffling slightly.

Dowd waited for a moment. Then, more gently, he said, "Please tell us what happened next."

"We . . . When it was . . . over, I . . . went into the bedroom. I locked the door."

"And when did your husband leave?"

"I don't know. I . . . didn't come out until the next morning."

Dowd nodded in silence. "Mrs. Fratt," he said finally, gently, "how did you feel after being raped?"

"What?"

"How did you *feel* after your husband raped you?"

Louann Fratt once again looked out at the audience, then dropped her head. She dabbed at her eyes with the handkerchief. "Horrible," she said. "Humiliated . . . filthy . . . I felt horrible."

"Did you tell anyone about the incident?"

She looked up, shook her head. "He called. . . . Poe called two days later. He said he was sorry. I told him . . . I told him, if he ever did that again, I'd tell the children."

"Why didn't you tell anyone, Mrs. Fratt?"

"I . . . It was so . . . filthy."

Dowd nodded again in silence, then walked across the room, away from the jury, his hand sliding along the audience railing.

"Now, I'd like to take you to November twenty-first, Mrs. Fratt," he said. "I'd like to take you to the evening that you stabbed your husband."

Louann Fratt straightened her posture slightly, lifted her chin. The handkerchief had disappeared.

"Do you recall what you had done that afternoon?"

"Yes. Peggy Keating and I had gone to the Museum of Natural History, for the lighting of the *origami* tree. Then we went to her apartment. We made some *origami* sculptures. After that, we went to my apartment and I loaned her a crystal bowl for the holidays. She left about six o'clock."

"How did you feel that afternoon?"

"How did I feel? I felt fine, I felt very good."

"Mrs. Fratt, I understand you had been seeing a man, is that right?"

"Yes. Bob Ault."

"Is it fair to say that this was a . . . close relationship?"

"Yes."

"A romantic one?"

"Yes."

"Then you and Mr. Ault were still seeing each other at this time?"

"Yes. In fact, Mr. Ault and I had just been to a benefit at the Waldorf two or three nights earlier."

"And . . . Please excuse my indiscretion, Mrs. Fratt, but where did Mr. Ault stay after this benefit?"

"He spent the night in my apartment."

Dowd hoped that the jury would think that a woman happily involved with another man would not feel homicidal toward an estranged husband. But he could not help remembering the telephone conversation he had had with Bob Ault. He wondered if Louann realized what kind of a relationship it had really been. He wondered if she realized how very much alone in the world she really was.

Looking at her now on the stand, Dowd suddenly understood Louann Fratt knew that loneliness all too well. But it was a loneliness that had begun many, many years before meeting Bob Ault.

"So," he continued, "you were feeling pretty good on the evening of the twenty-first?"

"Yes, I was."

"Do you recall receiving a phone call from Poe Fratt that evening?"

"Yes. It was sometime around six-thirty, seven-thirty. He wanted to pick up his mail. He hadn't picked it up in two weeks."

"And what did you say?"

"I agreed. There were some financial matters I wanted to discuss with him, some oil investments I didn't understand. He said he would be gone until eleven o'clock that evening, to call back then."

"And did you?"

"Yes. But he wasn't back. I called my daughter, Laura, in California, and we talked for a while. Then I called again, at about eleven o'clock. This time, the line was busy."

"Did you finally reach your husband on the phone?"

"Yes. About one o'clock, Poe answered."

Dowd leaned back against the audience railing. "Please tell us what you talked about."

"Poe asked me to bring the mail to his apartment."

"What did you say?"

"I didn't want to do that. But he said he'd be going out of town the next day. He . . . he insisted that I bring the mail over right away."

"And?"

"And I said I would."

"What happened next?"

"I got dressed, in a sweatsuit and sneakers. . . . I put the mail in a bag, along with the knife, and some cigarettes. . . . I put a leash on our dog. . . . And I left."

"You had a knife in the bag?"

"Yes, for protection."

"And your husband's mail."

"Yes."

"Nothing else."

"No."

"All right. What happened when you got to the apartment?"

Louann Fratt paused for a moment, the memory playing back in her mind like an old movie.

"Poe answered the door. He offered me a glass of wine. I accepted. I put the mail on the table. Then I sat down on the couch."

"Where was your husband?"

"He was on the bed. With the dog."

"What was he wearing?"

"Poe was in his pajamas."

"Uh-huh." Dowd stepped away from the railing, began walking toward the jury. "And where was the bag?"

"The bag?" She looked back at the movie. "It was on a stack of books, next to the sofa, where I was sitting."

"What did the two of you talk about?"

"Poe was talking about the game, the Cornell-Penn game. And he asked me how I liked his new comforter. He had just bought a new comforter for the bed."

"Uh-huh. And at some point, your husband stopped talking, is that right, Mrs. Fratt?"

The woman nodded.

"What happened?"

"Poe got up from the bed. He grabbed my right arm, he just grabbed it and pulled me off the sofa. He . . ."

"Did he say anything at this time?" Dowd once again had walked to the only place in the courtroom that forced his client to face the jurors.

"He said . . . Poe said . . ." The woman looked down at her hands, then up again at the ceiling, her jaw clenched tightly. "Poe said . . . 'I'm going to . . . I'm going to fuck you like you should be fucked.' "

"Go on, Mrs. Fratt."

The woman was silent for a moment, once again fighting for control, fighting to keep from showing feelings, any feelings.

"He . . . pulled me onto the bed. He . . . began to pull my sweatpants off. . . ."

"What did you do?"

"He . . . I . . . scratched him, I scratched him in the face. With my fingernails. I was trying to get away. . . ."

"What did you think your husband was going to do, Mrs. Fratt?"

"He was . . . Poe was going to . . . was going to rape me again."

"How did you feel?"

"I was terrified."

"And then what happened?"

"Poe . . . hit me, he hit me on the side of the head."

"What did you do?"

"I . . . the knife, I had the knife in my hand, and he grabbed me, and pulled me back. I said, 'Let me go, Poe, I've got a knife, I've got a knife.' "

"Did he stop?"

Louann shook her head, almost violently. "I . . ." She looked out at the audience again, out toward her children, her eyes filling with tears. "I stabbed him. I stabbed him."

"Mrs. Fratt," Dowd said slowly, "when you stabbed your husband, did you intend to kill him?"

Louann Fratt again shook her head, the tears now beginning to run. "I was trying to get away from him. I was trying to get out."

"What happened after that?"

"He . . . he hit me again, in the face. And he said, Poe said, 'You're not getting out of here alive.' "

" 'You're not getting out of here alive.' "

The woman nodded. "He turned, he reached for something on the table. A letter opener, I think. And I . . . I stabbed him again, in his back."

"And were you trying to kill him this time, Mrs. Fratt?"

"I was trying to get out. He was . . . Poe was blocking the way out. I was trapped. I . . . He was going to kill me."

"Kill you?"

"I thought he was going to kill me."

Dowd looked at the jury. Fifteen sets of eyes were riveted on his client. What were the jurors thinking? Dowd wondered. Did they believe her? Could they *see* what had happened? Could they *feel* what it had been like for this woman? Could they begin to understand the sheer terror? Or did they see it as nothing but a charade, a cheap drama?

"What happened next, Mrs. Fratt?" Dowd asked, his eyes still on the jurors.

Louann Fratt again shook her head. "I don't . . . I remember I was swinging the knife, swinging it back and forth. . . ." She squeezed her eyes tightly shut for a moment, then opened them. "He fell. Poe fell."

"Your husband fell to the ground?"

"Yes. I . . . I left. I grabbed the dog and I left."

"You recall the testimony of the medical examiner, that the lethal wound was to the heart?"

Dowd's client nodded. She dabbed the handkerchief to her eyes. Her hand was trembling.

"Do you recall stabbing him in the chest area?"

"No," she said, shaking her head.

"All right. What did you do after you left the apartment?"

"I don't . . . What happened after that, I'm not sure."

"You don't recall?"

"Some things, I can remember some things."

"What do you remember?"

"I . . . got back to my apartment somehow, I don't remember how. There was blood on me. I changed into another sweatsuit. I didn't know what to do. I called my son, I called Poe Junior. Then I thought that maybe Poe was alive." She was watching the movie again, her eyes transfixed on the invisible drama. "I went back. I went back to Poe's apartment. I unlocked the door. He was just inside, behind the door. On the floor. I think he was dead. Then I want back to my apartment. I didn't know what to do. I didn't know what to do."

"What *did* you do?"

"I . . ." She shook her head helplessly. "Then I called the police. And they came, the police came."

"When they came, you didn't tell them about Poe trying to rape you."

Louann Fratt shook her head.

"Why not?"

"It was . . . humiliating, and disgusting, and filthy, and dirty."

The courtroom was still hushed as Dowd stepped away from the railings and walked in silence toward the swinging gate, his gaze on the floor. He turned, looked up at the woman sitting so alone on the witness stand.

"Did you intend to kill your husband?"

"No," she said, again shaking her head back and forth. "I didn't want Poe to die. He was the father of my children. I didn't want him to die."

"Then . . . What *were* you trying to do when you stabbed him, Mrs. Fratt?"

"I . . . I was trying to get out of there alive."

Dowd stared at the woman in silence, then nodded slowly. He walked toward his chair, put his hand on the backrest.

"Nothing further," he said quietly.

"Mr. Brownell," Judge Goodman said.

Daniel Brownell pushed back his chair and rose slowly to his feet. He walked to the jury box without saying a word, his head bowed in thought. When he reached the railing, he turned toward the witness stand and looked at Louann Fratt. Still he said nothing, his eyes locked on his prey.

"Mrs. Fratt," he said finally, "do you know Joan Clark?"

CHAPTER 25

"Joan Clark?" Louann Fratt repeated.

Brownell studied the witness in silence for a moment. "Joan Clark," he said quietly.

"Yes. I've met Mrs. Clark."

"When was that, Mrs. Fratt?"

"I . . . It was in January, I believe, January of 1987."

"And where was this?"

"At the New York Public Library," the woman said, shifting slightly in her chair. "We were both attending a dinner there."

"This was shortly before your husband told you he wanted a divorce."

"It was before that, yes."

"Now, you ran into Joan Clark a second time, didn't you, Mrs. Fratt?"

"I believe I did."

"Where was this?"

"Again, at the public library. I was attending a lecture, with Peggy Keating. And my son William."

"And when did this . . . encounter take place?"

"It was sometime in 1987, I don't recall exactly when."

"Do you remember whether it was before or after your husband told you he was leaving you?"

Louann Fratt's jaw visibly clenched. "I really don't recall."

"You don't recall."

"No."

"Now . . ." Brownell rested his hand on the jury railing. He looked down at the dark polished wood, stroking it gently with his hand. "Did you have occasion to run into Joan Clark again, at another library dinner?"

"No."

"You did not encounter her at another library dinner, this time at the Hilton?"

"No."

"Mrs. Fratt—"

"It was a Stanford dinner."

"I'm sorry?"

"The dinner at the Hilton, it was a Stanford alumni dinner."

"I see. And when was this, Mrs. Fratt?"

"It was . . . I believe it was sometime in the spring of 1988."

Brownell looked up at the woman. "This was soon after Poe Fratt had left you?"

"A few months later, yes."

"And Joan Clark," he said, continuing to press on in his deceptively calm, courteous, low-key style, "was she alone at this dinner?"

"No."

"No," the prosecutor repeated quietly. "And who was she with, Mrs. Fratt?"

"She was with Poe."

"I see."

Brownell leaned against the railing. He stood there silently for a moment, seemingly digesting this new information. But of course, he was digesting nothing: Like Dowd, he knew never to ask a question when you didn't already know the answer. The pause was part of the young prosecutor's own unique style—a chance to let the jury absorb the fact and the implications, a chance to let them watch the witness grow uncomfortable in the unnerving silence.

"And isn't it true," Brownell finally continued, "that you and your husband had angry words about bringing Joan Clark to the alumni dinner?"

"No, it is not."

"It is not?"

"No."

"You and your husband never argued about his taking Joan Clark to a dinner where many of your old friends would be attending?"

Louann Fratt looked away from the assistant D.A. for a moment. She seemed to be looking out the windows at the dark winter sky. Dowd realized, as he watched his client, that it was difficult to tell whether she found these memories painful or simply distasteful.

"I had planned to attend the dinner," she said finally, her gaze still on the bleak grayness outside. "Poe called our son William the day of the dinner. He told William that if I went to the dinner that night, it would be a disaster. He told him to tell me not to go."

"But you *did* go."

"Yes," she said, looking back at Brownell. "And I did talk with Poe at the dinner. But I did not have an argument with him."

"I see."

Brownell walked very slowly toward the counsel table, again seemingly lost in thought.

"Mrs. Fratt," he said at last, "did you know at that time that your husband and Joan Clark were having a . . . romantic relationship?"

Louann Fratt's chin raised slightly. "I assumed they were."

"And when," the prosecutor said, "did you start assuming that?"

"In the summer of 1987."

"Soon after your husband told you he was leaving you."

"I suppose so."

"But while he was still living with you."

"Yes."

Brownell nodded his head very slowly, appearing to ponder this. "And did that . . . relationship continue up until November of 1988, when you stabbed your husband to death?"

The woman sat there silently, just staring at the young prosecutor. Then she looked across the room at her attorney, seated at the counsel table.

Dowd knew she was looking to him for help. He knew she wanted him to protect her, to do something, anything. And as he looked at this woman desperately reaching for him, he wanted nothing more in life than to help her. But there was nothing he could do. If he tried to protect her by throwing up constant objections, the jury would resent the obvious obstructionist tactics. Worse, they would think —rightly—that he was giving his client breathing room, a chance to come up with a deceitful answer. Dowd could give her some protection from the prosecutor's cross-examination, but the cost would be too high. The fact was, Louann Fratt was on her own.

"Mrs. Fratt?" Brownell said.

The woman looked back at the assistant D.A.

"Did that relationship continue—"

"Yes," she said.

Brownell nodded. He turned, his eyes again on the floor, his hand holding his chin, as if he were lost in thought.

"Two days before you stabbed your husband," he said finally, "he was at a football game at Cornell, is that right?"

"Yes."

Here it comes, Dowd thought, feeling a sickening sense of helplessness as the drama slowly, inevitably unfolded.

"And your son Poe Junior was at that game?"

"I believe so, yes."

"Joan Clark was with your husband at that game, wasn't she?"

"I really couldn't say."

"I see." Brownell smiled again, an almost imperceptible smile but one that seemed dramatic on his normally serious, deadpan face. "Do you know the Gradys, by any chance? Jerry and Susan?"

"Yes, of course."

"How long have you known them?"

"For about twenty years. Jerry Grady was a classmate of Poe's, and we've spent many, many weekends together."

"At Cornell football games?"

"Yes, among other things. The Gradys always had a tail-gate party at the games."

"But *this* football weekend, your old friends were with your husband and his . . . girlfriend."

"I couldn't say."

"And with your son."

"I couldn't say."

Brownell turned, walked slowly away from the witness stand, his chin again resting in his right hand.

Here it comes. . . , thought Dowd again.

"Mrs. Fratt," the prosecutor said quietly, "did you talk with Susan Grady at any time after the football game?"

"I beg your pardon?"

"Did you talk with Susan Grady at any time after the football game?"

Dowd felt his heart quicken, felt it pounding against his chest. It was coming, and there was nothing he could do. Nothing.

"Yes, I did."

"Oh?" Brownell looked up at the witness. "When was this?"

"I don't know. I talk to her all the time, two or three times a week."

"Mrs. Fratt—"

"I believe it was on a Monday."

"On Monday?"

"Yes."

"And did you talk about the football game?"

"I believe we did. I seem to recall that she mentioned something about the tailgate party, something about a Hawaiian theme to the party."

"Did Susan Grady tell you that your husband had been to the game with Joan Clark?"

"I . . . I don't believe she mentioned Poe. I believe she said she had seen Poe Junior."

"And you didn't ask her anything about your husband, or Joan Clark?"

"No, I did not."

"This telephone call, Mrs. Fratt, this call where Susan Grady told you about the football game . . ."

"Yes?"

"This call took place on Monday."

"Yes, I believe I've already said that."

"November twenty-first."

"I believe so, yes."

"And it was later that same day that you went over to your husband's apartment."

"That night, yes."

"And stabbed him to death with a kitchen knife."

Louann Fratt clenched her jaw, looked away from the young man.

There it was, Dowd thought to himself. All neatly wrapped up and presented to the jury with a bright pink bow. The motive. The timing. All that was left was the opportunity. And this, Dowd knew, would be next.

Brownell walked over to the swinging gate. With his back to the witness stand, he studied the brass hinge for a moment, calmly running his fingers over the smooth metal.

"How did you get into your husband's apartment that evening, Mrs. Fratt?" he asked, his back still to her.

"How did I get in?"

"Yes."

"Why, Poe let me in. I believe I've already testified to that."

"Yes. And, as I understand it, you went over to his apartment at . . . what time was it?"

"About one o'clock, one-thirty."

"One-thirty in the morning."

"Yes."

"Alone."

"Yes."

"On the streets of New York."

Louann Fratt did not answer.

"Because . . ." Brownell slowly turned around to face the woman. "Because the man who had left you . . . wanted his mail."

Again Louann Fratt did not answer.

Brownell sighed deeply, then took the two or three steps to his chair.

"Did you have a key to your husband's apartment, Mrs. Fratt?"

"No, I certainly did not."

"You did not."

"No."

"Didn't you testify on direct, Mrs. Fratt, that you *un-locked* the door when you went back the second time?"

"I . . . Yes, I did. I unlocked the door."

"With what?"

"With a set of keys. An extra set Poe kept in his car."

The opportunity, Dowd realized with a sick feeling. The final nails in the coffin.

"You got this extra set of keys from your husband's car?"

"Yes, the Ford Taurus."

"And this was on your way back to his apartment the second time?"

"Yes."

"Where was this car," Brownell asked, the vaguely amused smile returning, "this Ford Taurus?"

"It was parked out in front of his apartment building. I remember I saw it, and I couldn't recall the combination. I thought I was going to faint, and I sat down on the curb. And then the combination came back to me."

"I see. And the spare set of keys, they were inside the car?"

"Yes, in a wooden box, in the trunk. He always kept them there, the spare keys and some cassettes."

"I assume this car, parked on the street late at night, was locked?"

"Yes, but it had a combination."

"A combination?"

"Yes, on the door. You enter the combination, and the door opens. And then you can get into the trunk, where the keys were."

"And you knew the combination?"

"Of course. I drove the car, too."

"I see. And this is what you did, to get into the apartment

the second time—entered the combination on the car door, opened the trunk, and got the keys?"

"Yes."

Dowd could see it coming. Worse, he realized, every one of the jurors could see it coming.

"Tell me, Mrs. Fratt, was the car parked in front when you came over the *first* time?"

"I believe so, yes. I recall thinking how lucky Poe was to have gotten such a good parking spot."

"Did your husband usually park his car in the street?"

"Not always in such a good location, but somewhere on the street, yes."

Brownell nodded, then walked slowly to the jury box. He stopped, looked at some of the jurors.

"Mrs. Fratt," he said quietly, still looking at the jurors, "do I understand, then, that you could have obtained a key to your husband's apartment whenever you wanted it?"

"Whenever I . . ." Louann Fratt had a quizzical look on her face, as if she did not understand the question.

"You could have gotten into your husband's apartment anytime that night you wanted," Brownell repeated, turning now to look at the woman. "Isn't that true, Mrs. Fratt?"

Louann shook her head. "No, I . . . I mean . . ." Again she looked across the room at Dowd, then back at the prosecutor. "I don't . . . I wouldn't . . ."

"Your husband was in his pajamas when you stabbed him, wasn't he, Mrs. Fratt?"

"He was . . . Yes, in his pajamas."

Brownell turned and began walking away from Louann Fratt, his dark brow furrowed deeply as if seriously considering this answer.

Dowd knew, of course, that the young prosecutor was simply giving the jury time to absorb the implications of this line of questioning. Brownell wanted the jurors to reach the obvious conclusions by themselves. A good trial lawyer was well aware that conclusions reached independently by jurors were far more deeply imbedded in their minds than those spelled out to them. And the conclusions here were all too clear: Louann Fratt, jealous, bitter, and furious over the football incident, and perhaps braced with a few drinks, had waited until her estranged husband would be asleep and had then walked to the parked car, taken the keys, slipped into the apartment, and, while he slept, stabbed him to death.

The assistant D.A. suddenly stopped, turned around. "Do you know a Deborah Emory, Mrs. Fratt?"

"Deborah? Of course."

"She is the wife of Meade Emory, one of your husband's best friends, is that right?"

"Yes. They're cousins, and they grew up together."

"You and Deborah Emory have known each other for quite some time, haven't you?"

"Yes," Louann Fratt said, shifting uncomfortably in the chair. "We've known each other for thirty years, for as long as I was married to Poe."

Where was this going? Dowd thought to himself. He knew of Meade Emory, and his activities in trying to organize friends and relatives against Louann. But what did his wife have to do with it?

"Where was Mrs. Emory living in the year before you stabbed your husband?" Brownell asked.

"In Seattle."

"And didn't you have a number of telephone conversations with Mrs. Emory during that year?"

"I may have. I don't really recall."

"You don't recall?"

"I don't recall."

"Isn't it a fact, Mrs. Fratt, that you called Deborah Emory on exactly ten occasions during that year?"

"I really don't recall."

"And isn't it a fact that during each of these calls, you told her how much you hated your husband?"

"No, it is not."

"And isn't it a fact, Mrs. Fratt, that you were usually intoxicated during these—"

"Objection!" Dowd yelled, jumping to his feet. He glared at Brownell, then looked at the judge. "May we approach the bench?"

"No, you may not," Goodman growled.

"But—"

"Objection is overruled," the judge said. "But I'll instruct the jury that the mere asking of a question does not give rise to any inference suggested by the question." Goodman looked down at Louann Fratt. "You will answer the question."

"The answer is no," she said.

Brownell nodded to himself again, then turned away from the witness. He walked along the railing separating him from the audience, his hand again trailing along the smooth dark wood.

"Mrs. Fratt," he said finally, "you haven't worked since 1959, isn't that true?"

"Nineteen fifty-nine?" She thought for a moment. "Yes, I believe that's true. Except for volunteer work, of course."

"You have not worked for about thirty years now."

"About that, yes," she said, a quizzical look again on her face.

"Since about the time you married Poe Fratt."

"Since shortly after that, yes."

"I assume it has been some time since your three children graduated from high school?"

"Yes."

"But you haven't chosen to work since then?"

"No, it wasn't—"

"When did the last of your three children move out of the apartment?"

"William moved out about a year ago."

"And you still have not chosen to work."

"No, I have not."

Dowd felt himself beginning to grow angry. Brownell was obviously trying to prejudice the jury by portraying Louann Fratt as a freeloader, a woman who married for money and then rode the gravy train. It was a cheap trick, and legally impermissible. But was it worth objecting to? Dowd wondered. Or would the tactic backfire against the prosecutor—especially among some of the female members of the jury?

"Mrs. Fratt," Brownell continued, "would you please describe for us the co-op you owned and lived in at the time you killed your husband?"

"Describe?"

"How many rooms does it have?"

"There are thirteen rooms."

"In fact, it takes up the entire floor of the building, doesn't it?"

"Yes."

"And the apartment that your husband lived in, the one he rented on Seventy-eighth, this was a small studio, wasn't it?"

"Yes, of course."

"Furnished?"

"Yes."

"In fact, when he left, he only took his clothes and his personal possessions, isn't that true?"

Dowd couldn't take it anymore.

"Objection!" he said loudly, again jumping to his feet. "May we *please* approach the bench!"

Goodman grumpily waved the two men toward him. Dowd and Brownell walked to the side of the bench farthest from the jury. When the court reporter had set up his machine on the bench next to them, Goodman looked at Dowd expectantly.

"My God, Your Honor," the lawyer said, straining to keep his voice down, "of what possible *relevance* is all of this?"

The judge looked at Brownell. "What is the purpose of asking her the dimensions of her apartment, Mr. Brownell?"

"Your Honor," the prosecutor said in a hushed voice, "I want to establish the deceased's actions during the year after the separation, the financial support he gave her."

Dowd looked up in despair. "Oh, for Christ's sake!"

"Mr. Dowd!" Goodman barked. Then he thought for a moment. "I will allow it," he said finally. "But let's not go overboard."

The reporter and the two lawyers returned to their positions.

"You may answer," Goodman said to Louann Fratt.

"Yes," she said. "He took only his personal things."

"Mrs. Fratt, once your husband moved out of the apartment, how did you support yourself?"

"Poe gave me a certain amount of money."

"How much is 'a certain amount'?"

"I believe it was two thousand dollars a month."

"Didn't he increase that amount a few months after moving out?"

"Yes. I believe it increased to thirty-five hundred a month."

"And this was over and above paying the mortgage on the co-op, and other expenses?"

"Not everything. I had to pay for the cleaning lady, for example."

The vague smile crossed the assistant D.A.'s face again. "The cleaning lady," he repeated.

"Yes."

Brownell turned away from the witness, walked quietly toward the huge television camera that was trained on him. He looked around the courtroom at the sea of faces. Some of the faces were fixed on him, waiting anxiously for the next question, the next blow, the next revelation. Others still looked fixedly at the figure seated rigidly on the witness stand, much as passengers in a car stare in morbid fascination as they slowly pass by the scene of a fatal accident.

"Mrs. Fratt," Brownell said without turning around, "do you recall the police officers testifying that they found a bloody nightgown in the bag you had taken to your husband's apartment?"

Dowd only half heard the question. The prosecutor's voice had begun to fade into the distance. He could still hear it, and he could hear Louann Fratt's answers, but they seemed far away, very far away. The words were there, in the back of his mind, waiting to set off a trigger that would cause him to jump to his feet with an objection. But the lawyer's mind was drifting now to how to go about picking up the pieces caused by the havoc Daniel Brownell was wreaking on his client.

Dr. Lois Veronen had flown in from South Carolina the previous day, and was waiting at her hotel room for a phone call from Debbie Cohen to come to the courthouse. Dowd figured Brownell's cross-examination would take the rest of the afternoon, so there was no reason to make the psychologist wait outside in the corridor. He would put her on the stand tomorrow morning.

"... washed my hair, I believe. I'm not really sure."

"Is it your testimony, Mrs. Fratt, that you don't even know whether you ..."

The key was the knife, Dowd thought to himself. He *had* to convince the jury that Louann Fratt's unlikely explanation of why she took a knife to her estranged husband's apartment was true—that, hard as it was to believe, this woman *always* carried a kitchen knife at night in a bag for protection.

"... and there was blood all over the sweatsuit, so I threw it in the washer...."

The voice droned on in the distance as Dowd thought of another witness waiting in another hotel room. His surprise witness—one who had just flown in all the way from San Francisco to testify. Who could corroborate Louann Fratt's story about the knife. Who could very possibly save his client's life.

"... can't really recall."

"Well, Mrs. Fratt," another voice was saying, "can you explain to us how the shoes got into the bag?"

"I don't recall ..."

CHAPTER 26

Dowd slouched in the chair, sleepy-eyed and sipping from a Styrofoam cup of hot black coffee, as he watched Judge Goodman finish reading the documents spread across his desk. At 8:45 on this cold, dark morning, the big Irishman was still only half awake. He had stayed up most of the previous night preparing his closing argument and putting together the defense set of jury instructions.

Dowd looked over at Brownell, standing at the window of the judge's chambers, his darkly handsome features impassive as he stared out into the shadowy skyline. He wondered what kind of a night his enemy had had. Then he looked back at the judge.

At the conclusion of Louann Fratt's cross-examination the previous evening, Goodman had told the two lawyers he wanted their proposed jury instructions on his desk by the following morning. When both sides had rested and the lawyers had given their closing arguments, or summations, the judge would read a long, complex series of instructions to the jury, telling them what the applicable law was and how they were to apply it. The judge would decide *which* instructions to read to the jury; some were required to be given by law,

312

others would be given because the judge wanted to, and still others were instructions drafted and proposed by the prosecution and defense. These proposed instructions tended to interpret the law in ways favorable to the side offering them, of course, and the judge had to decide which ones to give and which to reject.

Dowd knew that the jury would ignore most of the instructions: They were simply too lengthy and technical for the average nonlawyer to understand. Very few jurors could maintain interest and comprehension through a monotonous reading of thirty-two pages of deadly legalese. But the instructions were still critically important. For although the jury might not pay attention to or understand the judge's reading, they *would* pay attention to Dowd and Brownell when they gave their closing arguments. It was during these arguments that the two men would present the facts and explain the law most favorable to their side. And it was the instructions selected by the judge and read to the jury that determined what the law was that had to be followed—and what the lawyers could argue.

The most important instruction that Dowd was now proposing to Judge Goodman related to self-defense. Under the old law, the use of deadly force—such as a knife—was justified only if the attacker was also using deadly force. However, New York had recently joined a number of other states in revising this to permit the use of deadly force to counter either deadly force *or* rape. Without an instruction reflecting the revised law, Louann Fratt would very quickly be convicted: Dowd would not be able to argue that the stabbing was self-defense, since even by her own testimony Poe Fratt had not attacked her with a deadly weapon (although it was remotely arguable that he was about to stab her with a letter opener).

Testimony in the trial was still not over, of course. Dowd had two witnesses yet to call, and the prosecution would then be permitted to offer further evidence as part of its rebuttal case. But judges and lawyers always had to think two steps ahead, or the trial would proceed in fits and starts. Dowd had spent much of the night working on his closing argument, despite the fact that the time for giving the summations was still a long way off, and there was a lot of evidence yet to be offered that would affect the summation. But the defense lawyer knew that he could not afford to wait. Brownell could rest his rebuttal case at any moment, possibly not even present one, which would force Dowd to immediately give his argument. From years of experience, however, Dowd had developed the ability to draft a summation that was flexible enough to adapt to unexpected developments in trial.

As Dowd sipped at the scalding coffee, he thought once again, as he often did, how very much a trial was like a play. The jury and audience watched as the carefully staged drama was acted out for them. But the public never saw what went on behind the curtain. They never saw the playwright laboring over the script, never saw the auditions and casting, the building of the sets, the endless hours of rehearsal, the lighting, the props, the costumes. . . .

He thought again of the nearly sleepless night he had just spent. It was always like this during a trial—long, hard days filled with tension and combat, followed by even longer nights preparing for the next day. It was no wonder that so few criminal lawyers lasted more than five or ten years. But the public never saw any of that. The public never saw the hundreds of hours of preparation before trial; they never saw the sleepless nights during trial, patching up wounds and scrambling frantically to get ready for the next day's battle. The public only saw a fresh, well-rested Perry Mason magically pulling brilliant cross-examination out of thin air, then suddenly turning to the jury and spontaneously delivering a stunning summation.

Dowd smiled to himself at the image of the fictional lawyer. Where the hell did the television audience think Ol' Perry got all those clever questions and arguments from? And *when*?

"All right," Goodman growled, looking up from quickly scanning the proposed instructions submitted by both Dowd and Brownell. Later, with more careful reading, he would decide which, if any, to read to the jury. "Anything else?"

Dowd shook his head.

"No, Your Honor," Brownell said, returning to the second chair arranged in front of Goodman's desk.

"All right." Goodman looked at Dowd. "How much longer for the defense?"

The lawyer shrugged. "A day, maybe. I've got two more witnesses. They're both waiting out in the corridor."

"This Dr. . . . What's her name?"

"Veronen," Dowd said. "Dr. Lois Veronen."

"That syndrome stuff."

"Uh-huh."

Goodman nodded, a look of disgust on his face. "And . . ."

"And I've got a corroboration witness."

Dowd took another sip from the white plastic cup, glanced to his left at Brownell. The expression on the assistant D.A.'s face had not changed; he was trying hard not to look too interested. Dowd looked back at the judge. He knew Goodman had no right to force the defense to divulge who its witnesses were or what they would testify to. But Dowd also knew it was time for yet one more tough decision.

Louann Fratt had testified that she routinely carried a knife in a bag for protection when walking the dog late at night. Dowd had tried to find some way to corroborate this, of course—someone who had seen his client carrying a knife in a bag long before November 21. There was no such witness. However, Louann did remember a friend who had flown out from San Francisco to stay with her for a few days. And she remembered that when she was getting the dog ready to go out late one evening, the friend's daughter expressed surprise at her lack of fear of New York's streets. Louann had explained to the daughter that she always carried a knife with her. And this was eleven months before the death of Poe Fratt.

Dowd had tried to ask his client on the stand about the conversation, but Judge Goodman had sustained an objection. The testimony would be self-serving hearsay, he had ruled. So Dowd had contacted the daughter in San Francisco, and she had agreed to fly out and testify to Louann's statement. Which now presented the defense lawyer with both a tactical and an ethical problem.

Underlying the problem was a legal question: Was Louann's statement still hearsay, though clearly no longer self-serving, if the friend's *daughter* testified to it? Given this, Dowd realized he had a more immediate dilemma: Should he bring the problem up before putting her on the stand, or wait for Brownell to object during her testimony?

Tactically, of course, it was far better simply to put the daughter on and ask the question. First, Brownell might not even object; tipping off the prosecutor by raising the issue in advance, however, almost guaranteed an objection. Second, as every lawyer knows, the question itself was almost as damaging as the answer. Asking a question like, "Didn't Mrs. Fratt tell you in January of 1988 that she always carried a knife?" inferred the facts it contained; many jurors would accept the inference even if there was no answer because of a sustained objection.

Ethically, however, Dowd was well aware that a lawyer was not supposed to offer evidence he knew was probably inadmissible. This placed the ethical question in a gray area, for although Dowd felt the answer was admissible, he knew the judge's previous ruling placed the question very much in issue.

"This witness," Dowd said finally, "will corroborate Mrs. Fratt's testimony that she always carried a knife when she went out at night with the dog."

Goodman said nothing.

"She will testify that during a visit to Mrs. Fratt's apartment," the lawyer continued, "eleven months before the stabbing, Mrs. Fratt told her that she always carried a knife when she walked the dog at night."

The room was still silent.

"As you may recall, Judge," Dowd said, "I tried to ask my client about that statement during direct examination. It was objected to, and you sustained it." He took another sip of coffee. "Now I have the witness she made the statement to."

Goodman suddenly shook his head. "No," he said, "it's not appropriate. You can't ask that question."

"What?"

"You can't ask that question. It's hearsay."

"Judge," Dowd said, growing angry, "my client made this statement to an independent witness. She made it eleven months before the stabbing. Eleven months before there was any motive to make up a story . . ."

Goodman shook his head again. "A witness can't get up on the stand and testify that Mrs. Fratt told her that she carries a knife because that is hearsay, and it is not admissible."

"This woman has flown all the way out here from San Francisco, and she's waiting outside."

"It is hearsay."

"Judge . . ." Dowd looked at Brownell, then back at Good-man. "The prosecutor has inferred in his cross-exam that this was all a story, that it's ridiculous to believe she carried a knife. And he's going to say that in argument. So he's opening the door—"

"Mr. Brownell is free to comment upon any of the evidence, counsel," the judge said sternly. "He cannot, of course, get up and say, 'She never told anybody that she carried a knife.'" He looked at the prosecutor. "I won't permit that." Then he looked back at Dowd. "But I'm not going to tell him how to try his case. If he wants to argue that it's ridiculous to believe that the defendant always went out alone and carried a knife in a bag . . . Well, he can say whatever he wants to say."

"Judge—"

"You can call any witness you want. If the witness says *she* advised Mrs. Fratt to carry a knife, that's fine. But she can't testify as to what Mrs. Fratt told her. That's hearsay."

"This witness—"

"Anything else?" Goodman said, looking at Brownell, then back at Dowd.

"No, Your Honor," the prosecutor said.

"Good," Goodman said, slamming his outstretched hands palm down on the desk. "Then we can finish this afternoon." He looked again at Brownell. "Rebuttal?"

"Yes," Brownell said. He shrugged his shoulders. "A couple of days maybe, no more."

"Fine." Goodman stood up from behind his desk and, his black robe streaming behind him, began to hurry out of the room. "Let's get the jury in."

Brownell and Dowd quietly rose from their chairs. They glanced at each other briefly, then followed the judge out of the haven of chambers and into the milling tumult of the courtroom.

Dowd felt as if he had hit bottom. First, he thought to himself, there was Poe Jr. and the "other woman." Then he had lost Dr. Rosen. And then the hatchet job on Dr. Veronen.

Followed by his own client providing the prosecution with proof of motive and opportunity. And now this, his corroboration witness knocked out of the game before she even got in. What else could go wrong with a defense case?

The crowd in the courtroom, conditioned by now to Goodman's threatening glare upon mounting the bench, quickly took their seats and quieted down. The reporters pulled out their notepads, and the television camera began scanning for a target. Within seconds, the jurors were filing in behind the bailiff and finding their chairs in the jury box.

"Call your next witness," Goodman said to no one in particular.

"Dr. Lois Joan Veronen," Dowd said, standing next to his seated client.

He looked across the table at Debbie Cohen. The young lawyer sensed something wrong, and there was a question on her face. But Dowd just frowned at her darkly, then looked away.

The doors at the rear of the courtroom opened, and Dowd glanced back as a woman walked in. A stunningly beautiful woman. The psychology professor whom the lawyer had never actually met was a classic Finnish beauty, complete with pale blue eyes, alabaster skin, delicately chiseled features, and fine blond hair that swept across her forehead and then cascaded straight to her shoulders. At perhaps forty years of age, Lois Veronen looked more like a gracefully aging fashion model than a renowned academic.

Yet, the Nordic beauty of the woman was in odd contrast to her clothing. She wore a plain black two-piece business suit, stark and somber, with a simple white blouse and functional low-heeled black shoes. A small gold brooch off her left shoulder was the only concession to appearance. The psychologist seemed intent on doing everything possible to hide her natural beauty. Dowd wondered if perhaps she had tired of that beauty causing her not to be taken seriously.

Dr. Veronen followed the bailiff uncertainly up the aisle, a ten-inch-thick file tucked tightly under one arm. She smiled hesitantly, trying to ignore the silent stares of the audience and the huge glass eye of the television camera trained on her. Dowd opened the swinging gate for her. She looked quickly at him, then at the jury as she passed them on her way to the witness stand. The psychologist gave the immediate impression of a competent professional, but one who was a bit nervous at the prospect of testifying in court for the first time.

After taking the oath, Dr. Veronen looked around the courtroom, not sure what she was supposed to do next. Then she saw the stranger who had opened the gates walking slowly toward her, a friendly smile on his face.

"Good morning, Dr. Veronen," Dowd said.

"Good morning," she replied with a polite nod, thinking this must be the lawyer she had talked to.

"Doctor, you are an associate professor of psychology, is that correct?"

"Yes, I am."

"And this is at Winthrop College in Rock Hill, South Carolina?"

"Yes."

"Would you please give us some idea of your educational background."

"Of course." Veronen looked directly at the jurors. "I received my B.A. from Marquette University, then my master's and a Ph.D. in clinical psychology from North Texas State. After that, I . . ."

The defense lawyer proceeded to "lay the foundation" for his expert witness—to ask a long series of largely boring questions concerning the witness's education, experience, publications, honors, professional memberships, and so on. Once the individual's expertise was sufficiently established to qualify her legally as an expert, a different set of evidentiary rules kicked into gear which permitted the attorney to ask questions that would not be permitted other witnesses.

When Dowd had finished qualifying Dr. Veronen, he launched into the area of her nationally recognized expertise.

"Now, Doctor, what does the term 'rape trauma syndrome' mean?"

"Rape trauma syndrome . . ." Lois Veronen sat up, cleared her throat. She was off and running. "This is a term that refers to a cluster of characteristics, characteristics that are commonly found among the victims of rape."

"Uh-huh."

The psychologist glanced quickly back at the lawyer. Then she returned to the jury, much as if she were lecturing a class of graduate students. "The phenomenon was first studied by Ann Burgess and Linda Holmstrom, in Boston. One is a nurse, the other a sociologist. They noticed that rape victims being treated in hospital emergency rooms appeared to have similar symptoms. And later, in subsequent visits, there were still similar symptoms. These symptoms related to physical, psychological, and social dysfunction. This initial work by Burgess and Holmstrom was followed by—"

"Objection, Your Honor," Brownell said.

"Yes," Goodman said. "Beyond the scope of the question."

"Well, Doctor," Dowd said, turning to the jury, "can you tell us whether there has been research done into the response of victims of sexual assault?"

"Yes. Since 1979—"

"Objection," Brownell said again.

"Sustained," Goodman said. "She has answered the question. Next question."

"Doctor," Dowd said, a touch of anger creeping into his voice, "has there been research done on the incidence of women not reporting the fact that they were a victim of sexual assault?"

"Yes. It is estimated that somewhere between three and ten times as many rapes occur as are actually reported. The reasons for this—"

"Objection," the prosecutor said.

Dowd raised his hand in acknowledgment before Goodman could say anything. He knew that Brownell and Goodman were letting him know early in the game that they were not going to let him cut this witness loose. The judge had severely limited what she would be permitted to testify to, and he would not let her ramble on. If Dowd wanted *any* of her testimony in, he would have to keep very tight reins on her.

"I'll rephrase the question," Dowd said. He looked at the psychologist. "This research on the incidence of reporting sexual assault . . . What are the specific reasons that have been found for the high incidence of failing to report?"

"There are a number of reasons," Dr. Veronen said, looking now uncertainly at the lawyer. "A belief by the victim that she will not be believed, fear of the victim, lack of police sensitivity . . . But one common reason is that the woman simply does not acknowledge that she has been raped."

"Acknowledge?"

"Yes. Rape, or attempted rape, is an abhorrent, violent, painful experience. Many women will simply repress the incident, or engage in minimization. They will block it out, deny to themselves that it ever happened. So, first, a woman must acknowledge that she has been a victim of rape. And many will not."

"Uh-huh."

"The act of rape is also an extremely degrading experience. Commonly, there is a sense of shame, of guilt. A powerful sense that it was . . . 'dirty.' The woman is ashamed, and wants desperately to forget the experience, to deny it ever happened. Again, there is repression, denial. And the rape is not reported."

"Could you explain this 'repression,' Doctor."

"Yes. Repression, or 'blocking,' is a protective mechanism, an unconscious process of self-protection. You might be more familiar with the term 'amnesia,' or simply 'going blank.' But the phenomenon is essentially the same."

"And that is?"

"Unconsciously, the victim protects herself, her emotional state, by simply blocking the memory from her mind. It is erased, in a sense, perhaps not permanently, but until her emotional condition is better able to handle the traumatic reality. Several hours after the incident, or several months, it may all come back. Or maybe only some of it, a bit at a time."

"You also mentioned 'minimization,' Doctor."

"Yes. This is a form of denial. Rather than being completely blocked out, the incident is unconsciously recalled or acknowledged in a way that minimizes the trauma. Many women, for example, when they are asked if they were physically attacked, will answer yes. But if they are asked if they were *raped*, they will say no."

Dowd nodded thoughtfully, then walked slowly away from the psychologist. When he reached the audience railing, he stopped and turned.

"You've talked about psychological reactions to being raped."

"Yes?"

"What about a woman's reaction to an *attempted* rape? What does the research show about that?"

"It's the same," Dr. Veronen said. "The research shows that an attempted sexual assault and a completed sexual assault are both experienced by the woman in much the same way. There is no difference in the severity of the trauma. It is the violence, the perceived threat to life, that constitutes the trauma, not the act of sexual penetration."

Dowd nodded again, then looked at the jury. Some of the faces were riveted on the psychologist. A few of the jurors, however, seemed to have tuned out.

"Dr. Veronen," he continued, "are there any *physiological* reasons why a victim of an attempted rape may not have a very good memory of the incident, and of the events surrounding it?"

"Yes, of course."

"And those are?"

The psychologist again turned to her students in the jury box. "Rape is perceived by the victim as a threat to her life. And certain physiological changes go on within any person in a life-threatening situation. A man, confronted by an armed robber, for example. A person involved in an automobile accident. The reaction is the same: The heart speeds up, the adrenaline shoots into the system, the blood is pumped away from the brain and out into the arms and legs. This is known as the 'fight or flight' response."

"Uh-huh."

"During that emergency response, perception is impaired. The individual does not always process events in a clear, coherent fashion. This is partly from the shunting of blood away from the brain, partly from the adrenaline's acceleration of physiological functions. Physiologically, the body's resources are marshaled to meet the threat, and perception and memory suffer. The person may only perceive and later recall isolated images, incomplete details."

Finished, Dr. Veronen looked back at the big man in the baggy gray suit.

"Okay," Dowd said. He walked over to the counsel table, placed his hands firmly on the back of his chair. "Doctor, what does the research show about repeated sexual assaults between the same two individuals?"

"I'm sorry?"

"Where women are raped by a husband or other person with whom they have some relationship, and then voluntarily put themselves in a position of risk with that same person again?"

"Yes, yes," Dr. Veronen said, turning again to the jury. "There has been research. Irene Freeze. Julie Doren has done a study. Haneke and Shields. Bowaker in Milwaukee . . ."

"And what does that research show?"

"There are several phenomena which operate to keep the woman locked into a relationship. One of those is what is called the 'cycle of violence.' Basically, after a sexual assault—"

"Objection," Brownell said.

Dowd looked up at the judge. "Your Honor—"

"Sustained," Goodman said. "Not relevant."

Dowd looked down at the table, trying to find some way to get the critical evidence past the objections and to the jury.

"Doctor," he said finally, "does research show what the psychological factors are which cause women to place themselves in jeopardy again?"

"The most important factors—"

"Objection."

"Sustained." Goodman looked down at the defense lawyer. "It is not responsive."

"Doctor," Dowd repeated doggedly, "how is it that a woman who has been victimized can voluntarily place herself in a situation where it can happen again?"

"Objection."

"Sustained." Goodman looked at the witness. "You can merely answer whether there has been research that shows women do place themselves in jeopardy, but you cannot say why."

Dr. Veronen nodded, a look of confusion on her face. "Yes, there is research in that area."

"Let me ask you this," Dowd said. "Is there research explaining why they do it?"

"Yes."

"And is that related to blocking, repression, and minimization?"

"Objection."

"Sustained."

Dowd spun around angrily and faced the judge. "May we approach the bench?"

"No," Goodman replied, "you may not."

"In light of your rulings," Dowd said, jerking his chair out from the table, "I have no further questions."

Goodman looked at the assistant D.A.

Brownell rose, walked across to the jury box. "Good morning, Dr. Veronen."

"Good morning," the psychologist said with a flash of a smile.

"Doctor, you are testifying to some *general* findings about rape, is that correct?"

"What I am testifying to is the scientific research that has been conducted on sexual assault victims over some twelve years."

"The fact is," the prosecutor said, turning to look at some of the jurors, "you have never examined the defendant in this case, have you?"

"No, I have not."

Brownell walked toward the witness stand, his left hand trailing along the jury railing. "Tell me, Doctor, has there been any research in the area of women *falsely* reporting sexual assaults?"

"There has been some research."

"And false reporting is done for a number of reasons, isn't that correct?"

"The incidence is so low as to be almost nonexistent."

"Oh?" Brownell stared at the psychologist. "And what about in marital relationships, say in cases of child custody battles? Are you saying that the research shows that false reporting does *not* take place where marital problems exist in a relationship?"

"Clinically," Dr. Veronen said reluctantly, "the phenomena have been reported."

"Thank you, Doctor," Brownell said, walking back to his seat. "I have nothing further."

"Doctor," Dowd said, almost jumping up, "would you be *willing* to examine the defendant?"

"Objection," Brownell said.

"Sustained," Goodman said.

Dowd sat down. "Nothing further."

The judge looked at Dr. Veronen. "You may be excused now." As the psychologist stepped down gracefully from the witness stand, Goodman looked at Dowd. "Call your next witness."

Dowd rose to his feet. He and Veronen exchanged brief glances as the woman walked past him. He knew the psychologist had to be completely confused: Why had she not been permitted to tell the jurors the truth? Welcome to *Alice in Wonderland*, Doctor, Dowd thought bitterly to himself.

Dowd looked up at the judge, then across at the jury. "The defense rests," he said simply, then sat down.

As the camera followed the beautiful Dr. Veronen down the aisle and out of the courtroom, Goodman looked at the prosecutor. "Rebuttal?"

Brownell rose to his feet. With an almost imperceptible smile, he said, "The People call . . . Jean Ayer."

Dowd was perplexed. Jean Ayer? He could not recall the name. There was nothing in any of the police reports about any Jean Ayer. He was quite sure none of the witnesses had ever mentioned the name. He looked across the table at Debbie Cohen. She looked back, shrugged slightly. Who was Jean Ayer? What was Brownell pulling out of his hat?

Dowd knew that the young assistant D.A. had been sandbagging him. He knew that he had put on a skeleton case-in-chief, holding back his bigger guns until after the defense had taken its best shot. Dowd fully expected to see Joan Clark called as a "rebuttal" witness. Maybe Susan Grady. Possibly an officer or two to contradict Louann Fratt's testimony. But who was this Jean Ayer that Brownell had been keeping in reserve?

What Dowd did not know was that the most important witness in the entire trial was about to testify.

Brownell had found a witness to the stabbing.

CHAPTER 27

The doors to the courtroom opened. A small, stocky woman in her forties with short gray hair walked in. She was wearing a midlength gray skirt and a plain white cotton shirt, with black walking shoes and black stockings. A small leather purse strapped across her chest completed the no-frills effect of a Catholic girls' school uniform.

The woman walked quickly down the aisle, pushed open the swinging gate, and strode confidently toward the witness stand as if she owned it. There was a practical, no-nonsense air about this plain, prim little woman. More than anything else, she reminded one of a humorless Mary Poppins.

When she reached the witness stand, she turned immediately and raised her right hand as if on command.

The clerk nodded. "Do you swear to tell the truth, the whole truth, and nothing but the truth, so help you God?"

"Of course," the woman said.

"Please state your full name, spelling the last."

"My name is Jean Ayer," she said, inspecting the witness chair as she settled herself into it. "That's spelled A-Y-E-R."

She looked up at the jurors seated in the box, studying each of them as if they were awaiting inspection.

"Mrs. Ayer," Brownell said, walking toward her.

Her gaze shifted to the prosecutor, studying him as well. "*Miss* Ayer," she said.

"Excuse me. Miss Ayer. Would you please tell us how you are employed?"

"I am a freelance translator. And I'm presently working on a graduate degree at Columbia."

"And where do you iive, Miss Ayer?"

"Fifty-two East Seventy-eighth Street."

Poe Fratt's address, Dowd thought. This woman lived in the same building as Poe Fratt. Had she been living there when he died?

"What apartment number?"

"9A."

"When did you move into that apartment?"

"November third, 1988."

"I see," the assistant D.A. said. "Now, what floor is your apartment on?"

"The ninth floor."

"And how many other apartments are there on that floor?"

"Four."

"What are the numbers of those apartments, Miss Ayer?"

"Mine is 9A. Next to me is 9B. . . ."

She lived next door to Poe Fratt. She had moved in on November 3—eighteen days before the stabbing. What had this woman seen that night?

". . . At the back end of the hall are 9C and 9D."

"So . . . your apartment is right next to apartment 9B, is that right?"

"Correct," she said. "In fact, our doors are approximately five feet from each other."

"Five feet from each other," Brownell repeated. "Then I assume there is only one wall which separates your apartment from 9B?"

"A very *thin* wall," the woman said.

Brownell walked toward Jean Ayer, then reached behind the witness chair and pulled out the same easel he had used before, this time with a large sheet of plain white paper tacked onto it. He handed a black felt marker to the woman.

"Miss Ayer, would you please step down here and draw a diagram of the ninth floor for the jury?"

The woman got out of the chair, took the marker, and quickly began sketching a floor plan.

"This is 9A," she said, drawing "9A" on one apartment, "where I live."

"Would you please indicate where apartment 9B is?"

"Right . . . here," she said, drawing "9B" on the adjacent apartment.

Judge Goodman looked down from his bench at the drawing. Then he looked at the jury. "Ladies and gentlemen," he said, "I will instruct you that this is just to show approximate locations. This drawing is not to scale."

Jean Ayer quickly looked up at the judge. "No," she said indignantly, "but I think the scale is pretty good."

There was loud laughter from the audience.

"Please, madam," Goodman said, "don't volunteer."

The woman shrugged, then turned back to the prosecutor.

"You may take your seat," Brownell said.

Jean Ayer sat back down in the witness chair, then again looked around, her chin held high.

"Miss Ayer," Brownell continued, "had you met the occupant of apartment 9B?"

"No."

"Did there come a time when you learned what his name was?"

"Fratt."

"And what about the other two apartments?"

"9C was occupied by a Melinda Pillon. 9D was vacant."

"I see. Now, I'd like to call your attention to the evening of November twenty-first of last year."

"Yes."

"This was about three weeks after you moved into your apartment?"

"Yes."

"What were you doing that evening?"

"I was at the Nineteenth Precinct station house."

"At the station house."

"Yes. I was an auxiliary police officer. I logged in at seven o'clock, and logged out at eleven."

A bloody auxiliary police officer, Dowd thought to himself. Why was he not surprised? He leaned forward slightly, trying to hear everything this woman was saying without giving the jury the impression that he was particularly concerned with her testimony. He was listening for every subtle nuance, looking for any expression or body language that might give away deceit or uncertainty. The only problem, he realized, was that there was absolutely nothing subtle or uncertain about Jean Ayer. She was direct, blunt, and completely confident.

"And after eleven o'clock?" the prosecutor continued.

"I came home."

"And then?"

"I watched television. I watched *Casablanca* on PBS."

"At some point that evening you went to bed, is that right?"

"Correct. It must have been around midnight."

"And where is your bed, Miss Ayer? Where in the apartment?"

"I have a Murphy bed. It folds down from a free-standing arrangement in the middle of the room."

"This is a studio apartment, like 9B next door?"

"Correct."

"So the bed is in the main room, the living room?"

"Correct."

"Near the wall adjoining apartment 9B?"

"Correct."

"All right," Brownell said, turning away from the witness. He dragged his hand along the smooth wood railing as he walked past the jury. "Did there come a time that night when you were awakened?"

"Yes."

"Can you tell us when this was?"

"It was at two-twenty A.M."

Brownell smiled knowingly. "How do you know that, Miss Ayer?"

"I looked at my watch."

"And where was your watch?"

"I always wear my watch to bed."

It fits, Dowd thought to himself again. Something caught his attention out of the corner of his eye. Debbie Cohen was pushing a document across the table toward him. Dowd picked up the document, glanced at it. It was an N.Y.P.D. follow-up report. Made out by a Detective Ferrell. An interview with . . .

Dowd suddenly sat straight up. He was holding a police report of an interview with Jean Ayer. Where had it come from? He looked across the table at Debbie Cohen. She shrugged slightly, looked at Brownell, then back at Dowd. Dowd knew she could not say or do anything to attract the jury's attention, but he badly wanted to know where the report had come from. He studied it again. It was a short report, with very little in it. Had he overlooked it in the piles of paperwork he had had to sift through in the previous months? Had Brownell held it back until the last minute?

"Now, Miss Ayer," the prosecutor said slowly, "can you tell us just exactly what it was that woke you up at two-twenty that morning?"

"A door shutting."

"A door shutting."

"Yes. The door to apartment 9B."

"You have heard the door to 9B close before?"

"I have."

"So you are familiar with how it sounds?"

"I am."

"And what was the next thing you heard, Miss Ayer?"

"I heard a man say, 'Hey, hey.' "

Dowd realized there was no time to find out where the report came from. The witness was on the stand and the only potential weapon Dowd had was the piece of paper in his hand. As so often happened in the course of a trial, the lawyer found himself trying to do two things at once—each of them critical. While keeping one ear carefully tuned to the testimony, he quickly read through the document, trying to find some ammunition to use on cross-examination.

"And then?" Brownell asked.

"You want to hear what I heard next?"

An amused smile crossed the young prosecutor's face. "Yes."

"Then I heard a door shut again. Then again, it shut again. And then I heard feet running."

"Feet running."

"Yes."

"I see." Brownell looked at the jurors in silence, then turned to the witness. "Miss Ayer, could you tell us where you heard the male voice coming from? The one that said, 'Hey, hey'?"

"It was coming from the direction of 9B." The woman paused. "It was either 'hey, hey,' or 'here, here.'"

"Did you hear a male voice say anything else during this time?"

"No."

"Nothing like, 'You're not getting out of here alive'?"

Jean Ayer shook her head pugnaciously. "No."

Brownell nodded slowly. "How much time passed between when you heard the door first open, and when you heard the voice say, 'Hey, hey'?"

"Less than a minute."

"Less than a minute."

"Yes."

"And how much time passed between when you heard the voice, and when you heard the door shut?"

"Two minutes."

"And between that, and the door shutting the second time?"

"Seconds."

"Now, you say you heard footsteps running."

"Correct."

"Could you tell in what direction they were running?"

"From 9B to the fire door."

"Where is the fire door?"

"Right across the hall from 9B."

"There is an elevator in that building, isn't there, Miss Ayer?"

"There is."

"And where is the elevator door on your floor?"

"Right across from my apartment."

"Can you normally hear the elevator doors open and close, from inside your apartment?"

"I can. In fact, it sometimes keeps me awake, makes me lose sleep."

"And when you heard these running footsteps, you never heard any elevator doors opening or closing soon afterwards?"

"No."

"They ran to the fire door, not to the elevator?"

"Correct."

"Now," Brownell said, looking at the jurors, "did you hear anything else?"

"No."

"At any time did you hear a dog barking?"

"No."

"Did you hear a woman's voice?"

"No."

"You heard nothing that sounded like, 'Let me go, I've got a knife'?"

She shook her head again. "No."

"And what did you do after hearing the footsteps?"

"I went back to sleep."

The assistant D.A. walked over to the swinging gate and looked out over the audience. Seated almost in front of him were the three Fratt children, Laura, Poe, Jr., and William. They were all in the pew staring straight ahead, their faces empty of expression.

Brownell turned back to the witness. "Did there come a time when you woke up again that night, Miss Ayer?"

"Yes."

"When was that?"

"Four o'clock."

"And what caused you to wake up?"

"I heard a door being broken down."

"Where was this?"

"At first, I thought it was my door. But it was the door to 9B."

"Thank you, Miss Ayer," Brownell said, walking back to his chair. "No further questions."

Dowd rose slowly to his feet. He realized that Jean Ayer's

testimony had been devastating. Brownell had produced a witness to the stabbing—if not an eyewitness, then an "*ear*witness." Worse, she was a disinterested witness with no apparent motive to lie. And she had testified that there had been no sounds of a struggle, no threats by Poe Fratt, no protests yelled out by Louann. She had testified that the incident took place exactly as Brownell was theorizing it: a silent entry, the surprised exclamation of a man being stabbed in his bed, and a quick and silent retreat.

Dowd had his work cut out for him.

As the defense lawyer slowly walked toward the jury box, he was still trying to decide how to deal with this tough little woman. He knew she would pugnaciously refuse to be budged. She had been clear, concise, and certain during her testimony. There was no room for error. And that, Dowd suddenly realized, was the answer.

If there was a key to Jean Ayer, he decided, it was that very attitude of absolute certainty. *Nobody* could be that precise, that confident. Human beings were simply not that infallible in their perceptions and memories. But this woman was trying hard to appear that way. Why?

Dowd sensed that Jean Ayer was a sad figure—a lonely, frightened, aging spinster who wanted to be noticed, to contribute, to feel important. That was why she had volunteered to be an auxiliary police officer. And that was why the interview with Detective Ferrell and her testimony here today were probably the most important things that had happened to her in many years.

The lawyer had a gut feeling that this woman lived in a world alone, afraid, filled with doubt and insecurity. She desperately needed the world around her to be ordered, definite, predictable, controlled. Her clothes were functional, utilitarian. She wore a watch to bed. The purse, already strapped across her chest, was clutched tightly with one hand. Everything about this woman said she could not afford to be fallible.

Dowd knew that Jean Ayer would never budge on the important parts of her testimony. And if he tried to attack this aging Mary Poppins, the jury would strongly resent it. The key to cross-examining her was to look to the small things, the details.

It never even occurred to the lawyer that the woman's testimony might be accurate.

"Good morning, Miss Ayer," Dowd said pleasantly.

Jean Ayer nodded her head reluctantly. This was the enemy.

"My name is Michael Dowd, and I'd like to ask you a few questions, okay?"

The woman nodded again.

"Now, you say you left the precinct station and went home and watched *Casablanca*?"

"Correct."

"You left around eleven o'clock?"

"That is when I was logged out."

"Logged out?"

"My logbook, my auxiliary police logbook," Jean Ayer said confidently.

"To your knowledge, then, you were logged out at eleven?"

"To my *certain* knowledge."

"And you watched the movie, the entire movie, before going to sleep?"

"Correct."

"I believe you testified you went to sleep around midnight?"

"I . . . yes."

"The movie is about an hour and a half long, isn't it?"

"Something like that, yes."

"Yet, you say you left the station at eleven o'clock?"

Jean Ayer shifted slightly in her chair, looked at the jury, then back at the lawyer.

"I may have left a little earlier," she said. "Yes, I recall now. I left in time to get home when *Casablanca* started. Ten-thirty-five P.M."

Dowd smiled at her renewed certainty. "The movie started at ten thirty-five . . . exactly?"

"Correct."

"So, I assume you had to leave the station earlier than that, to get home in time?"

"Probably . . . ten-fifteen."

"You are quite sure now that it was ten-fifteen when you left the station that night, and not eleven o'clock?"

"Yes."

"To your certain knowledge," Dowd added with a slight smile.

"Yes."

Dowd walked back to the counsel table, picked up the police report. He looked back at the witness.

"Miss Ayer," Dowd continued, "you testified that you heard a male voice that said either, 'Hey, hey' or 'Here, here.'"

"It was one of those two, yes."

"You're certain?"

"I am certain."

"Do you recall being interviewed by a police officer, a Detective Ferrell?"

"I do."

"And isn't it true that you told him you heard the voice say something *like*, 'Hey, hey' or 'Here, here'?"

Dowd looked down at the report, appearing to read it as Jean Ayer watched him. He was not really reading it, of course. He only wanted the woman to know that he had the report in his hands, ready to prove his point if he had to.

"I may have used words like that," she said reluctantly.

"So the voice may have said something *else*?"

"It was something like, 'Hey, hey' or 'Here, here.'"

Dowd walked over to the jury box, leaned back against the railing. Jean Ayer's veneer of infallibility was beginning to crack, he thought to himself.

"You also testified, did you not, that you heard running?"

"Correct."

"And you heard this outside of your apartment, in the hallway?"

"Correct."

"Miss Ayer, that hallway had just recently been carpeted, hadn't it?"

"I believe so, yes."

"But you could still hear the footsteps, from your bed inside your apartment."

"Yes."

"And you could tell in which direction they were going?"

"Yes."

Dowd looked down at his shoes for a moment, then back at the witness.

"You mentioned that you heard a door shutting?"

"I did."

"Again, do you recall telling Detective Ferrell that you heard a *bang*?"

Jean Ayer watched the lawyer as once again he looked down at the document in his hands.

"I . . . may have said something like that."

"And didn't you tell him that you heard a bang *like* a door shutting—rather than actually telling him that you heard a door shutting?"

"I . . . I don't remember."

Dowd looked at the jurors. Did they see the point? he wondered. Did they realize that the sound Jean Ayer heard—the bang she had thought was a door shutting—might have been from the struggle between Louann Fratt and her husband? Or did they need to have it spelled out for them with more questions? A trial was filled with hundreds of small tactical decisions like this, any of them potentially critical.

Dowd decided it would be more effective if he left it to the jurors to reach the conclusion. If some of them missed the obvious, the others would, hopefully, point it out to them during later deliberations.

"Miss Ayers," he continued, "you said you heard the door closing three times, is that correct?"

"Three times, yes."

Dowd held the document up. "Didn't you tell Detective Ferrell you heard the door close only *twice*?"

"I . . . don't remember."

"You have testified that you heard the door close. But you told the detective that you heard it *slam*, or *bang*."

"It is a weighted door," Jean Ayer said. "They all sound the same in this building."

Dowd looked surprised. "You're saying that all of the doors on the ninth floor sound exactly the same when they close?"

"They are weighted."

"If a door to apartment 9C closes, it sounds exactly like the door to 9B?"

"9B is closer to me. It sounds different because it is closer to me."

"Then you can tell which door on the floor is closing?"

"Correct."

Dowd took two steps toward the woman.

"And you could tell which door the police were breaking down at four o'clock that morning?"

"I . . ."

"You thought it was *your* door, didn't you, Miss Ayer?"

"Correct, but . . . but there is a reason for that."

Dowd was not going to give her the chance to explain the reason. Don't ask the question if you don't know the answer.

"Melinda Pillon," Dowd said quickly.

"Yes."

"You testified that she lives in apartment 9C."

"Correct."

"Are you sure," he asked, glancing at the report, "that she doesn't live in 9D?"

Jean Ayer paused for a moment, her confidence now shaken.

"Isn't it true," Dowd pressed on, "that Melinda Pillon lives in apartment 9D?"

"I . . . don't . . . know."

It was time for a shot in the dark, Dowd thought. Melinda Pillon. A studio apartment—she was probably single. It was time to gamble, time to violate the rule.

"Miss Pillon is single, isn't she?"

"Yes."

"From time to time, she had male visitors, didn't she?"

"Correct."

Bingo.

"And this happens at different hours of the day and night."

"It does."

"Including late hours?"

"It does."

"As late as two o'clock in the morning?"

"Sometimes."

Leave it right there, Dowd thought to himself. He looked at the jurors. They were still watching the witness, but he could almost hear their minds grinding away. They were wondering if maybe it wasn't Melinda Pillon's door Jean Ayer heard that night, possibly even one of her male visitors who had said, "Hey, hey" out in the hallway.

"No further questions," he said, walking back to his chair.

Dowd knew he had succeeded in casting doubt on Jean Ayer's testimony. He had shown that her perception and memory were not as clear as she would have the world believe. But he knew that her story remained essentially intact. Jean Ayer was a flawed witness, but an impartial one: She had not been lying. Just how faulty she had been in her hearing and later recall was for the jury to decide. The simple fact remained that Jean Ayer *was*, in all probability, a witness to the homicide. And if her testimony were to be believed, it had not happened the way Louann Fratt said it had.

CHAPTER 28

"And for how long have you known the defendant, Mrs. Grace?"

"I have known Louann Fratt for approximately fifteen years. I met her once briefly before that when she and her husband were at Stanford, but I have known her for approximately fifteen years."

"And her husband?"

"I first met Poe Fratt at Stanford, when we were both students. Later, I also knew him as a business associate. I did some consulting work for Peat Marwick."

"I see," Brownell said. He leaned back against the audience railing.

Kay Sprinkle Grace fit the mold of so many of the supporting cast in the Fratt trial—a sophisticated, articulate, very gracious woman in her early fifties, with shoulder-length blond hair and a little too much makeup covering the truth of age. Like the others, she wore the uniform of the class, in this case a very expensive-looking medium blue wool suit, black pumps, and a pink silk scarf.

"Mrs. Grace," the prosecutor said, "did you have occasion to call Poe Fratt sometime on November twenty-first, 1988?"

"Yes, I did," she said, recrossing her legs discretely. "I placed a call to Poe in the morning, West Coast time. I called his office first. They said he wasn't in, so I called his apartment."

"And did you reach him there?"

"No. But I left a message on his answering machine."

"What was that message?"

"I asked him to call me back."

"And did he?"

"Yes."

"What time was that?"

"Let me see, it was eight-thirty in the evening in San Francisco . . . It would have been eleven-thirty in New York."

"Eleven-thirty in the evening."

"Yes."

"Mrs. Grace, perhaps you can tell us how Poe Fratt *sounded* that night."

"He sounded very happy."

"Very happy."

"Yes."

"Incidentally, Mrs. Grace . . ."

"Yes?"

"Have you ever been with Mr. Fratt when it was obvious he had had too much to drink?"

"Actually, I have."

"Then you know what he sounds like when he has had too much to drink?"

"I believe so."

"And how does he sound?"

"His voice is slurred."

The assistant D.A. turned to look at the jury. "When you spoke with Poe Fratt that night, the night of November twenty-first, was his voice slurred?"

"No," Kay Grace said, shaking her head slowly, "no, it was not."

"I see." Brownell brought up his right hand and rested his chin in it, a look of reflection coming over his face. "Just one other thing, Mrs. Grace . . ."

"Yes?"

"Would you please tell us how the conversation ended?"

"How it ended?"

"Yes. What was the last thing Poe Fratt said to you?"

"Oh, yes. He told me at the end of the conversation that he was very tired. He was going to bed."

"This was at eleven-thirty on the evening of November twenty-first?"

"Yes."

Brownell again looked at the jurors with dark intense eyes. "At eleven-thirty that night, Poe Fratt told you he was very tired."

"Yes."

"And he was going to bed."

"Yes."

"Thank you, Mrs. Grace," he said, not taking his eyes off the jurors. Then he turned and walked back to his chair. "No further questions."

Dowd started to rise, then sat back down. "I have no questions, Your Honor."

If you've got nothing to say, shut up and sit down.

"You may be excused, madam," Goodman said to Kay Grace. Then, looking at the prosecutor, "Call your next witness."

"Deborah Emory," Brownell said.

The young prosecutor held the swinging gate open for Kay Grace as she walked past him with a polite nod. She walked up the aisle toward the doors, smiling to some of the friends and relatives on the left side of the audience.

Within seconds, another member of the clan walked through the doors and down the aisle to the witness stand.

In her early fifties like Kay Grace, Deborah Emory was handsome rather than pretty, tall and slender, with a long, thin patrician face and very short, coiffed platinum blond hair. She wore a simple, elegant dark blue wool dress, highlighted by a long necklace of gold chain, and black pumps.

Deborah Emory approached the witness stand, took the oath, and quickly sat down in the chair. She looked at Daniel Brownell with a direct, unwavering gaze that held little humor.

"My name is Deborah Carley Emory," she said. "That is spelled E-M-O-R-Y."

"Mrs. Emory," Brownell said, "where do you live?"

"I live in Seattle, Washington."

"Do you know the defendant in this case, Louann Fratt?"

"Yes, I do."

"How long have you known her?"

"I have known her for approximately thirty years."

"And how is it that you know Mrs. Fratt?"

"Louann is . . . *was* married to my husband's cousin."

"What is your husband's name?"

"Meade Emory."

Dowd had already figured out that this woman was probably the wife of the man who had been giving so much help to the prosecution. But he had no idea of what she would be testifying to. Brownell had done a good job of sandbagging the defense; very little of the "rebuttal" testimony had anything to do with rebutting defense evidence, and most of it was coming as a complete surprise. The young prosecutor was landing some good blows, and Dowd had been unable to see them coming.

"Mrs. Emory," Brownell continued, "during the year prior to November of 1988, did you have occasion to receive telephone calls from the defendant?"

"Yes, I did."

"And can you tell us how many calls you received from her during that year?"

"I received a total of twelve calls."

"Can you tell us how long those calls were?"

"They ranged in time, perhaps thirteen minutes to about sixty-two minutes."

Pretty damned exact, Dowd thought to himself. Too exact. He remembered Brownell's cross-examination of Louann Fratt, remembered the questions he asked about her having told Deborah Emory over the phone that she hated Poe. This must be what the woman was here for.

"And can you tell us what the nature of those calls was?"

"The conversation had to do with Poe."

"Can you tell us what was said?"

"She complained about her husband's lack of provision for money for her support during their separation."

"As best you can remember, what did she say about that?"

Deborah Emory's gaze continued to be locked onto the prosecutor's eyes, never wandering to the left, to her old friend seated stiffly at the far table.

"She said she thought he was hiding money and spending it so that there would be less for him to have to give to her in their divorce settlement."

"Did she make any other complaints about her husband?"

"Yes, she did."

"What else did she say?"

"She complained that he called her frequently on the telephone. She characterized that as harassment."

Brownell walked over to the place where the jury and audience railings met, then looked studiously down at the floor.

"Did she express any feelings towards her husband during any of those phone calls?"

"Yes, she did."

"What were those?"

"A number of times she said she hated him. She wanted him out of her life. She wanted to get on with her own life."

"She wanted him out of her life," Brownell repeated ominously.

"Yes."

"Tell us, Mrs. Emory, what was the tone of her voice during these conversations?"

"Agitated. And she slurred her words."

Damn it! Dowd thought angrily, rising quickly to his feet. "Objection!" Brownell would not quit trying to get in evidence of Louann Fratt's drinking habits.

"Yes," Goodman said. "Strike it out. The jury will disregard it."

Yeah, Dowd thought to himself, go ahead and unpaint the picture.

"Nothing further, Your Honor," Brownell said calmly, pulling out his chair to sit down.

Dowd stood up, walked over to the jury box, and stopped. He looked at his client's former friend and smiled.

"Good morning, Mrs. Emory. My name is Michael Dowd and I'd like to ask you a few questions."

"Good morning," she replied with no hint of a smile.

"These phone calls Mrs. Fratt made to you, have you used anything to refresh your memory about how long they lasted?"

"Yes, I have."

"What is that?"

"Copies of her telephone records, the long-distance records."

"Copies of *Mrs. Fratt's* telephone records?"

"Yes."

"And where did you get these records from?"

"From Mr. Brownell."

"Uh-huh." Dowd took two steps toward the woman. "So, correct me if I am wrong, but Mr. Brownell gave you Mrs. Fratt's telephone records, and you looked at these records, and then you testified."

"Yes."

"And before you looked at these records, did you know how many times you had spoken to Mrs. Fratt?"

"I could not have said that I spoke to her twelve times," Deborah Emory said in a perfectly calm and controlled voice, "but I know that I spoke with her on a number of occasions."

"Uh-huh." Dowd turned around and walked away from her. When he reached the audience railing, he stopped. "You and your husband were rather close to Mr. Fratt, isn't that true?"

"It is."

"And in fact," Dowd said, looking out into the audience at the bald man with the red bow tie sitting in the last pew, "hasn't your husband been sitting here during the entire trial?"

"I haven't been present. I assume he has been here."

"And hasn't he come home every day with notes he has taken of the trial?"

"He may have notes, but I haven't seen any."

Dowd turned to face Deborah Emory. "You are saying," he said, anger creeping into his voice, "you are unaware that throughout this trial he has been taking notes every day of what is being said?"

"I didn't say that."

"So you are aware of that?"

"I presume he has," she said very calmly, almost indifferently. "He is a note taker."

"And he is out there right now, isn't he?"

"Yes, he is."

Dowd turned, looked out again at the elderly man. "Could I ask him to stand up, please?" he asked, challenging the man.

"Objection!" Brownell said.

"No," Goodman said, "I will allow it."

Meade Emory rose slowly to his feet, his chin thrust out pugnaciously. A pen and a pad of paper were in his hands.

"Would you give us your name, please," Dowd demanded.

"Meade Emory," the man replied calmly.

The two men just stood there for a long moment, staring at each other. Finally, Dowd turned around to face Deborah Emory.

"Isn't it a fact that for the past few years you and your husband have been calling friends and family of the Fratts to try to find any derogatory information you could about Mrs. Fratt?"

"That is not correct," Deborah Emory replied.

Meade Emory sat down quietly.

"You do know that your husband has been in contact with Mr. Brownell on a regular basis, don't you?"

"Objection," the prosecutor said.

"Overruled."

"My husband has told me that he has talked with Mr. Brownell," Deborah Emory said casually, "but I don't know that I could say with what regularity or with what frequency."

"Uh-huh." Dowd walked over to the counsel table and pulled out his chair. He looked back at the woman. "Mrs. Emory, after Poe Fratt's death, there was a memorial service for him in New York, was there not?"

"That's correct."

"You and your husband flew back here for it?"

"Yes."

"At that memorial service, Mrs. Emory, did your husband not take notes of everyone who was there?"

"I do not know."

"You don't know."

"I do not know."

"Nothing further," the lawyer said, sitting down.

As Deborah Emory stepped down from the stand, Goodman turned to Brownell. "Call your next witness."

"Margie Hascup," the prosecutor announced loudly.

Dowd jumped to his feet. "Objection!" he yelled out angrily.

Goodman glared at the big defense lawyer for a long moment, then turned to the jury. "Ladies and gentlemen," he said with a forced calm, "it's time for a brief afternoon recess. Please be back in your seats in exactly ten minutes."

Dowd remained standing in silence as the jurors slowly got up and filed out of the box, down the aisle and out through the doors into the corridor. When the last of them was gone, Judge Goodman turned to Dowd.

"Well, counsel?" he asked.

"I move to strike the testimony of Kay Grace and Deborah Emory," Dowd said, trying hard to control his Irish temper.

"What!" Goodman said.

Brownell, still standing near the jury railing, remained silent.

"Judge," Dowd continued angrily, "this is supposed to be a rebuttal case. But these witnesses don't rebut anything we raised during the defense case."

Goodman said nothing.

"Like the testimony from Kay Grace," Dowd railed on, "about Poe Fratt sounding sober. There was no evidence offered by the defense that Poe Fratt was drunk."

"Your Honor," Brownell said calmly, "Mr. Dowd raised the issue of the victim's sobriety during the medical examiner's testimony. He even asked for judicial notice of New York's drunk driving law."

Goodman looked from the prosecutor back to Dowd. "I assume the purpose of that was to prove that the deceased had been drinking, counsel. Mr. Brownell is permitted to rebut that."

"Sure," Dowd said, "but that was during the People's case. They should have brought in witnesses on that during their case-in-chief."

"Your Honor—" Brownell said.

Dowd suddenly pounded a fist on the table. "There was no evidence on Poe Fratt's sobriety during the defense! The prosecution is not permitted to rebut something that was not raised during the defense case!"

"I think, Counselor," the judge said slowly, "that sometimes maybe you have had some dealings with D.A.s in Queens County, or other counties, but I find that in New York County most of the assistants stick to the rules of evidence and try not to sandbag people."

"Judge—"

"Your motion is denied," Goodman growled, threat in his voice.

"Judge," Dowd pressed on, "none of these witnesses are proper rebuttal witnesses. They—"

"I have ruled."

"Judge," Dowd said furiously, "is there anything you're *not* going to allow on rebuttal?"

Goodman glared at him. "I'm not here to teach you the rules of evidence, counsel."

"And I just hope we're following them!" Dowd retorted angrily.

The courtroom was hushed as the two antagonists stared at each other in the tense silence. Dowd knew that Goodman was very close to throwing him in jail for contempt. But he also knew that Goodman, like all judges, was concerned with being reversed on appeal—and throwing a defendant's lawyer in jail in the middle of a murder trial was a risky thing to do. Further, if he did not raise the issue of Brownell's sandbagging on the record, his client would lose this as a possible grounds for appealing a conviction. In any event, if he did not stand up and fight back, Brownell and Goodman would roll right over him.

Those were the legal rationalizations. But the truth was that all the frustrations, setbacks, sandbagging tactics, and bad rulings had finally gotten to Dowd.

Without taking his eyes off the big Irishman, Goodman said to his bailiff, "Bring in the jury."

The bailiff quickly stepped outside and called the jurors back from their short recess. As they began filing in one by one, the judge leaned back in his chair and studied Dowd as if trying to decide something. Dowd dropped into his own chair with a dark expression on his face.

When the jury was seated, Goodman looked at Brownell. "Proceed."

"Margie Hascup," Brownell repeated.

The doors opened and a young woman, about twenty-eight, stepped into the courtroom. She was very pretty, with large brown eyes, thickly billowing auburn hair, and a bright red silk blouse. After the parade of aging thoroughbreds, Margie Hascup was a refreshing breath of vitality and color.

The young woman walked self-consciously down the aisle and through the gates held open by Brownell. Quickly taking the oath, she walked to the witness stand, sat down, and spelled out her last name. Then she looked around expectantly.

"Ms. Hascup," Brownell said, walking toward her, "how are you employed?"

"I am a secretary with Peat Marwick."

"During the time you have been a secretary at Peat Marwick, did you have occasion to work for someone named Poe Fratt?"

"Yes. I was Poe's secretary."

Poe, Dowd thought to himself. Not Mr. Fratt.

"For what period of time did you work for him?"

"From March of 1987 to, I guess, November of last year."

"I would like to call your attention to November twenty-first, Ms. Hascup . . ."

"Yes."

". . . and ask you if there was anything you were involved with that evening."

"Yes. There was a dinner for some executives that Poe had set up."

"This is at a restaurant called La Colombe d'Or?"

"Yes."

"You were helping set up the dinner?"

"Yes, Poe and myself."

"What time did you get to the restaurant that evening, Ms. Hascup?"

"Between six-thirty and seven, I believe," she said. "The reservations were for seven."

"When did Mr. Fratt arrive?"

"I believe between seven and seven-thirty."

"How many people were at this dinner, if you can recall?"

"Yes, I would say about twenty-five."

"I see." Brownell wandered over to the jury box, his dark, brooding eyes seemingly lost in thought. "And what time did you leave the restaurant that night?"

"About ten-thirty."

"When you left, was Mr. Fratt still there?"

"Yes, he was."

"Now . . . you were pretty much in Mr. Fratt's presence throughout that evening, isn't that so?"

"Yes."

"During the course of the evening," the prosecutor said, looking up at Margie Hascup, "did you observe Mr. Fratt consume any alcoholic beverages?"

"Yes, I did," the young woman replied. "I didn't watch him the whole evening, but I only saw him with about four glasses of wine."

"Four glasses."

"Yes."

"Tell us, Ms. Hascup, did Poe Fratt appear to you at any time to be intoxicated?"

"No," she said, shaking her head, "he did not."

"Thank you." Brownell walked back to his chair. "Nothing further."

Dowd stood up, walked over to the jury railing.

"Good afternoon, Ms. Hascup."

"Good afternoon," she said, smiling brightly.

"My name is Michael Dowd and I'd like to ask you a few questions, if that's okay."

"Sure."

"Have you ever seen Mr. . . . . Poe Fratt intoxicated?"

"What?"

"Have you ever seen Poe Fratt intoxicated before?"

"No," the young woman said, shaking her head. "He was always a gentleman."

"Then . . . you really don't know *what* he looks like when he's had too much to drink, do you?"

"I . . . I guess not."

Dowd nodded pleasantly. "Well, this dinner at the Colombe d'Or . . . it got started around seven o'clock?"

"Seven or seven-thirty, yes."

"Isn't it a fact that there were was a cocktail hour *before* the dinner?"

"Yes."

"And when and where was this?"

"At the Marriott Marquis, between five-thirty and six-thirty."

"Uh-huh. And were both you and Poe present during this cocktail hour?"

"Yes, we were."

"And how many people were at this cocktail hour?"

"I don't know," she said thoughtfully. "All the people who had been at the conference. There had been a business conference earlier that day. Plus the twenty-five who were going to the dinner."

"Was it more or less than a hundred?"

"Less."

"And I assume you were not watching Poe all this time?"

"No, I wasn't."

"So it would be fair to say that you don't really know *how* much he had to drink?"

"Not at the cocktail hour, I suppose not."

"Uh-huh."

As he stood there, Dowd glanced down at his feet. For some reason his mind suddenly could focus on nothing but his old mud-stained shoes. He noticed that the sole of the left shoe was beginning to peel slightly in the front. And the left cuff of his baggy dark gray trousers had slipped down, as it always did, so that he was walking on the bottom inch or so of material. He found himself grinning foolishly, and everything seemed ridiculous and very, very funny. The questions, the witnesses, the judge's rulings, the war with Brownell, the cops, and the medical examiner and Mary Poppins and the whole damned trial. He wondered what Irene was going to fix for dinner tonight. . . .

All of a sudden, Dowd looked up. Everyone was staring at him. *My God*, he thought, *I did it again*. He looked at the pretty young woman sitting in the chair in front of him. What was her name?

"Ms. Hascup . . ."

"Yes?"

"Ms. Hascup, uh, do you know how many bottles of wine were served at the cocktail hour or at the dinner?"

"No, I do not."

"Or other drinks?"

"No."

"Do you know how much the final bill was?"

"No, I don't."

Dowd nodded. "Let's just take the dinner. How much was the food, just the dinner, do you recall?"

"I'm not really sure."

"It wasn't more than fifty dollars per dinner, was it?"

"No, no."

"Poe had an American Express gold card, didn't he?"

"Yes."

Dowd walked over to his table, picked up a small piece of paper.

"Your Honor," he said, showing the paper to Brownell, "I'd like this marked defense exhibit N."

"It will be marked," Goodman growled.

Dowd walked up to Margie Hascup and showed her the piece of paper.

"Do you recognize this?"

"It's an American Express receipt."

"Notice the dates."

"Yes."

"Isn't it a fact, Miss Hascup, that the bill for the dinner portion of the evening, at the Colombe d'Or, was $3,139?"

"I didn't receive the bill, so I wouldn't know."

Dowd stepped back, looked at the jury.

"If there were twenty-five people at the dinner, and the dinners cost no more than fifty dollars, then the food portion of the bill would have been no more than . . . $1,250, right?"

"Maybe."

"Plus tax and tip."

"And appetizers."

"And appetizers," Dowd said. "Leaving somewhere around . . . fifteen hundred dollars for alcoholic drinks?"

"I can't say."

"That's a lot of alcohol for only twenty-five people, isn't it?"

Margie Hascup just shrugged.

"Thank you, Ms. Hascup," Dowd said, returning to his seat. "Nothing further."

The young woman looked questioningly at Brownell, then at the judge.

"You may step down," Goodman said. "You are excused."

As Poe Fratt's secretary stood up and walked past the jury, Goodman looked at Brownell.

"Call your next witness."

The assistant D.A. rose slowly to his feet. He looked at the judge, then turned to look at the jury.

"The People rest," he said.

CHAPTER 29

"Louann Fratt stands accused of the act most condemned by her fellow human beings, and that is the intentional act of taking the life of another without justification. We call it murder."

Dowd walked along the jury railing, looking from one face to another. Seven women and five men. Young and old. White, black, and Hispanic. Beards and button-downs, sweatshirts and designer labels. Twelve.

Dowd had wondered once why a jury had twelve people on it. Why not a round number, like ten? He had asked many of his fellow attorneys, and was surprised to find that no one seemed to know; they simply accepted the fact that there must be a good reason for having twelve. But he kept digging and had finally stumbled across the answer in an old history book. We have twelve jurors, he found, because there were twelve apostles. The biblically significant number was used in the old English courts and eventually passed on to the colonies.

In other words, like so many other things in the criminal justice system, there was no good reason for having twelve people on a jury.

"I want to take you back to November twenty-second of

354

last year," Dowd continued, "to an apartment on Seventy-eighth Street. I want you to go back to that time, to sometime after two o'clock. I want you to go back to the time when Louann Fratt sat on that small couch at the foot of the bed. Take yourselves back to that time, to when Poe Fratt came down the side of that bed and grabbed her by the arm, yanked her to her feet, and said, 'I'm going to fuck you like you need to be fucked.'

"I want you to go back there, and in those seconds, those few quick seconds that it took for everything to happen, I want you to watch. Watch as this two-hundred-and-twenty-pound former football player grabs this woman, begins tearing her clothes off. I want you to remember what he had done to her once before, how he had ripped her clothes off and violently raped her in her own apartment, how she had hidden in her bedroom afterwards, afraid to come out until the next morning.

"I want you to watch, as this small, frail woman tries to resist, begs him to stop. Watch as she reaches frantically for the knife, the knife she carried for protection. Watch as she pleads with her husband to let her go. Watch as this man hits her in the face, then hits her again. Try to picture it, this woman wildly waving the knife in terror, trying desperately to get to the door, to escape, and Poe Fratt standing in her way. Poe Fratt, hitting her with his fists, telling her, 'You're not getting out of here alive!' "

Dowd looked into the eyes of each of the twelve jurors, one at a time, as he walked along the railing. One at a time he met their eyes, seized them, would not let them go.

"I want to take you back and then I want to ask you a question. The central question in this case. The *only* question in this case . . ."

He suddenly stopped his slow pacing and scanned all twelve faces.

"Has the prosecution proven . . . that Louann Fratt . . . was unreasonable . . . in believing . . . that her husband . . . was going to . . . rape her?"

Dowd was silent for a moment, letting the critical issue sink in.

"And have they proven it . . . *beyond a reasonable doubt?*"

The lawyer continued staring at the twelve men and women in silence.

Dowd had to be realistic in recognizing the strengths and weaknesses of the case. If the prosecution had built a brick wall, it made no sense to ram your head against it trying to knock it down. Winning an acquittal lay in learning to go *around* the wall. Winning lay in sidestepping the opponent's strengths and in playing to your own strengths.

And Dowd's strength lay in one simple fact. In many states, the defendant had the burden of proving self-defense; if the person did not convince the jury that the killing was in self-defense, he or she was convicted. The law in New York, however, stated that once a defendant presented clear evidence of self-defense, the prosecution was required to prove that the homicide was *not* committed in self-defense—and it had to be proven *beyond a reasonable doubt*.

Those beautiful words: beyond a reasonable doubt.

Dowd was aware, then, that the path to an acquittal lay in getting the jury to focus upon self-defense and upon the burden of proof.

Focus.

"Ladies and gentlemen, you all took an oath. You took an oath to test the evidence that Mr. Brownell presented to you, to weigh it, to ask yourselves: Has he convinced me beyond a reasonable doubt? I know that it is an incredibly difficult thing, to be asked to judge another human being. We know the Bible says, 'Judge not, that ye be not judged.' But we do it. We do it in our system of criminal justice. We ask it of you. *Before* you do this, however, before you accede to the prosecution's demand that you wrench this woman from her family, we only ask that you be absolutely certain, that you be convinced . . . beyond a reasonable doubt."

Focus.

The secret to an effective summation was in directing the *focus* of the jurors. There were many different issues in the Fratt case, many different ways of looking at things. Dowd knew, for example, that a juror could look at the case and focus on the question "Do I believe Louann Fratt?"; if he did not, the juror would likely vote to convict. To win an acquittal for his client, Dowd knew that he had to get the jury to focus on the question "Has Mr. Brownell convinced me *beyond a reasonable doubt* that Poe Fratt was not trying to rape his wife?" For the simple fact was that there would be jurors who did not believe his client—but who might vote to acquit anyway if they were not absolutely convinced there was no rape attempt.

But the big Irishman also knew that relying on reasonable doubt would not be enough. He knew instinctively what many lawyers never learn—that in every trial you must have facts, a central theory, and a consistent approach to win. It is not enough to rely upon legal niceties like presumption of innocence and burden of proof. It is not enough to point out the flaws of the prosecution's case, to try to prove what did *not* happen. The reality was that the defense must tell the jury what *did* happen. Nor is it enough to say that *either* this, or that, happened: The jury would see this as lack of conviction. So Dowd knew that he had to present one single version of the facts. He had to believe in it, and stick to it, both in testimony and, now, in argument.

Dowd stepped back from the railing, turned to look at Louann Fratt still seated rigidly in her chair at the counsel table, staring straight ahead. He looked down for a moment, seemingly lost in thought. Then he looked back up at the jurors.

"I told you at the beginning of this trial that it was a long and winding road that brought Louann Fratt to this apartment that night. I told you she was a woman from a different time and a different place.

"One can perhaps wonder if it is wise in 1989 for a woman to let her husband make all of the decisions in her life. One can question whether it is wise to be financially dependent on a man, dependent on him for security. To be so much under his control that you must ask permission to use the car. One can question whether it is wise to follow this man all over the world, to go where he says, to live in Manhattan, where she didn't want to live. But her husband chose Manhattan, and so that is where she lived. Because that is how she was raised. That is who she is."

Dowd looked back again at his client, compassion in his eyes as he studied the sad figure.

"One can perhaps question whether it is realistic after being raped by your husband to go over to his apartment alone. One can wonder why, today, a woman would still obey a man who has abandoned her and raped her."

Dowd looked back at the jury. An elderly woman in the front row was unconsciously nodding her head in sympathy.

The lawyer looked at Brownell seated in his chair, gazing vacantly at the ceiling.

"The prosecutor cross-examined Louann Fratt. And what did he ask her? 'Mrs. Fratt, isn't it true that you never worked again after you married Poe Fratt?' No, she did not work. Of course, 'work' meant you were employed by someone, it meant you had a job somewhere. Of course, 'work' did not mean raising three children. 'Work' was not providing a home, and cooking, and being the dutiful corporate wife, and following your husband all around the world. That was not 'work.' 'Do you work, Mrs. Fratt?' 'No,' she said, 'I only do volunteer work.' "

Dowd turned back to the jury, grabbed the railing with both hands, and leaned forward.

"Why do you think he asked those questions, ladies and gentlemen? What conceivable relevance does it have to whether she murdered her husband? I'll tell you why he asked her. The same reason he asked her to describe the kind of apartment she lives in, then describe the small studio her husband had. The same reason he asked her how much money she was getting from Poe Fratt. He asked her because he was trying to convince you that Louann Fratt is a *parasite*, an ungrateful woman, a woman who does not appreciate all the wonderful things her fine husband has done for her! And so she should be convicted of murder! What is the purpose of those questions if not that?"

The lawyer's voice was rising, and his Irish complexion turning even redder. He stopped, took a deep breath, and forced himself to relax for a moment. Then he let go of the railing and stepped back, shaking his head slowly.

"Ladies and gentlemen," he said, his voice returning to normal, "you have taken an oath. In that oath you have prom-ised not to be influenced by passion or sympathy. You have promised to consider only the facts, and apply the law. So let's take a look at those facts. . . ."

Dowd began pacing slowly back and forth in front of the jury.

"Louann Fratt testified that her husband was trying to rape her, and that she tried to fight him off, that she scratched him with her fingernails. Fact: There were five fingernail scratches on Poe Fratt's chin. How did they get there? Fact: Photos show that Louann Fratt had bruises and swelling on her face and head. Where does the prosecution think these injuries came from? Fact: There was enough alcohol in Poe Fratt's body to qualify him as legally intoxicated. Yet, the prosecution is trying to convince you that he was stone sober and that Louann Fratt was the heavy drinker.

"Of course, Mr. Brownell will argue to you that she just made everything up, that she is on trial for her life, and that she would say anything to save herself. She would say *anything*. But ladies and gentlemen, let me ask you a question. If she had just made all of this up, don't you think she could have done a better job?"

Dowd stopped, looked at the jurors, letting the concept sink in before going on.

"Don't you think she could have made up a better story than taking her husband's mail to him at two o'clock in the morning? Don't you think she could have come up with something *better* than carrying a knife over with her—and then obligingly turning the knife over to the police, rather than getting rid of it? Would this woman say, 'I had a glass of wine with him and we had a pleasant chat just before he tried to rape me'? Why didn't Louann Fratt say that her husband was raving drunk, that he was out of control when she arrived? And why did she say she went back to the apartment that second time? How did that help her cause any?"

The big lawyer paused again, then resumed his slow pacing back and forth.

"Mr. Brownell will remind you that Mrs. Fratt never mentioned anything about a rape, either to the nine-one-one operator or to the police. He will tell you that this story was made up later, that if there had been an attempted rape, she would

have said something. And, of course, it's true she said nothing.
Oh, yes, oh, yes, she never told those kind and gentle and
sympathetic officers that her husband had tried to rape her.
She said nothing. And, of course, as Mr. Brownell knows, this
simply means that there must not have been an attempted
rape. Because, as every *man* knows, something like that would
be reported."

Dowd stopped again, scanning the twelve faces that were
riveted to him.

"Louann Fratt was frightened. She was scared to death.
But she was not afraid of the police after stabbing her husband. She was not afraid of being prosecuted. She was frightened because her husband had just tried to rape her, her
husband and the father of her children, and she had stabbed
him to death. She was terrified, and hurt, and confused.

"You heard the testimony of Dr. Veronen. The emotional
trauma of an attempted rape . . . The repression, the denial,
the refusal to admit even to yourself that your husband has
tried to rape you. It takes time, she said, time before the reality
can be acknowledged, time before the soul is strong enough
to deal with the truth. And it took Louann Fratt time."

Dowd stopped and thought for a moment. The image of
Jean Ayer suddenly came into clear focus. Jean Ayer. Should
he talk about her, point out the problems with her story? Or
would this only serve to emphasize the importance of the prim
little woman's testimony?

As with most good trial lawyers, Dowd used few if any
notes in giving his summation, and followed no rigid outline.
He had an overall picture of what he wanted to do, a rough
organization that he had sketched out on paper. But he firmly
believed that to be effective, he must develop a rapport with
the jurors—and this could only be done by *talking* with them,
openly and spontaneously, not by lecturing to them from
notes. He had long since learned that once outlines or notes
or any other signs of a "sales pitch" are pulled out, the jury
begins to withdraw.

Dowd found it a bit unnerving at times to face a jury
without any props, without anything to fall back on for guid-
ance. It was not unlike an acrobat performing without a safety
net. But for the lawyer with the skill to pull it off, the benefits

were considerable. Besides permitting a closer rapport with the jury, the unstructured approach gave Dowd freedom—freedom to create, to sense and adjust to the reactions of the jury, to follow the instincts of the moment, to genuinely feel and express feeling. And, of course, freedom to fall flat on his face.

Jean Ayer. A rigidly prepared closing argument would deal with how to handle her testimony in advance. With Dowd's approach, however, he was aware only that the issue of Jean Ayer existed. What he did about it, if anything, would depend on how he felt at the time. Dowd had developed confidence in his method. Her name would come to him at the right time in his argument, and he would know then how to deal with it.

"Mr. Brownell will tell you that there is a witness to the homicide, a woman who was listening next door."

Dowd slowly shook his head.

"We are fallible, ladies and gentlemen. We are all fallible. We can't see everything, we can't hear everything, we can't remember everything. We are not cameras, we are not tape recorders. We make mistakes. We are human.

"Most of us, of course, acknowledge this fallibility. Most of us recognize and admit that we are less than perfect. Most of us . . . But not Jean Ayer. I suggest to you that Miss Ayer desperately wants to feel that she is helping, that she matters, that she is important. She volunteered to be an auxiliary police officer. And when there was a homicide right next door, she desperately wanted to be a part of the investigation, desperately wanted to testify in a real murder trial.

"But I also suggest to you that Miss Ayer's life is a rigid one, a life where precision and certainty are necessary to any sense of control, of security. There is no room in Miss Ayer's life for mistakes, no room for human error.

"What did she testify to? She left the police station at eleven—she was quite certain. Except that it turned out to be more like ten-fifteen. She heard a door close—she was quite certain. Except she told the detective that it was a bang that sounded *like* a door. She heard this three times—she was quite certain. Except that she told the detective she only heard it *twice*. She heard a man say, 'Hey, hey' or 'Hear,

hear'—she was quite certain. Except that she told the detective it was something that sounded *like* 'Hey, hey' or 'Hear, hear.' Melinda Pillon lived in apartment 9C—she was quite certain. Except that she actually lives in 9D. What else was she wrong about?

"What did she really hear? We'll never know. Maybe she heard Melinda Pillon and a boyfriend, talking in the hallway, opening and closing the door to 9D, saying good night. Maybe the bangs she heard were from the deadly struggle in Poe Fratt's apartment. We'll never know."

Dowd walked over to the counsel table, placed his hands on his chair, and leaned forward. Then he turned and looked out at the audience, at the sea of faces and cameras. He could not recognize any of them, though. They all seemed part of a huge blur.

"Joan Clark," he said suddenly, turning back to face the jury. "The prosecution has to explain *why* Louann Fratt killed her husband, of course. Mr. Brownell has to explain to you why a fifty-five-year-old mother of three would suddenly go berserk and attack her two-hundred-and-twenty-pound husband with a kitchen knife. And the reason is the old standby—the 'other woman.' Joan Clark. Louann Fratt was so insanely jealous that she planned out the murder of her husband.

"Except that it doesn't make sense, ladies and gentlemen. It just doesn't make sense. Louann Fratt knew about Joan Clark in the summer of 1988—months before the stabbing. Does a woman wait five or six months before suddenly becoming insanely jealous?

"None of it makes sense. Does she spend a happy afternoon with a friend, making paper sculptures—hours before carrying out an assassination? Does she attack a man twice her size with a kitchen knife, rather than a gun—and then save the knife for the police? Does she make up a story that is so obviously going to be hard for most people to swallow?"

Dowd looked down for a moment, then back up at the jurors, once again making contact with each of the twelve pairs of eyes.

"And where *is* Joan Clark?" Dowd asked quietly. "Why didn't she testify?"

He would like to have had the answer to that question himself, Dowd thought. Why *had* Brownell not called Poe Fratt's girlfriend?

It would be some time before Dowd would learn that Brownell had, in fact, issued a subpoena for Joan Clark. The wealthy socialite had shown up at the assistant D.A.'s office with her attorney; while she sat silently in a chair, the high-priced lawyer had explained to the young prosecutor that his client would say nothing unless ordered to, and then only with the assistance of counsel. In what may or may not have been a break for the defense, Brownell had decided against taking the risk of putting an uncooperative witness on the stand in front of a jury and gambling on what she would say.

Dowd stepped back, looked once again at his client. He stood there like that for a long moment, as if trying to understand who she really was. Then, sighing deeply, he turned back to the jury.

"You heard Louann Fratt testify. You watched her as she sat on that stand, you watched her testify. You have every right to measure her as a witness. You have every right to judge her. And maybe she didn't use the best judgment. Maybe others would have seen it more clearly, that long, winding road that brought her to her husband's apartment on that fateful night. But that road was a part of her life, it made her what she is. It made her human, and perhaps it made her foolish in the eyes of some. But it did not make her a murderer."

Dowd sighed again, a sigh of deep weariness. He knew he had reached the end. The end of his argument. The end of the trial. The end of his strength. He had given everything. There was no more to give. It was over.

"Ladies and gentlemen," he said quietly, with a tired smile, "do you know what is happening inside of a lawyer at this point? You are scared to death. I don't care how many times you've done this, you're scared to death. You are responsible for another person's life, another human being. You have that person's life in your hands, and the responsibility . . . the responsibility is awesome."

Dowd continued to look deeply into the eyes of each of the jurors.

"I hand that responsibility now to you, the responsibility for this person's life. The responsibility of judgment."

The lawyer bowed his head for a moment, then turned and walked quietly back to his chair.

"I am not so arrogant as to stand here and tell you what that judgment must be. My conscience, and yours, must rest with the evidence."

Dowd quietly pulled out the chair and sat down.

The strange hush in the courtroom was broken by Judge Goodman's voice.

"The People may proceed with summation," he said.

"Thank you, Your Honor," Brownell said, rising quickly to his feet.

Each lawyer had only one opportunity to present argument to the jury. Under New York law, the defense gave its summation first, followed by the prosecution. This gave an obvious advantage to the prosecutor, since he could reply to whatever was said in the defense summation—leaving the defense lawyer powerless to reply in turn to the prosecution's arguments. The justification for this arrangement, at least in theory, was that since the prosecution had the burden of proof in the case, it should get the benefit of arguing last.

Daniel Brownell would have the final word before the jury began to deliberate the fate of Louann Fratt.

"Ladies and gentlemen," the young prosecutor began in his calm, low-key manner, "Mr. Dowd told you that what you have heard was a long and winding road that led to November twenty-second, 1988. I suggest to you that what you heard was nothing more than the complaints of a woman about what a lousy husband Poe Fratt was during their thirty years of marriage.

"But this case is not about the history of that marriage. From all the evidence, it is clear that marriage was dissolving with a lot of bitter feelings. The defendant was careful not to show any of that bitterness and anger in her testimony—because she didn't want you to think this played any part in what happened on November twenty-second. But as we heard from Deborah Emory and others, there *was* bitterness and anger. And *that*, ladies and gentlemen, is the 'long and winding road' that led to November twenty-second."

Brownell paused for a moment, his chin once again resting introspectively in his right hand. Then he turned and began to walk slowly back and forth in front of the jury, one hand sliding along the polished wooden railing, then the other.

"The defense that the defendant chose is very interesting. It is rape. Rape, more than anything else except possibly murder, invokes an emotional reaction in people. What is more disgusting than rape? How can anyone have any sympathy for someone accused of rape? It's a very easy allegation to make, very difficult for anyone to disprove. But I remind you that it comes from one source only. It comes from the woman who killed the supposed rapist. And it comes only *after* she killed him and *after* she was charged with murder. It was never reported to the police, she never went to a doctor, never told anyone about it until sometime after she was charged with the murder of her husband. Then, suddenly, she remembered he was trying to rape her."

The assistant D.A. stopped for a moment, as if he had just remembered something, then continued on.

"It's important to keep in mind that we are not dealing here with a rape victim. We are dealing with a woman who *claims* she was raped. And we are dealing with a woman whose testimony is contradicted by every single important witness in the case. In fact, the *only* evidence you have of self-defense is her own testimony. And that testimony is nothing more than self-serving fantasy.

"In fact, her story is so fantastic that even her own lawyer has suggested that it must be true because no one would make up anything so bizarre. *Why* would she say she went over to his apartment that night? he asked. The answer is that she *had* to admit that: She couldn't very well carry the two-hundred-and-twenty-pound body from his apartment to hers and then claim he came there to rape her. Of course, one of the most bizarre things is her explanation of *why* she went. We heard testimony that she thought Poe Fratt was cheating her financially. And yet she is still willing to run right over there late at night simply because he wants his mail.

"Let's take a closer look at this so-called attempted rape. Mr. Dowd took great pains to tell us what a big bruiser this Poe Fratt was—an ex-football player, two-hundred-twenty pounds, six feet four. He is *big*! And his client is small, fragile, only weighs a hundred and ten pounds. Well, ladies and gentlemen, if it was this giant's intention to hurt her, to rape her, or even kill her, he *would* have—whether she had a knife or not. There is just no way she could have gained the upper hand. It's just not possible.

"And another thing. The defendant tells us that she was shocked and terrified after her husband had tried to rape her, so much so that she blocked the incident out. Well, for someone who was so shocked and terrified, she did an awful lot of deliberate things before she finally called the police an hour and a half later. She stabs her husband in the heart. Then, strangely, rather than leave it in his body, she pulls it out and takes it with her. Somehow, she is able to grab the bag, and the dog, who just happens to be sitting calmly nearby, grab her coat, and get out of the door—before Poe Fratt falls against it, wedging it shut."

Brownell shook his head in disbelief.

"She gets back to her apartment. And there, the doorman notices nothing different about her. If she is in such terrible shock, and she has just been through a fight for her very life, why doesn't the doorman notice anything? Why does she seem so calm, so normal? Why aren't her clothes or hair or anything disheveled?

"So, she gets back to her apartment, and what does she do? Does she call the police? Does she call emergency medical services? No. She changes her clothes. *Then* she washes the blood out of the sweatsuit. *Then*, and only then, does she go back to save her husband."

The tall, darkly handsome lawyer stopped, smiled to himself in amusement.

"Now this is where it gets interesting. She goes back and just *happens* to see Poe's car conveniently parked in front of his apartment. She enters the combination, gets the keys out, and goes up to the apartment. She unlocks the door, opens it, and steps inside. And there she sees Poe Fratt lying face up on the floor. Except that she couldn't have opened the door and gotten inside. It took three big police officers to force the door open enough for anyone to get inside. And when they did get inside, the body was lying face *down*!

"So, what does this tell us? It tells us that Louann Fratt never went back to her husband's apartment a second time. She did go out; the doorman saw her. But she did not go back to the apartment to save her husband. If she had, she would have known she couldn't get in. And she would have known that her husband's body was lying face down."

Brownell looked across the room at Louann Fratt, still sitting without expression.

"All right," he said turning back to the jury, "so what *did* happen? Let's look at the timing. The defendant said she called the police at about three forty-five that morning, and that this was about an hour and a half after the stabbing. That places the time of the stabbing somewhere around a quarter after two. And that, ladies and gentlemen, fits perfectly with what Jean Ayer told you."

The assistant D.A. once again looked back at Louann Fratt. Every one of the twelve jurors followed his gaze. But the silently seated woman did not seem aware.

"Only two people actually *saw* what happened in apartment 9B that night, ladies and gentlemen. One of those is Louann Fratt. The other is dead. But we do have someone who *heard* what happened. We do have Jean Ayer. And Jean Ayer is, without doubt, the most important witness in this trial. She is an impartial witness, a witness who knows none of the people involved, a witness with absolutely no reason to lie. And what does this witness to murder say? At exactly two-twenty that morning—the very time the defendant herself says she was at Poe Fratt's apartment—she heard his door open. Notice that she did *not* hear a knock, or someone identifying herself at the door, or a conversation of any kind. Just a door opening. Then, a minute or two later, a man says something like, 'hey, hey' or 'here, here'—the kind of exclamation Poe Fratt might have made upon awakening to being stabbed. Notice that although she could hear this, she heard absolutely no other conversation, no other words. She never heard Poe Fratt tell the defendant that he was going to fuck her, or that she wasn't getting out of there alive. And she never heard any sounds that sounded like a fight. And she never heard the sounds of a dog barking—although I submit to you that if a dog sees its master being attacked, even if by someone it knows, it will bark. And finally, Ms. Ayer heard the door close, and the sounds of running—to the fire door, not the elevator."

Brownell walked over to the audience railing, turned, and leaned against it. Once again he assumed a contemplative posture, his right hand embracing his chin, his left arm supporting the elbow, with his intense green-brown eyes fixed, as if in a trance, on some unseen object. After a moment, he turned to the jury.

"I suggest to you, ladies and gentlemen, that if you look at all the evidence, if you look at the medical examiner, and at the crime scene evidence, and the police testimony, and you compare it with what Miss Ayer said on the stand, you can get a very good idea of what actually happened that night in apartment 9B.

"First of all, we know what the motive is. We know what Louann Fratt had been told earlier that day. We know she waited until very late at night, until she knew her husband would be asleep. And we know from Kay Grace's testimony that he *was* asleep, that he told her two or three hours earlier that he was very tired and he was going to bed. We know the defendant went over to that apartment at about two-fifteen in the morning, carrying a long, lethal knife. We know how she got into Poe Fratt's apartment: She found the car, entered the combination, and retrieved the keys from the trunk. Then she unlocked the door to the apartment, quietly entered, and delivered three carefully aimed thrusts to her sleeping husband, who cried out something like 'hey, hey!' "

Like Dowd, the young prosecutor studied the faces of the jurors, trying to read what was going on behind the nearly expressionless faces. And, as usual, there was nothing but enigma staring back.

"Mr. Dowd asked his client if she *intended* to kill her husband, and she tearfully told you that she did not. Of course not. Well, ladies and gentlemen, actions speak louder than words. And I suggest to you that the best evidence we have of what this woman's intent was, is . . . the placement of the three knife wounds. Those wounds speak volumes. Look at them. Recall the medical examiner's testimony. One knife thrust was to the neck, barely missing major veins and arteries. Another was to the back, perhaps while Poe Fratt slept on his stomach, or perhaps a coup de grâce after he had fallen. Had the wound been deeper, it could have penetrated to the lungs or other vital organs. And the third was the deadly thrust, six inches deep into the chest, passing all the way through the heart and coming to rest finally in the liver.

"Tell me, where are the nondeadly wounds, the wounds to the arms? The defendant testified that Poe Fratt was swinging at her, hitting her, and grabbing for the knife. Yet we have three potentially deadly wounds, carefully placed. Can you picture this two-hundred-twenty-pound man, standing six feet four, coming after her—and this tiny woman is able to sink a knife six inches into his heart?

"*There*, ladies and gentlemen, is your evidence of intent."

Brownell walked slowly back to his chair, his head bowed in thought. He stopped, looked back at the twelve men and women.

"In this case, the defense has used rape as a way to justify a cold-blooded murder. Don't allow that emotionally charged idea to interfere with your own common sense. And don't judge this woman's life, as Mr. Dowd would have you do, and give her the sympathy he wants. You are not the jury in a divorce case. Whether or not this was a good marriage or a bad marriage, whether or not Poe Fratt was a good husband or a bad husband, is irrelevant.

"You are not judging any lives here today, ladies and gentlemen. You are weighing the facts and determining guilt or innocence. And those facts are very clear.

"At two-fifteen in the morning of November twenty-second, 1988, Louann Fratt cold-bloodedly murdered her husband by stabbing him to death with a knife."

Brownell quietly pulled out his chair and sat down.

CHAPTER 30

At 2:00 in the afternoon of Thursday, December 14, the jury began its deliberations.

Dowd spent most of the next two days nervously pacing the barren, harshly lighted hallway outside the courtroom, a cigarette in one hand and a Styrofoam cup of watery coffee in the other. When the cigarette began to burn his fingers, he would pull another from a crumpled pack and light it from the still-burning stub. When the pack was empty, he went down to a tiny store on another floor of the courthouse and bought another pack, along with more tasteless coffee and a stale doughnut.

The hallway was almost empty now. The reporters and cameramen were gone, waiting for news that the jury had reached a verdict. And the thrill seekers had moved on to other courtrooms, other human tragedies. To find complete solitude, though, the defense lawyer would occasionally slip into the witness waiting room located just outside the court-room. There, alone in the tiny, cheerless cubicle, he would go back over the trial in his mind yet one more time, second-guessing the moves, analyzing the strategy, playing back the techniques. Wishing he had done this a different way, that another. Wondering if a certain decision had perhaps not cost his client her life.

It was a helpless feeling, this waiting for a verdict. The experience always reminded Dowd of one terrible night he had spent in a maternity ward, worrying and waiting anxiously for news of the birth of his first child. So much hanging in the balance. So little that could be done. Everything in the hands of others. The overwhelming feeling of impotence.

He recalled once again the long, tedious reading of the jury instructions by Judge Goodman. It was during this hour or two that Dowd and Brownell, finished with their work and now seated helplessly in their chairs at counsel tables, would furtively study the expressions and body language of the twelve men and women listening to the judge. The two lawyers would scan the twelve faces, looking for the slightest frown, the hint of a smile, the tiniest suggestion of a grimace. Was juror number eight glancing at Louann Fratt? Yes, there it was again. Why? What did her face say? What was she thinking? Had she already decided how to vote? And juror number eleven had his hands folded across his chest as the judge read the instruction on presumption of innocence. Was that a sign that he was rejecting the idea, that he had already decided she was guilty? A smile—number two had looked at the prosecutor and smiled. One vote for conviction?

At 4:00, the jury asked to have parts of Jean Ayer's testimony read back to them.

After the reading, Dowd agonized over the meaning of the jury's request. When a jury asked to have testimony read to them, it usually meant individual jurors were disagreeing over what that witness had said. And it meant the disagreement was important enough to influence votes. What part of her testimony were they fighting over? Which way would it go? My God, Dowd thought, why didn't I spend more time on Jean Ayer? I should have questioned her about the acoustics of the apartment. I should have brought out her motives for testifying. I should have subpoenaed Melinda Pillon. I should have . . .

At 6:30 that evening, Judge Goodman ordered the jury sequestered in a nearby hotel for the night.

Dowd spent a sleepless night at home.

At 9:30 A.M. on Friday, December 15, the jury resumed its deliberations.

The big defense lawyer was not alone in the hallways of the Criminal Justice Building's sixteenth floor. There was another person standing vigil with him in the echoing emptiness, another figure slowly pacing the cold waxed floors.

Louann Fratt.

Dowd's client was tastefully dressed in a dark gray wool suit, with a white blouse, red and black silk scarf, and black pumps. Like Dowd, Louann Fratt was a chain-smoker, but the ever-present cigarette was the only indication she would permit of what was going on inside of her. Constantly at her side was at least one of the three Fratt children. As always, the immaculately dressed Fratt clan kept their heads held high and their feelings to themselves.

Yet, there was a deep sadness in Louann Fratt's face that could not be disguised. For all the stiff-upper-lip affectation, her eyes could not hide the sorrow, the emptiness, the feeling of being infinitely alone and cold.

At 10:00 A.M. the jury asked the judge to reread the instruction on self-defense.

After the instruction had been read, Dowd was seized with fear and doubt. Smoking furiously now, he tried to read the significance of this latest request from the jury chamber. The self-defense instruction was critical—Dowd's entire defense rested on it. Just before closing arguments, he and Judge Goodman had fought over the wording of that critical instruction. Goodman had been going to give an old instruction which told the jury that deadly force could be used in self-defense only when countering deadly force—in other words, if Poe Fratt had not used a weapon against Louann Fratt, she could not use a knife to defend herself against him. Dowd had patiently explained to the judge that fending off a rape attack was now recognized in New York as justification for using a knife. But Goodman had insisted that "rape, which is a conclusion, does not give rise to the use of deadly force." Trying to control his temper, Dowd had pulled out the law books and pointed to the new statute. Goodman read the statute, then reluctantly agreed to give the instruction requested by the defense lawyer.

But the jury had asked that the instruction be read a second time. Dowd frantically pondered the significance of this in the waiting room. Why had they asked for the rereading? Were they confused about the wording? Was there still some doubt about whether rape justified using a deadly weapon? *I should have spelled it out*, Dowd thought to himself. *I should have spent more time in summation explaining the law of self-defense. That's my job, that's what summation is for. Damn! If only I had spent more time on that . . .*

But maybe it was a good sign, Dowd suddenly thought. If the jurors were arguing about the self-defense jury instruction, didn't that mean that they had accepted the fact that an attempted rape *had* taken place? No, he thought, no, it could just as easily mean they had rejected the rape—and were now trying to decide whether the fists of a two-hundred-twenty-pound man constituted "deadly force." In which case, Dowd had lost.

Or could it possibly mean. . . ?

Dowd took another deep drag of the crumpled cigarette, then pulled out a fresh one and lighted it from the old one. He absently dropped the burning butt into his half-empty cup of coffee, then picked up the cup and sipped at the brown water. The big Irishman did not notice anything different.

Dowd knew that as a general rule, the longer that jury deliberations went on, the more likely that the verdict would be an acquittal—or at least a hung jury. My God, he thought to himself, a hung jury! If there was no unanimous verdict either way, there would have to be a second trial!

A second trial. The lawyer thought for a brief moment of the possibility of having to go through this all over again, but it was too much, and he tried to put it out of his mind. A second trial. No, that was not thinkable.

At 12:30 that afternoon, the jury announced that they had reached a verdict.

Dowd sat nervously in his chair at the counsel table as the twelve men and women filed slowly into the jury box and found their chairs. Again, he searched their faces for some telltale sign of the secret they carried. But there was nothing. Twelve cold, impassive faces.

There had been some difficulty locating Brownell in the district attorney's office, but the prosecutor had finally rushed over and was now sitting in his chair. His attitude was one of apparent calm and nonchalance. As with Louann Fratt, however, this appearance was carefully maintained for show. The young assistant D.A. had worked hard, fought hard, and, like Dowd, there was a small piece of his soul riding on this verdict.

There had not been enough time for the two camps of friends and relatives to get to the courthouse, but the reporters and cameras were back, along with the gawkers and thrill seekers. It always amazed Dowd that within minutes of an announced verdict, the newspapers and television stations had crews on the scene. He suspected that the media had paid informants among the various courthouse employees. What was even more impressive, however, was the courthouse grapevine. How could the spectators, who had converged so quickly on the available pews, have heard about the verdict? Where had they all come from?

Dowd looked again at the jurors. He noticed that none of them were looking in his direction. They're avoiding eye contact, he suddenly realized. A bad sign. A very bad sign. They don't want to face me. They don't want to face the woman they've just condemned. My God, they've done it! he thought, his heart pounding now. They've found her guilty!

He glanced quickly at his client seated next to him, her head held high, her posture perfect, her eyes fixed straight ahead as always. The lawyer felt a sudden twinge of sadness, almost of pain.

He leaned over to Louann Fratt. "No matter what happens," he whispered to her gently, "try to stay calm."

The woman's shoulders seemed to sag almost imperceptibly. Without looking at her lawyer, she nodded slightly.

When the last of the jurors had taken their seats, Judge Goodman looked at them sternly.

"Will the foreperson please stand," he demanded.

A middle-aged woman stood up in the front row.

The clerk, a harried-looking man in a white shirt and tie, stood up from behind his desk across the room from the jury.

He held a sheet of paper in his hand and, after glancing at the foreperson, began to read from it.

"In the case of *The People of the State of New York* versus *Louann Fratt*, number 10810-88 . . ."

Dowd tried hard to take a deep breath, to keep control. God, he thought to himself, what a miserable, sadistic ritual.

As the man read, Judge Goodman looked down at Louann Fratt, his dark eyes burning under furrowed black eyebrows.

". . . as to count one, murder in the second degree . . ." The clerk stopped, cleared his throat.

Dowd felt something welling up inside of himself, something dark and ugly and clawing to get out. *Read* the goddamn thing! it was screaming. *Read* it!

". . . how does the jury find, guilty or not guilty?"

The silence that followed seemed to last forever. Time was suspended in those few seconds as every eye in the courtroom turned and bore into the lone figure standing in the jury box.

The woman looked from the clerk to the judge, then to Louann Fratt.

"Not guilty."

Dowd felt a chill, then a huge, overwhelming weight suddenly lifted and, in its place, came a sense of wonderful lightness. His vision began to blur, and his throat seemed to be constricting, and he was trying to get air. At the same instant, he heard what sounded like a gasp, almost a small cry. He turned to his client.

Louann Fratt had collapsed in her chair.

EPILOGUE

After the trial, Louann Fratt sold the condominium on Seventy-ninth Street and moved back to the San Francisco Bay area where she and Poe Fratt had spent the early years of their marriage.

She lives well. With $1.3 million from an insurance policy on her former husband's life, $500,000 from their security portfolio, and slightly over $2 million cleared from the sale of the condominium, Louann Fratt's lawyers set up a $4 million trust fund to permit her to live in comfort for the remaining years of her life. The trust purchased a large house in the exclusive Piedmont section of the Bay area for $700,000; the lawyers arranged a life estate for her, with the property going to the children after her death.

Louann Fratt spends much of her time now playing bridge at the elegant Francesca Club in San Francisco. She continues to live alone in the large house in Piedmont.

Laura Fratt married a Stanford business graduate soon after the trial and moved to New York City. Poe Fratt, Jr., completed his master's degree at Cornell and also married and moved to New York City, where he is a securities analyst for

376

the stock brokerage firm of Shearson Hammill. William Fratt
works with a venture capital firm in San Francisco.

Judge Budd Goodman continues to preside in Part 62 of
the Supreme Court of New York. In his typically blunt manner, he still recalls the Fratt verdict with considerable surprise.
"I was in a state of shock," he says. "I just didn't believe her.
I found it incredible that a woman on Park Avenue would walk
around with an eight-inch butcher knife in her pocket. And it
was incredible to me that a husband who had a gorgeous
girlfriend like Joan Clark would have any need to rape his
wife."

Daniel Brownell prosecuted nine more cases after the
Fratt trial, winning convictions in all of them. But it is the
Fratt verdict that he continues to remember. "I was frustrated,
really depressed for a long time," he recalls. "I just couldn't
prove the motive." He had tried. But Joan Clark had refused
to cooperate. And Susan Grady—the friend who had told Louann Fratt about Poe bringing "the other woman" to the football game—had gone to South America during the trial.
Brownell is now a supervisor in the district attorney's office,
training new assistant D.A.s how to try cases.

Michael Dowd is no longer an attorney. On August 7,
1990, he was suspended from the practice of law for five years.
The grounds given by the five judges of New York's Appellate Division who signed the order were two: First, Dowd had
"engaged in conduct adverse to his ability to practice law" by
paying extortion to Queens Borough President Donald Manes
during the Parking Violations Bureau scandal of 1982—1984.
Second, since Manes was technically a member of the bar,
Dowd had failed to immediately report the ethical violations
of a fellow lawyer.
The reaction of the New York media to the announcement
of Dowd's suspension was immediate and forceful.
From the *Daily News*: "The two-page decision banning
Dowd from the courtroom has the aroma of the political system striking back at a whistleblower whose testimony ended
the careers of two corrupt kings of the system—Donald Manes

and Stanley Friedman. . . . There is no other way to explain such a grossly excessive punishment."

From *Newsday*: "[The suspension] has raised more questions about politicized judges than about the lawyer himself. . . As long as [Dowd's] brilliant career is ruined, the bench itself will remain on trial."

From *New York*: "There has been extraordinary violence in the streets recently . . . And now we have violence committed in the dark corridors of power. A man who did wrong—who was the first to rectify it, who tried to do good—has been ruined."

And from the lawyers' journal, *Manhattan Lawyer*: "Dowd did not get a fair deal from the judges of the appellate division, in a decision that was at least as political as it was judicial. . . . The message their ruling sends is: Keep your mouth shut."

A number of reporters pointed out that the investigation of Dowd had not begun until 1989—when U.S. Attorney Rudolph Giuliani resigned his position to run for mayor. Giuliani had been Dowd's protector. He recognized that Dowd had not offered bribes, but rather had been a victim of extortion. And he knew Dowd had been alone in voluntarily stepping forward at a time when no finger of suspicion pointed to him. "If Michael didn't have the courage to do that," Giuliani later testified at Dowd's suspension hearing, "I don't know if [the exposure of corruption] would have happened." So long as Giuliani was U.S. attorney, then, Dowd was safe. As Pulitzer Prize-winning journalist Jimmy Breslin later wrote, "The [city politicians] wouldn't have the guts to go against anybody holding that office on the best day they ever saw." But Giuliani resigned. And the investigation began.

At the hearing, conducted on March 1 and April 6, 1989, by referee Stanley Buchsbaum, no witnesses appeared to testify against Dowd. Dowd's attorney, however, produced dozens of witnesses, including federal and state judges, lawyers, prosecutors, law professors, and journalists. As Buchsbaum noted in his report to the Appellate Division, "the wide variety and prominence of his witnesses comes close to being astonishing."

Buchsbaum's fifty-six-page report was not completed until April 4 of the following year. The findings in the report were inconclusive. "Whether the making of extorted payments should be considered wrongful or improper depends on the nature of the threats . . . in the circumstances," Buchsbaum wrote. He noted the evidence of imminent financial ruin, and of Dowd's fear of Manes's power and influence. "Here, the threat, direct or implicit, was substantial. . . . [Dowd's fears] were substantially valid." And, he concluded, if the threat was enough to excuse the payments, then it would also be enough to excuse reporting Manes. Nevertheless, the referee chose not to make a finding of whether the payments *were* wrongful, leaving that final determination up to the Appellate Division. If the judges should determine that the payments *were* wrongful, however, Buchsbaum noted that "the testimony is replete with circumstances which may be regarded as mitigating."

Dowd and his attorney were relieved when they finally heard about the findings of the referee. And Buchsbaum, in a subsequent interview, stated that he felt he had written a report sympathetic to Dowd. Nevertheless, the five judges of the Appellate Division voted to suspend Dowd for five years.

Two of the reporters covering the story pointed out that all five judges were products of the political patronage system. The presiding judge, Guy Mangano, was a close associate of Brooklyn boss Meade Esposito, who was convicted in 1987 of corruption; Mangano's father before him had been a district leader in Brooklyn for twenty years. Judge William C. Thompson, a former city councilman, was another member of Esposito's political machine. A third judge, Stanley Harwood, was the former political boss of Nassau County.

"Dowd blew the whistle on the system that produced the appellate division judges," Jimmy Breslin observed in his column. "The message from the [five judges] was as clear as a gangland murder: Don't talk. . . . The only thing that didn't come with the court opinion was a dead canary."

The reporters pointed also to the apparent discrepancy in treatment received by other attorneys. In the first of the three cases found to be similar to Dowd's, attorney Walter O'Hearn was caught in 1983 paying bribes to labor leader Anthony Scotto; O'Hearn was subsequently convicted on eight criminal counts. The Appellate Division, with Guy Mangano a member, voted merely to censure his conduct.

The second case involved a Bronx lawyer and politician, Ivan Warner. Warner failed to object to, or report, a state senator who tried to fix a drug case for $100,000 in his presence. The attorney was charged with professional misconduct, but the Appellate Division failed to take any action. Instead, Warner was himself soon after appointed to the bench.

Finally, the clearest parallel involved two other attorneys who made payments to Manes's Parking Violations Bureau at the same time Dowd did. Manhattan lawyers Bernard Sennet and Samson Jochnowitz also owned a collection agency, which was heavily dependent upon a contract with the bureau. As with Dowd, they agreed to make payments to Manes; Jochnowitz even bought Manes a clock the political boss had admired in a store window. Unlike Dowd, however, neither attorney ever voluntarily reported anything. In fact, both lied when interviewed by F.B.I. agents working with Giuliani.

To date, the Appellate Division has taken no steps to discipline either of these two members of the bar.

Dowd's suspension became effective on February 1, 1991. He closed his offices and began looking for a job. His constant representation of indigents has left him almost penniless. As *Newsday* columnist Jack Newfield noted, "Dowd has defended a series of indigent battered women, a *pro bono* practice few lawyers can match; he is the only lawyer I know who owns no stock and has less than $1000 in the bank."

On March 14, 1991, New York Governor Mario Cuomo appointed Michael Dowd Director of Special Projects in the State's Office for Prevention of Domestic Violence. His primary assignment: develop legal programs to deal with prosecuting men who beat up their wives.

Ten days later, on March 24, 1991, Dowd was featured in a segment on the CBS television show *60 Minutes*. The segment, entitled "The Trials of Michael Dowd," dealt with the Parking Violations Bureau scandal and Dowd's suspension. In his introduction, Mike Wallace observed that "his license has now been taken away, not because he wasn't good at defending his clients, but because he's being punished for something he did—something that should have made him a hero, but didn't."

In the weeks following the airing of the television show, Michael Dowd has been deluged with offers of money—many of them from million-dollar trusts—to help him in his work on behalf of battered women. At the time of this writing, it is Dowd's dream to use the funds to establish a center for training lawyers—defense attorneys, prosecutors, and judges—to recognize and deal with cases involving abused women.